THE ANARCHIST'S DESIGN BOOK

EXPANDED EDITION

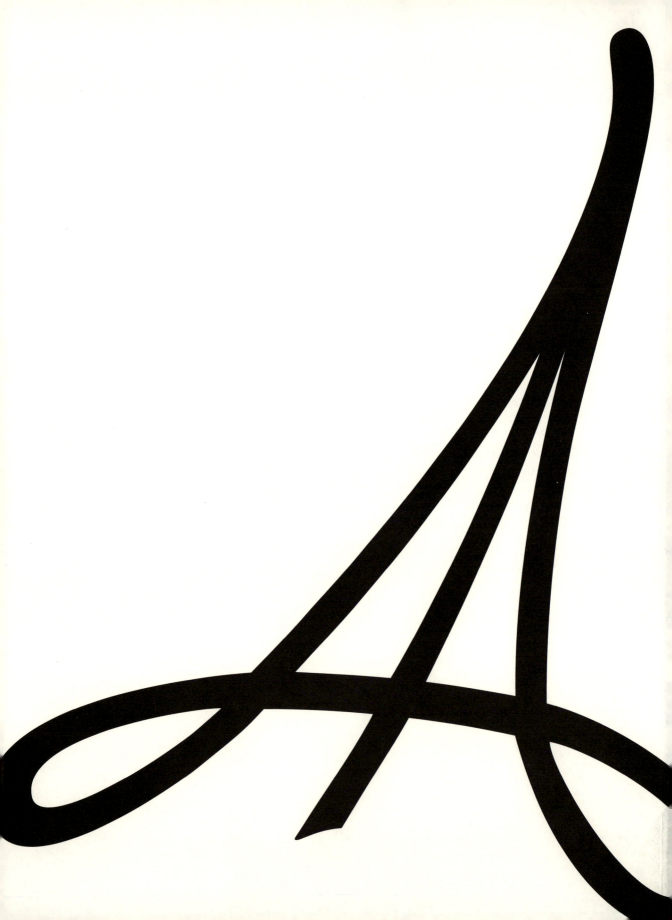

THE ANARCHIST'S DESIGN BOOK
EXPANDED EDITION

By Christopher Schwarz
Plates by Briony Morrow-Cribbs

First published by Lost Art Press LLC in 2019
837 Willard St., Covington, Ky., USA
Web: http://lostartpress.com

Title: The Anarchist's Design Book: Expanded Edition
Author: Christopher Schwarz
Plates: Briony Morrow-Cribbs
Copy editors: Megan Fitzpatrick & Kara Gebhart Uhl
Indexer: Suzanne Ellison
Distribution: John Hoffman

Text is copyright © 2019 by Christopher Schwarz
Plates are copyright © 2019 by Briony Morrow-Cribbs
Photography by the author, except where noted.

ISBN: 978-1-7333916-1-0

Third printing of the expanded edition.

ALL RIGHTS RESERVED
No part of this book may be reproduced in any form or by any electronic or mechanical means including information storage and retrieval systems without permission in writing from the publisher, except by a reviewer, who may quote brief passages in a review.

This book was printed and bound in the United States by:
Signature Book Printing
Web: http://signature-book.com

TABLE OF CONTENTS

Preface		viii
1: The Furniture of Your Gaoler		1
2: A Guide to Uncivil Engineering		6

STAKED FURNITURE

3: An Introduction to Staked Furniture		28
4: Staked Sawbench	*Plate 1, 46*	40
5: Extrude This		80
6: Staked Low Stool	*Plate 2, 86*	84
7: Staked High Stool	*Plate 3, 104*	102
8: Drinking Tables	*Plate 4, 122*	116
9: Furniture in the Water		138
10: Worktable	*Plate 5, 154*	146
11: Staked Bed	*Plate 6, 172*	168
12: Trestle Tables	*Plate 7, 190*	184
13: Seeing Red		228
14: Chairs! Chairs!		234
15: Notes on Chair Comfort		240
16: Staked Backstool	*Plate 8, 254*	250
17: Staked Chair	*Plate 9, 280*	276
18: Staked Armchair	*Plate 10, 298*	296

Continued on the following page....

...continued from previous page.

BOARDED FURNITURE
19: All Aboveboard		338
20: Bare Bones Basics of Nail Technology		348
21: Low Boarded Bench	*Plate 11, 370*	368
22: Boarded Tool Chest	*Plate 12, 384*	382
23: To Make Anything		404
24: Six-board Chest	*Plate 13, 412*	408
25: Mule Chest	*Plate 14, 444*	440
26: Boarded Settle Chair	*Plate 15, 468*	466
27: Boarded Bookshelf	*Plate 16, 486*	484
28: Aumbry	*Plate 17, 502*	500
29: Fear Not		522
30: Coffin	*Plate 18, 530*	526
31: The Island of Misfit Designs		544

Afterword — 566

APPENDICES
A: Tools You Need	570
B: On Hide Glue	586
C: On Soap Finish	590
D: On Milk Paint	602
E: Tenons by Hand	606
F: Machine Tapers	612
G: Seat Templates	618

Acknowledgments	624
Supplies	627
Index	629

By hand. A stone dovecote in Cornwall, England.

PREFACE

ANARCHISM

To build rather than buy.

On the surface, the words "anarchist" and "design" don't belong together in a sentence. Most woodworkers think of "design" as a way to organize the visual elements of a piece of furniture and "anarchism" as something akin to chaos.

Once you understand a bit about the American brand of anarchism – a non-violent and anti-consumerist approach to living – I think these terms are allied.

Contemporary North American anarchism (which I wrote about in "The Anarchist's Tool Chest") is a tendency among individuals to eschew large organizations, corporations, governments and religions. It is a preference for individual action as opposed to mandates, mass-manufacturing and canonical law.

I think those who care about craft will agree that our furniture – and much of our material culture – has been nearly ruined by mass-manufacturing. In the span of two generations, we have gone from a time when a newlywed couple would buy a dining room set that would last their whole lives, to a time when it's accepted (even necessary) to replace your furniture every few years.

Anarchism in this context is a tendency to build rather than buy, to create rather than consume. You can call it self-sufficiency or DIY. But when you make something that does not have to be replaced in a few years, you throw a monkey wrench into a society fueled by a retrograde cycle. It begins with an advertisement of something you don't need,

"(E)veryone should have a project: after all it is the best way to avoid being designed yourself."

— *G.C. Argan, "A Critical and Artistic Evaluation" in* L'Espresso, *May 5, 1974*

which leads to the manufacture of an object of the lowest common denominator and ends with the object at the curb. Then there's a new advertising campaign.

This book is an attempt to show you how to design and build furniture that will last generations. But I hope it's also something more.

Among furniture connoisseurs in North America, the "best" objects are highly ornamented and elaborate, using expensive veneers, carving, inlay and a high-style finish.

I contend that striving to make this kind of high-style furniture isn't the only path in our craft. Individuals have built furniture for themselves for hundreds of years, but these simple forms have mostly been ignored by historians.

I call these pieces "the furniture of necessity," and I think they are the perfect furniture form for the amateur woodworker. The pieces are straightforward, attractive and stout. They answer the call of "necessity" in some obvious ways. They hold your food off the floor, prop up your backside and protect your things from being stolen or ruined.

They also are "necessary" in the sense that we have to make things – anything – to preserve both the craft and our humanity. The history of civilization and woodworking are the same.

Making things makes you human.

That idea might seem overwhelming. Who has time to make all the furniture in the house? I think that you do.

In researching early furniture I found that many "necessary" pieces were built using just two simple techniques – the staked tenon and the tapered iron nail – that fell out of favor as the more ornate furniture styles demanded more technical and difficult techniques to build them.

Once you understand the basic principles of these two joints, which are detailed in this book, I think that you – anarchist or not – can design and build a whole houseful of furniture.

Christopher Schwarz
October 2015

For Lucy

*Without you,
none of this would be possible.*

DIE TRYING

The Muses Almanac. "The 1572 siege of Naarden" by Johannes Christiaan Bendorp (circa 1825). Spanish forces attack a blacksmith shop.

"What knowledge is this which thieves may steal, mice or moths eat up, fire or water destroy?"

— *13th-century Parisian preacher in a sermon on elaborately bound books*

Too much. A table leg from "The Cabinet Maker's Assistant: Original Designs for Furniture" (Blackie & Son, 1867).

THE FURNITURE OF YOUR GAOLER

CHAPTER I

Imitate the taste of your boss's boss's boss?

We came in through the basement door of George Reid's tidy ranch-style house. Like most basement workshops, George's was a dark cave. As I put down my photography gear, my eyes adjusted to the dimness and I found myself staring at a full-scale drawing of a Chippendale chair that was tacked to the wall.

"Hmm," I thought. "Nice poster."

For the next two hours, a co-worker interviewed George about his lifetime of work. How he built his first milking stool on his family farm, constructed miniatures while he was working at Wright Field and fell into making furniture for clients by building hi-fi cabinets.

We looked at his exquisitely cared-for machines. We admired his carving tools, which he bought from a guy who worked on Pullman train cars. I was there to take photos, and what I remember most is how I just couldn't see anything in the low light.

At his workbench, George showed us two of his miniature pieces – quarter-scale chests of drawers with bow fronts. It was nice work, we said. Do you have any other of your pieces here?

"Oh yes," George said. "Let's go upstairs."

George lived on a nice middle-class street in Kettering, Ohio, in a compact, mid-century ranch home. He led us around the house from the shop, through the front door and into a state of speechlessness.

All I remember was that every wall was painted brilliant white, and every bit of space was occupied by amazing pieces of dark 18th-century-style furniture in mahogany. I almost kicked a Newport kneehole desk. There were highboys, lowboys, carved chairs and corner cabinets in every corner. All in Chippendale, Hepplewhite, Sheraton and Queen Anne styles. And they were all perfect, like they were fresh from the tool of the maker.

I have never seen anything like it since.

George Reid was one of the most talented makers I have ever met. Yet, I'll never forget how wrong his beautiful pieces looked in the living room of his humble Ohio home.

This is Not for You

While the work itself is amazing, most of the American furniture we celebrate as the pinnacle of design can be overbearing, over-embellished and a monument to waste and excess.

It also represents the furniture of people you probably dislike.

These high styles of furniture took hold in North America in the 18th century and persist to this day as both cult objects for collectors and as rites of passage for artisans. These are precious pieces that are auctioned, collected, reproduced and written about in exhaustive detail.

We call them by the names of their champions or designers – Chippendale, Sheraton and Hepplewhite to name a few.

And while I am quick to admit these pieces were made using exquisite materials by talented hands, I want to add an asterisk to the discussion of high-end furniture: This stuff was built for the ultra-rich to satisfy their whims and fancies.

Or, to put it a slightly different way, the people who could afford this furniture also owned mega-farms, factories and (sometimes) entire towns. This is not a knock on their wealth. But it is a simple way of asking a question that rarely gets asked among amateur makers: Why would you want to imitate the taste of your boss's boss's boss?

Is it because their elaborate furniture is the peak of design? Or is

"New, new, new, just for the sake of newness, for the sake of the sales curve, in order to make people throw away the old things before they have served their time. Not so long ago we looked for a better form, now we only have to find a new one."

— *Poul Henningsen (1894-1967), Danish author, architect & critic*

it because it's put on display by institutions that are supported by the generous wealthy patrons – foundations, trusts, museums and cultural heritage centers?

Here's how I see the equation: Because the wealthy were (as always) scarcer than the rest of us, there simply aren't a lot of these pieces extant. It's their rarity more than anything that makes them expensive and desirable. Yes, the furniture is nice. But don't confuse a price tag with beauty or utility.

So if every log cabin on the frontier wasn't decked out with a set of Robert Manwaring chairs, then what were most people sitting on, eating off of and sleeping in during the last 500 years? After years of researching this question for myself, I think the answer is this: furniture that doesn't have a name, a museum or many champions.

> *What seems to have happened is this. Certain pieces of furniture, because of their essential practicality and usefulness, began during this period [the 17th century] to achieve definitive forms for which they were to retain for many years. Skilled but unsophisticated country craftsmen, usually joiners rather than cabinet-makers, repeated the same designs again and again, without changing them much, because they had been found to be the best for a particular purpose. A good deal of furniture thus escaped from the influence of fashion and, however unconsciously, responded only to the principle of fitness for use.*
>
> — Edward Lucie-Smith, "Furniture: A Concise History" (Oxford University Press, 1979).

The Furniture of Necessity

Among furniture historians, little has been written about this so-called "vernacular" furniture in comparison to the mountains of scholarship on high styles. There are a few books here and there (thank you Christopher Gilbert), plus magazine articles tucked between the gilded and carved masterworks. But the furniture of necessity is, for the most part, invisible.

Why? To be honest, vernacular items are tricky to study. They can be difficult to date because they don't change much – many of these forms are still made today in the same way they were built in the 1600s. Most of their makers are anonymous. These pieces, by and large, were built by amateurs or part-time, self-taught woodworkers.

This book does not pretend to be a proper study of Western vernacular styles from 1300 to present. I'll leave that to someone who is better at formatting footnotes. Instead, I want only to introduce you to pieces of furniture – some of them shockingly unfamiliar at first – that represent the core of our common furniture history.

This is the furniture of the people who work for a living. It is sturdy, made from everyday materials and isn't orchestrated to impress you with ornament. Instead, it is designed to keep you dry, comfortable and safe.

Also – and this is important – this furniture is largely disconnected from fashion. It cannot be labeled as a particular style, so it does not fall in or out of fashion. It looks at home in a log cabin, ranch house or an industrial loft. In fact, the only place it looks out of place is a high-style parlor or drawing room.

> *I admire the everyday ordinary furniture from the past, particularly from before the Industrial Revolution, what's known as vernacular furniture. The makers are usually unnamed, often not professionals. I like it because of its directness, honesty and functionality. It tends to be kind of minimal and spare for reasons of cost. It is striking how the dictates or slogans of Modernism align with those of the vernacular or craft: less is more," "form follows function," and so on. It's ironic because Modernism typically saw itself as release from the bondage of tradition.*
>
> *— Laura Mays, a furniture maker and graduate of College of the Redwoods.*

About this Book

In the 18th century, there was an explosion of so-called "pattern books" that were stuffed with illustrations of fashionable architecture, interiors and furniture. One count from the Metropolitan Museum of Art estimates there were 250 pattern books for architecture and 40 for furniture.

These books were usually gorgeous, oversized and expensive. Their copperplate engravings regulated and transmitted fashion throughout England, the United States and other parts of the world. In fact, the books are so influential that many are still in print (though usually as falling-apart paperbacks, which amuses me).

But there's never been a pattern book for the furniture of necessity.

This book, in a small way, is designed to echo those pattern books. Each of the furniture forms has a full-page illustration by Briony

"Of splendid books I own no end. But few which I can comprehend."

— Sebastian Brant (1457-1521), "Narrenschiff" (Strassburg, 1494)

CHAPTER 1

Morrow-Cribbs, a Vermont artist who specializes in intaglio printing.

Following the plate is an explanation of the piece – how it is constructed and its general features – much like the explanation you might find in André-Jacob Roubo's "l'Art du menuisier" or any other 18th-century text. Then each chapter departs from this historical format.

Vintage pattern books don't tell you how to build a Chippendale chair. The local cabinetmaker was supposed to be able to reproduce the particular set of details to suit the fancy of the customer. But unlike high-style pieces, the furniture of necessity was usually built by its designer and end-user. So I offer step-by-step instructions for constructing the pieces featured in the plates.

I hope you will find these pieces liberating in several ways. Like many furniture makers, I spent my adult life in the shadow of the 18th-century masterworks. I was told that to be a real furniture maker, you needed to build these high-style pieces. You needed to learn veneering, carving, turning and even gilding. Otherwise, you were just a glorified trim carpenter.

That is complete crap.

Beautiful, durable and useful furniture is within the grasp of anyone willing to pick up a few tools and learn to use them. It does not require expensive materials or a lifetime of training – just an everyday normal dose of guts.

Millions of people before you – and just like you – built all the furniture in their homes. They might not have left pattern books behind, but they left clues sprinkled through paintings, sketches and the furniture record. That is where our design ideas will come from. And that is where we will begin.

In all its horrible eccentricity of non-descript Gothic, worse Chinese, and inane rococo, combined though they be with the most exquisite workmanship and occasionally a quaint gracefulness, Chippendale's style is not in favour with those whose training enables them to discriminate between the true and false in design.

— *D. Adamson, "A Chat About Furniture,"* Work *magazine, March 23, 1889.*

I've half a mind. Frontispiece to *"Jack Sheppard"* (Geo. Barrie & Sons, 1898) by William Harrison Ainsworth. Etching by Leon Lambert after a painting by Hugh W. Ditzler.

A GUIDE TO UNCIVIL ENGINEERING

CHAPTER 2

Cut furniture down to the bone.

The dining table that Steve Shanesy sketched for us had an edge-banded plywood top, simple maple aprons and four tapered legs that were rotated 45° from what was typical in a traditional table.

It also had a clever mechanism to attach the legs to the aprons.

At the time, I was the managing editor of Steve's magazine. My job was to write the headlines for the articles. What, I wondered, were we going to call this table? So I asked him: "What style is this built in?"

"It's Shaker Millennium," he replied (I could hear the capital letters in the tone of his voice).

"What's that?"

"It's Shaker (a pause for Steve doing jazz hands) Millennium," he said. "It's going to be the new style for the new century."

Were our readers ready for us to create a new furniture style in a two-page article tucked in the middle of a mid-sized woodworking magazine? Probably not.

Furniture styles are not like magic tricks. It's not like: Bang – here is the Early Tim Style. As far as I know that has never happened – not successfully, anyway (sorry, Timmy).

"New" furniture styles are almost always reactions to an older style or adaptations of an even earlier style. Classicism and Gothic regularly spar like flabby wrestling veterans. The Functionalism, Arts & Crafts and Modernism styles were all reactions to Victoriana or the Aesthetic Movement. Chippendale was a whack-doodle sympathetic reaction to Chinese forms. Danish Modern and Shaker were an attempt to improve English vernacular forms and reject an ornamental style.

In fact, almost every book I own about a specific furniture style begins by exploring the previous furniture movement that was then victoriously flushed down the commode.

What about the furniture of necessity? It's also a reaction – a reaction to a wet backside, a need to protect your property or a place to eat that's not the floor. But not much else.

If both of your neurons are firing today, then you know that a Rococo chair, a Federal nightstand and a Regency dining table will also do these necessary things, yet I am calling them out as costume jewelry. So what makes the furniture of necessity different? How can we find it? How will we know it when we see it?

We have to cut our furniture down to the bone.

> *If ordinary applied art has a personal stamp, this means that it is incomplete. The artist has not gotten past his mistakes or arrived at the typical solution that is just as ordinary and natural in form as a Yale lock, a fountain pen, a bicycle, a scythe, a shovel. Imagine if a bicycle bore the mark of the artist who had designed it!*
>
> — *Poul Henningsen (1894-1967), Danish author, architect and critic.*

On the outside, we are all different organisms. Different hair, skin, weight, height, clothes and surface decorations (tattoos, makeup, scars). These differences gives clues as to our age, gender and place in society.

If you strip us naked and shave us bald, our differences fade. Slice away the flesh and muscle, and you would be hard-pressed to tell your mother from your worst enemy.

It's the skeleton – the framework upon which all of our personal ornament hangs – that is most like the furniture of necessity.

This might seem an obvious observation, but I think it is a useful tool

CHAPTER 2

Not natural nature. Examples of columns from "The Handbook of Ornament" by Frank Sales Meyer (Dover, 1957).

when looking at or designing furniture. When you can see the skeleton, then you can design furniture that is functional and, with a little more work, beautiful. You just have to start thinking like an orthopedist instead of an oil painter.

The first step is to accept the following statement as fact: Most of the problems in designing and building furniture were solved brilliantly thousands of years ago. The human body is still (Golden Corral excepted) the same, as are our basic spatial needs.

Therefore a real study of furniture should focus first on the things that haven't changed – table height, chair height, the human body, our personal effects, the raw materials, joinery etc. Intense study of ornament is interesting, but ultimately that will make you an expert in bell-bottom jeans, things that have been Bedazzled™ and feather boas. (See also: props in a Glamour Shots franchise.)

Where should you begin this study? Luckily for us, there is a group of scientists who has done all the work for us: the anthropometry engineers. The bible of this field of science is also my bible of furniture design: "Human Dimension & Interior Space" by Julius Panero and Martin Zalnik (Whitney Library of Design, 1979).

This widely available and inexpensive book (about $6 used) is everything a furniture maker needs to know about the spatial needs of the human body. What are the ranges for chair height among children and adults? Where should you put chair slats to offer proper back support? At what angle?

How big do tables need to be to seat a certain number of people? What are the important dimensions for an office workstation? A closet? A kitchen?

If a dimension isn't listed in "Human Dimension & Interior Space," then you probably don't need it.

Get the book. You don't have to read it – it's a reference work that will stay with you the rest of your life. Every designer should have a copy.

Aside from anthropometric texts, early pieces of furniture can tell us a lot about basic furniture design. These pieces were far simpler – I would say "elegantly Spartan" – than what is typical today, even in an Ikea store. But there aren't many of these early pieces left to study.

We have some beds, stools and thrones from the Egyptians, but we have no way of knowing if these were in widespread use. Egyptian tomb paintings offer additional details, but it's important to remember that these are mostly depictions of royalty and the things they made their slaves do while dressed in their underwear.

"I believe more in the scissors than I do in the pencil."

— *Truman Capote (1924-1984)*

CHAPTER 2

2.2 DINING SPACES

The relationship of the chair to the dining table is an important consideration. The top drawing explores two basic aspects of this relationship. The first is the various locations of the chair in relation to the table during the course of the meal and the clearances involved; the chair may be relocated as many as four times during the dining process. At the beginning, it is much closer to the table. Near the end of the meal, perhaps while the person is sipping coffee and attempting to relax by changing body position, the chair may be moved away from the table about 24 in, of 61 cm. Intimate conversation may cause the chair to be brought closer to the table than at the beginning. Finally, as the person rises from the chair at the conclusion of the meal, its final location may be as much as 36 in, or 91.4 cm away. The drawing indicates that the edge of the table should be at least 36 in, or 91.4 cm, away from the wall or nearest obstruction to accommodate all these movements. The height of the seat above the floor should allow the foot to rest firmly on the ground. If the seat height is too great, the foot will dangle and the area of the thigh just behind the knee will become pinched and irritated. A seat height of 16 to 17 in, or 40.6 to 41.3 cm, should be adequate to accommodate most people. Adequate clearance for the thigh should also be provided between the top of the seat and the underside of the table. As indicated on the drawing, 7.5 in, or 19.1 cm, is the minimum required. The backrest of the chair should be properly located to give support to the lumbar region of the back. The height of the table top from the floor should be between 29 and 30 in, or 73.7 to 76.2 cm. The bottom drawing indicates that to allow sufficient clearance for someone to pass or serve, the table should be located between 48 and 60 in, or 121.9 to 152.4 cm, from the wall.

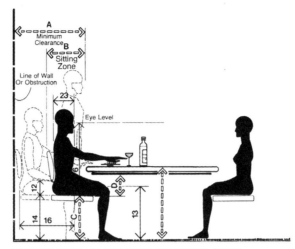

MINIMUM CHAIR CLEARANCE / NO CIRCULATION

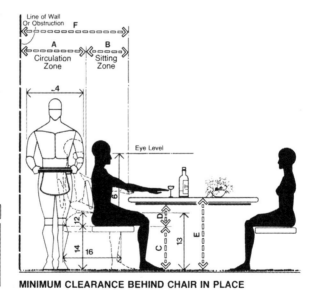

MINIMUM CLEARANCE BEHIND CHAIR IN PLACE

	in	cm
A	30–36	76.2–91.4
B	18–24	45.7–61.0
C	16–17	40.6–43.2
D	7.5 min.	19.1 min.
E	29–30	73.7–76.2
F	48–60	121.9–152.4

146 INTERIOR SPACE/DESIGN STANDARDS

Good guide. The book "Human Dimension & Interior Space" is the foundation of a good library on furniture design.

Thanks to a volcanic eruption in 79 A.D., parts of the Romans' physical culture – both high and low – have survived. And in the Middle Ages we can paint a picture of daily life thanks to paintings and drawings of everyday life. But it's not until the 1500s that surviving pieces of furniture start to tell their stories.

The stuff that survived is – no surprise – the furniture of the wealthy. It is elaborate, well-made, expensive and put into museums. Academics devote careers to studying it. Collectors hoard it. Furniture makers – both amateur and professional – study it and copy it.

Ordinary stuff was too ordinary to preserve or study, and so it ultimately became useful one last time, as firewood.

Not everyone was happy with the raw deal handed to simple furniture. Many reformers – William Morris and Gustav Stickley, for example – sought to bring good furniture to the masses. Their efforts were noble but doomed because we are natural cheapskates.

The Failure of Arts & Crafts & Other Modern Styles

"(O)ur society includes a great mass of slaves, who must be fed, clothed, housed and amused as slaves, and that their daily necessity compels them to make the slave-wears whose use is the perpetuation of their slavery."

— William Morris (1834-1896) from "Useful Work v. Useless Toil" (1888)

The idea behind the Arts & Crafts, utopian and democratic-reform movements was that common, everyday people deserve simple, well-made things. Some of these, such as the English Arts & Crafts movement, tried to accomplish this goal with handwork. Others, such as Danish Modern and American Arts & Crafts, attempted it with the help of machines.

All these movements failed. Well-built furniture – made by hand or power – has remained something only for the wealthy. Cheap, poorly manufactured furniture will always outsell expensive, well-made stuff. Our economy, at least at this particular consumerist phase, is ruled by price.

I have concluded that either most furniture buyers cannot tell the difference between crap and craftsmanship, or they do not care.

So – and this is important – we cannot look to furniture manufacturers to give us good places to sit, eat and store things. We need to look elsewhere.

I propose a new and most certainly doomed furniture movement. Here is the gist: The only way that most of us can own good furniture is to make it for ourselves.

The tools are widely available, inexpensive and useful in maintaining our homes. Common building materials – red oak, poplar and construc-

CHAPTER 2

13

English Arts & Crafts. Detail of a Sidney Barnsley "hayrake" table on display at the Cheltenham Art Galley & Museum.

tion timber – can be found at any lumberyard or home center.

The design of this furniture needs to be beautiful and simple. Who has the time or skills to build a highboy while raising a family and working? (That has been a paradox of the craft during the last century. People who have time to make furniture are retired and already have a houseful of it. People who really need furniture don't have the time or the money to set up a workshop and learn traditional joinery.)

To find this beauty and simplicity we need to look back in time – way back – for a solution. In a pre-industrial society, it was more common for common people to make their own common furniture. The joinery and furniture forms were simple. So simple, in fact, that they have remained invisible to most furniture historians.

> *This is such a familiar form of construction that a vocabulary of terms has hardly been found to describe it, but some early inventories seem to refer to it as "staked," or "with stake feet." Added to this is the fact that it*

has been largely ignored by serious furniture historians, though its place in the development of furniture design is so important that it is hard to account for this neglect.

— Victor Chinnery, "Oak Furniture: The British Tradition" (Antique Collectors Club, 1979).

If you seek to build simple stuff – the staked and boarded furniture used by common people during the last 500 years – you don't need a shop full of machines. You don't need years of training. You don't even need plans, really. You just need to understand the early pieces and the basic rules of anthropometry. This, of course, is not a new idea. Many of the best furniture designers were guided by history and the human body.

Last year we began by surveying two different groups of furniture. One comprises the forms that were created by important artists. I consider furniture in the other group (of furniture pieces) that, through the work of several people, and through evolution over a period of time, have achieved the simplest utilitarian form….

(This) other form, the one that was created over a long period of time and for ordinary use, is the one that we will be especially concerned with this year here at the school. You need not the distinctive, but the common and exceedingly utilitarian form.

From days past, we have furniture to which experience has given a form that has not been significantly changed over the ages and can be used to full advantage this very day.

The beauty of this furniture depends on its perfect, simple structure and utility. Although the pieces come from different periods, they have this in common….

We will find the best of old constructions and with recent experience seek to create furniture with the best possible craftsmanship.

— Kaare Klint's introduction to his class on draftsmanship for joiners at the Copenhagen Technical Society's School (1920-1921 school year). From "Kaare Klint" by Gorm Harkaer (Klintiana, 2010).

In the above quote, Kaare Klint, the father of Danish Modern furniture, was training professional joiners and designers to look backward for the foundation of their furniture designs. I propose that instead of asking the furniture designers and factories to make good stuff that we

CHAPTER 2

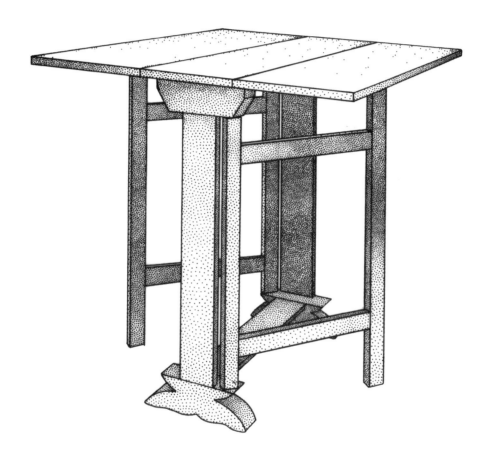

Early. Vernacular designs don't change much through the centuries. This is a joined gateleg table. English. Oak. Circa 1640.

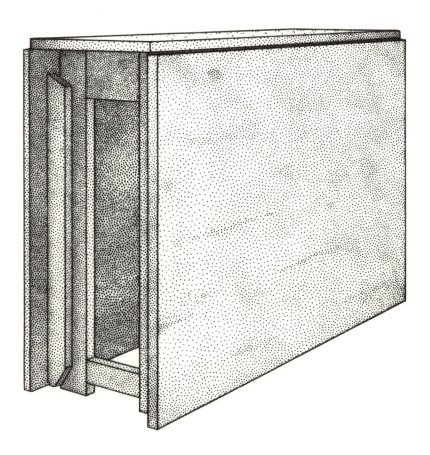

Still early. A joined gateleg table. Swedish. Circa 1800.

CHAPTER 2

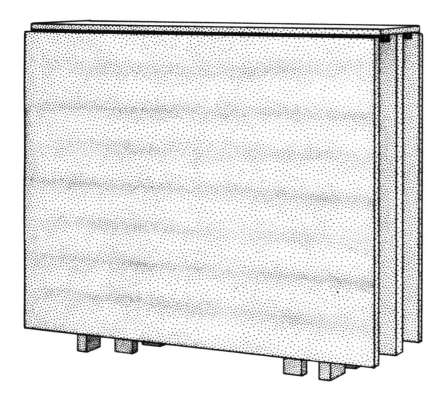

Later. A joined gateleg table. Denmark. Mid-20th century.

Today. A joined gateleg table. Swedish. 21st century.

can afford (a request that has yet to be filled in human history), amateurs need to take the wheel.

You can make any sort of platform with a staked joint: stools, chairs, beds, dining tables, desks, ottomans, sawbenches, workbenches and even couches. The trick is to understand how the staked joint works and to purchase a couple inexpensive tools that make the joint a lead-pipe cinch. You can make a good-looking stool in an afternoon with a broom handle and a 2x12. Staked furniture is covered in the first section of this book.

Likewise, you can make any sort of box with rabbet joints and fasteners – a special wedge-shaped nail or a tapered wooden peg. The trick is to understand how the fasteners work and to ignore some of the misguided and totalitarian commandments of wood movement. A boarded blanket chest, for example, can be made from dimensional pine in a day or two. Boarded furniture is the second section of this book.

What about wood-on-wood joinery, which is what most woodworkers consider the arterial blood of our craft – dovetails, the square mortise-and-tenon joint etc.? You don't need to know this stuff to fill your house with furniture. Every other significant woodworking book covers these joints – you don't need me to repeat it for you. If you ever decide to try it, I recommend "Woodwork Joints" by Charles H. Hayward and "The Essential Woodworker" by Robert Wearing as starting points.

When I embarked on the research and building for this book in 2011, I was unsure if these pieces of furniture were legitimate. Some of the techniques were downright odd to a traditional joiner like myself. Some of the forms were so stark – a three-legged chair? – that visitors to our house were afraid to use them.

As shocking as some of the pieces were to the eye, they quickly became commonplace and even beloved in my home. My kids moaned in protest when a three-legged backstool went to a new owner.

My response to them was honest: "You guys can build one for yourself. Anyone can."

So let's begin by talking about the design process in some detail.

"... (T)he end product, although usable, is only important because of its educational value."

— Enzo Mari (1932-) on his book of furniture designs for amateurs in "autoprogettazione?" (Edizioni Corraini, 1974)

Shortcuts to Good Design

All of the pieces in this book were designed using dirt-simple techniques that rely on photos of old furniture, a pencil, scraps of wood and wire clothes hangers.

It's in Chinnery. A staked backstool shown on page 77 of Victor Chinnery's "Oak Furniture: The British Tradition" (Antique Collectors' Club, 1979).

CHAPTER 2

Nice backside. When I began designing the staked side chair in this book, I started with rear legs that were angled 30° off the sightline. This angle gave the chair a wide stance that looked great from the rear.

The method allows you to stand on the shoulders of successful designs and alter them to fit a particular space in your home, to remove ornament or to even change the purpose of the piece (you can turn a stool into a desk).

It begins with finding a piece of furniture with an attractive form or, as I like to say, "good bones." It doesn't matter in what style or period the piece was built. What matters is that the piece's proportions and lines hit you in the gut.

Bambi? Is that you? But when I viewed the model from the front, the chair began to resemble a newborn fawn that was struggling to stand.

CHAPTER 2

The chair and backstool in this book both began with a piece from Victor Chinnery's classic "Oak Furniture: The British Tradition." I liked the rake of the legs, the four evenly spaced spindles and the smallish crest rail.

But there's a problem when starting with a photograph. As a photographer friend says, "Photos are lying bitches." Well-designed furniture looks good from almost every angle, and a photo shows only one viewpoint. The solution is to make a quick digital model or small mock-up.

To do this, you need some dimensions. I use a pair of dividers and a ruler to work these out. For example, I knew that the seat of the backstool in Chinnery was about 14" from the floor. That allowed me to figure out the width of the seat and the other relevant dimensions. Some dimensions, such as the depth of the seat, I guessed at using ranges from "Human Dimension & Interior Space."

If I'm building a case piece, I then make a quick 3D model in a computer-aided design (CAD) program. No joinery. No details. Just boxes that reflect the mass and major components of the piece. Then I rotate the piece and look at it from all angles to see if the photo was lying.

'Modeling' Projects in 'Wireframe'

Modeling chairs or any staked piece in CAD, however, is stupid. OK, "stupid" is a strong word. It's much faster to make a half-scale model using scraps and wire.

I epoxy the wire legs into the plank seat and bend them into position with pliers. As you'll see in the next section on staked furniture, this modeling process will also solve the geometry problems for you when building the piece.

Then I put the model on a table and walk all around it. I bend and snip the wire legs until the piece hits me in the gut the same way the original photograph did.

At this point I'll do one of two things: If I have the time, I build a quick full-size prototype from junk wood. This allows me to work out some of the joinery and construction problems that I might not have anticipated.

If I'm in a hurry, I take a picture of my wire model, print it out and draw on the printout. I might add bulk to the legs, scalpel bulk from the seat, add spindles and other details.

Then I head to the shop and build what I pretty much know is something that will work.

Fix you. Just like in nature, the answer was to help the model stand up a little more straight. In a chair, I usually make changes in 3° increments or so. But because this chair looked splayed like a squashed spider, I changed the angle by 5°.

CHAPTER 2

Run Forrest. The 5° alteration changed the stance significantly. Viewed from the rear and the front, the chair looks more like a bird dog in the field.

If this process sounds arduous, you might not be ready to design your own pieces of furniture. Stick to plans – there's no shame in that.

Design, like anything in woodwork, takes a little effort. I've never met anyone who can design a piece using pure inspiration and nail it on the first try. The process outlined above, however, is the shortest distance I've found between desire and satisfaction.

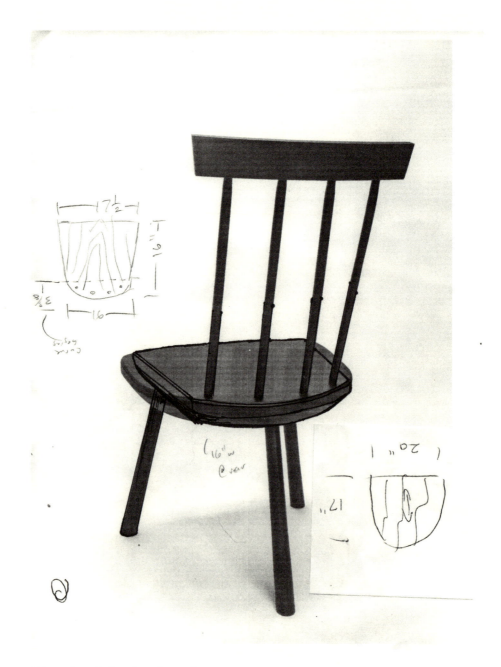

Photos & ink. I took a photo of a prototype of the backstool in this book and began to sketch changes to the seat and legs.

CHAPTER 2

Second prototype. After altering the seat, legs and spindles a bit, this prototype started to look like something I would want to sit in.

Tighten up. A staked joint can be as simple as a cylindrical mortise and tenon. Or it can be as complex as a tapered mortise and tenon that is back-wedged, as shown here. The advantage of this conical joint is that it gets tighter with use.

INTRODUCTION TO STAKED FURNITURE

CHAPTER 3

An almost-disappeared joinery technique.

The idea of "staked" furniture is one that is both foreign and familiar. The "stake" is literally the same thing you would pound through the heart of a vampire. It is a sharpened stick that does its job because of its shape and its strength.

Except that in this case, the victim isn't undead. It's an innocent piece of wood.

Furniture that has "staked feet" is made up of a thick platform of wood that is pierced by its feet. Aside from some details of angles and the occasional wedge or two, there isn't much more to know about this form of furniture.

What can you make with staked feet? Almost anything that makes a platform for your hinder, your food or your work. The earliest workbenches were made with staked feet. Our ancestors used the joint to make tables for dining, drinking and butchering animals. Plus stools for sitting, chopping and sawing (and drinking). You can hardly look at a medieval illustration without encountering a piece of staked work.

Making furniture using this simple technique fell out of favor as more sophisticated joints and furniture forms became popular. In fact, the staked joint has disappeared almost entirely from modern society with one notable exception: joinery in high-style Windsor chairs.

It took a while for me to accept that you don't need stretchers between the legs of a chair or stool to shore things up. And my slow embrace of this fact began with a Welsh chair class I took with David Fleming in Cobden, Ontario, in the middle of a Canadian winter.

After riving out the chair's ash legs and planing them to slightly tapered octagons, we started work on the seats. Wait. Why weren't we turning stretchers for the undercarriage?

"You don't need them," Fleming said.

I didn't believe him. So Fleming walked to the bookcase at the front of his cozy hand-tool-only shop and grabbed an old book. He flopped it open onto the bench to a page that showed Welsh chairs that were 300 years old. They were all well worn, more like geological rock formations that had been formed by erosion and the constant grinding of Welsh buttocks.

"You don't need them," he said.

A few years later, I took another Welsh chair class with bodger Don Weber. We rived out the oak legs then starting turning stretchers for the undercarriage. Wait. Why were we turning stretchers?

"We don't need them," I said.

Weber's reply went something like this: "The chair doesn't need them, but the customer does."

The modern eye expects the cross-bracing below the seat. It's a sign of quality – like spotting dovetails in the drawers of an antique dresser.

During the last 12 years, I've built, used and sold a lot of chairs without stretchers. And I've sat in dozens of antique ones (sometimes when the museum docents weren't looking). Now when I see old vernacular chairs with stretchers I see socks on a squirrel – cute, but unnecessary.

I contend that you can build almost any platform using this joinery. And you can do it without a single bit of math.

Before we get into details of angles and other minutiae, know this: The joint is forgiving. Even the most unsophisticated carpenter or joiner can make a chair, stool or table that will last hundreds of years because the joint is naturally robust. So if compound angles, conical tenons and differential shrinkage tables have you paging forward to the next section of this book, stay your hand. Once you understand a few basic ideas, staked furniture is ridiculously simple.

"Don't make a clock out of it."

— German woodworking instructor to students who fussed over their work.

CHAPTER 3

With & without. One of my Welsh stick chairs (left) built with staked joinery and stretchers in the undercarriage. A Welsh chair (right) without stretchers. And a three-legged backstool (below) without stretchers.

Roman workbench. Though this drawing is adapted from a 15th-century painting, the bench is Roman and uses staked joinery. The legs pierce the top without any stretchers or other reinforcement.

CHAPTER 3

A Soft but Cranky Top

Let's start with the part that is the seat, benchtop or tabletop – that's the easy bit. The platform should be thickish and in a species that ideally is both soft and difficult to split or rive.

The thickness of the platform can vary with what you are making. But I wouldn't want to make a piece of staked furniture with a platform that is less than 1-1/2" thick. Once you get to 4" thick, you can make almost anything with staked construction, including a dining table or workbench.

When it comes to picking a species, look for one that's difficult to split and has interlocked grain. If I could make every platform out of slightly wet elm I would. But elm is difficult to find where I live (21st-century Kentucky), and it's expensive when I can find it.

What else is difficult to rive? Poplar and white pine are both decent choices and easy to find at the lumberyard. Hickory, cottonwood, beech, cherry, sweetgum, eucalyptus and any other species with interlocked grain will also do admirably as your platform.

You want a species that is difficult to rive because driving a stake into its heart is like driving a spiral wedge into a stump when you split firewood. You want the wood to resist your efforts to cleave it in twain.

Also important: You want the species for the top to be softer than the species you pick for the legs.

Arrow-straight Legs

The legs, on the other hand, are best made from a stout species that is easily rived. Riving the stock will make its grain dead-straight and the legs incredibly robust.

Even if you aren't able to rive your legs, you should saw them so that the grain runs as straight as possible through the entire leg. There are a lot of good species for legs that can be rived, including oak and ash. If you are going to turn your legs, maple is ideal.

As far as the size of the leg components go, I think 1-1/2" square is a good starting point. As your legs get longer, the legs should get thicker.

If my argument still sounds mad, consider this: I think the French workbench is basically a piece of staked furniture (though the joints are square, which technically makes it a piece of joined furniture). And those legs are 6" wide. I don't think you need to use railroad ties to make the

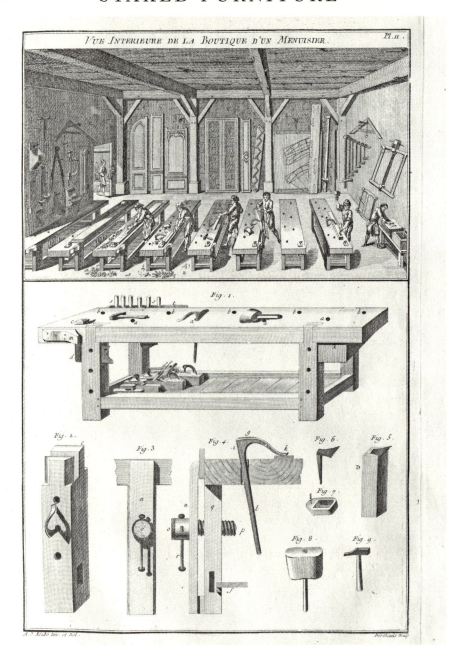

Square but staked. Early workbenches, including this French form from "l'Art du menuisier," derive all their strength from the joint between the top and the legs. The stretchers here help, but are more for creating a shelf.

CHAPTER 3

legs of a staked dining table, but 3" square isn't out of the question.

Oh, one more thing about the legs. When building staked furniture, it's always a good idea to make a couple more legs than you need for the piece. Sometimes things go bad when making the tenon, so it's nice to have a back-up leg on hand.

The Joint

The best way to join the top and the legs is to use a conical tenon and a mortise that is the same shape. Then you wedge the top of the tenon into the show surface of the top.

As you'll see in many cases in this book, the staked leg sometimes also passes through a batten below the top that is arranged cross-grain to the grain of the top. In other words, the tenon locks the batten and the top together. And because one piece's grain is 90° to its mate, the whole thing should explode. Or at least crack.

But they don't (always) do that. Why?

I think many woodworkers have a too-extreme view of wood movement. Either they think too little or way too much about it. The result is that some ignore wood movement and suffer the result. Others spend too much time trying to control it and complicate things needlessly.

If you take an evening to read chapter four of "The Wood Handbook: Wood as an Engineering Material," a free publication from the U.S. Forest Products Laboratory, you will be able to calculate how much your wood will move during the seasons.

And if you do some simple calculations, you might learn something shocking: Softwoods that have reached equilibrium moisture content don't move much compared to hardwoods. Most woodworkers think that softwoods will cast if we just look at them wrong. The truth is that most softwoods we buy are too wet for furniture, and the twisty movement is what happens as the wood reaches equilibrium.

Also important to know: Nails bend; screws don't.

With those two facts in your pocket, a staked joint won't look so crazy.

To make the joint, there's a little geometry to learn, but not much. The first project in this section of the book, the sawbench, introduces you to the angles, plus the processes used to shape the tenon and ream the mortise. After you make a pair of sawbenches, you'll probably wonder why you ever feared chairmaking.

I hope that the simple act of making a sawbench will also open your

"Leave your walls bare as a planed board, or build them of baked mud and chapped straw, if need be; but do not rough-cast them with falsehood."

—John Ruskin (1819-1900)

Moravian chairs. They appear to be a wood-movement nightmare. The grain of the seat is 90° to the battens below. Then the seat and battens are pierced by legs. Why do these not fail in every case? The image is from Frank Leslie's Sunday Magazine, *1883.*

CHAPTER 3

eyes as to how this joint can be applied to other forms of furniture. Today it's rare to see a staked table, but that's only because we have forgotten how to make them.

Good Wood for Staked Furniture

If I were writing this book in the 16th century, this chapter would most certainly be different. The wood used in making staked stools, chairs and tables was probably rived – especially the leg stock.

While there were saws available to early woodworkers, the most efficient way of processing lumber was with wedges, a beetle and a froe.

Today, however, I can't make the same statement.

Many woodworkers have limited access to green, rivable stock – especially if they live in the western half of the United States. Plus urban woodworkers, like myself, always struggle to find a good supply of logs from arborists and firewood piles. And when I do find some urban wood, the tree it came from usually sucks. Street trees are gnarly, filled with metal and many times rotted in some way.

So when I started building the projects for this book, I began with the assumption that you will buy your wood from the local lumberyard or the home center. That translates to this: legs from red oak and seats from poplar. No matter where you live in the United States, you should be able to find these two species for sale.

Tulip poplar (*Liriodendron tulipifera*) is soft, cheap, somewhat difficult to rive and can be found in thicknesses up to 4" at most lumberyards. It's fairly easy to work with hand tools and is quite paintable. So it's perfect for a seat or a tabletop.

For the legs you need something hard, readily available and cheap – red oak. While red oak might be the noxious weed of the fine-furniture world, it's perfect for staked furniture. You can buy tons of it for little money. It's readily available in 8/4 (2" thick), which is the perfect starting point for the legs of staked pieces.

When you shop for red oak, don't be beguiled by a pretty face. You're not looking for your typical clear stock. You are looking for straight grain on both the face and edge of the board. And the straight grain on the edges is more important than the grain on the face. If you can find a board with straight grain on its edges, buy it – even if it's butt-ugly overall. You can straighten out the grain on the face when you rip the legs from the board.

Poker straight. A shaving from a leg for a staked sawbench. The straighter the fibers, the stronger the component. This is true for chairs, ladders, tables and anything else that has to bear a heavy load.

CHAPTER 3

What about moisture content? If you work with green wood, you ideally want bone-dry legs and slightly moist stock for the seat or top. That way the seat will shrink on the legs and tighten the joint.

If you buy your stock from the lumberyard, you might not have much choice about the moisture content of your wood. So don't worry too much about it. Buy your red oak. Cut it into 24" or 30" lengths and let it sit until you are ready to use it. You want the leg stock to be dry.

Right before you build your staked project, buy the poplar and get to work. Whether it's dry or wet, things will be OK. Just make sure the legs are at equilibrium before you get busy.

You might have other options in your area. Seats can be basswood, white pine or cedar. Legs can be white oak, maple (soft or hard), hickory, ash or anything harder than the seat and tough enough to take a hard knock with a mallet.

But don't let the particular species available to you stop you from building something you need. It didn't stop woodworkers during the last 500 years or so.

STAKED SAWBENCH

CHAPTER 4

Where to begin.

If compound-angle joinery seems difficult, then building a simple staked sawbench will expand your woodworking consciousness in a snap, like a Zen koan.

Even if you have no intention of building a sawbench, I recommend you read this chapter before moving on to the other staked projects in the book. This chapter – more than the others – takes you through the process of understanding the geometry and joinery with baby steps.

The first and most important thing to remember is this: Every angle, compound or otherwise, is just as easy to accomplish as 90°. Nothing is special about a square.

Why this Sawbench?

Since I was a kid, I've built dozens of sawbenches and sawhorses of every common design. Most used dimensional lumber and nails to create a platform at a certain working height.

Sawhorses, in general, create a skinny platform – the edge of a 2x4 is typical – that's at table height, somewhere about 30" from the ground. Sawhorses are ideal for power-tool work. A couple sawhorses and a hollow-core door create a makeshift workbench. You can use circular saws, jigsaws and other power tools on top of sawhorses with ease.

Sawbenches, however, are a horse of a different height. They are used

Saw-somethings. All these forms are made for sawing. The sawbenches are for handsaws. The taller sawhorse is for electric saws.

with handsaws and mortising chisels in traditional work. They offer a platform that is about 7" wide and knee-high to the worker. This height is ideal for hand operations – ripping, crosscutting, mortising and sandwich-eating.

Most 20th-century sawbenches are built with dimensional softwood 2x4s and 2x8s. They are comprised of a top, legs and stretchers – like a sawhorse but lower and with a wider top. These sawbenches are nailed or screwed together like a modern job-site sawhorse.

But if you look at old drawings of shops, from the 16th century on, you see a different sort of sawbench. These are a made from a slab of wood that's pierced by four angled legs; many times the legs look like they curve out a bit.

Why do they curve? We don't know. Jennie Alexander has suggested that it is because the legs were rived from wood at the bottom of the trunk, which is usually unsuitable for high-class furniture.

These sawbenches are, without a doubt, staked furniture. The legs are angled to make the sawbench's top as stable as possible. The legs are

Der Zimmermann.

They're everywhere. Staked sawbenches – look to the left by the axe – are in many early illustrations of carpenters and joiners. This one has straight legs. From "The Book of Trades" by Jost Amman and Hans Sachs (1568).

Side, rake; front, splay. Chair geometry is like saw geometry. From the side of a saw or chair (left), the teeth or legs are raked, either forward or back. Looking at the front of the saw or the chair (right), the teeth or legs are splayed out; we call this "set" in a saw and "splay" in a chair.

joined to the top with some sort of mortise-and-tenon joint. This joint could be as simple as a plain old hole in the top or as complex as a conical tenon that has been wedged.

The legs are angled out to stabilize the top but also to stay out of the way of the worker. You don't want to nick a sawbench leg with your saw, and you don't want to trip over its legs when you walk around the shop. I have found that the rake and splay of sawbench legs are similar to the rake and splay of the rear legs of a Windsor chair.

Introduction to Leg Angles

"(Chairs) are too hard. Chairmakers are doomed to poverty."

— Gary Bennett (1934-) furniture maker and artist

Oh sorry. I introduced some chairmaking terms without lubrication. "Rake" and "splay" are terms chairmakers use to describe the compound angles of chair legs. If you look at the front of a chair (the elevation), the angle that the legs project out is called the splay. If you look at a chair from the side (the profile), the angle of the legs is the rake. (These angles are usually pretty low numbers – 5° to 15° – in typical work.)

I've built chairs for more than a decade, and I don't mess around with describing or measuring rake and splay much, except to explain it to

CHAPTER 4

One angle. The bevel gauge is set to 15° and has been placed on the sightline on the underside of this sawbench. This "resultant" angle allows you to drill the holes for your legs with one line and one setting of your bevel gauge.

Sawbench

Pl. I

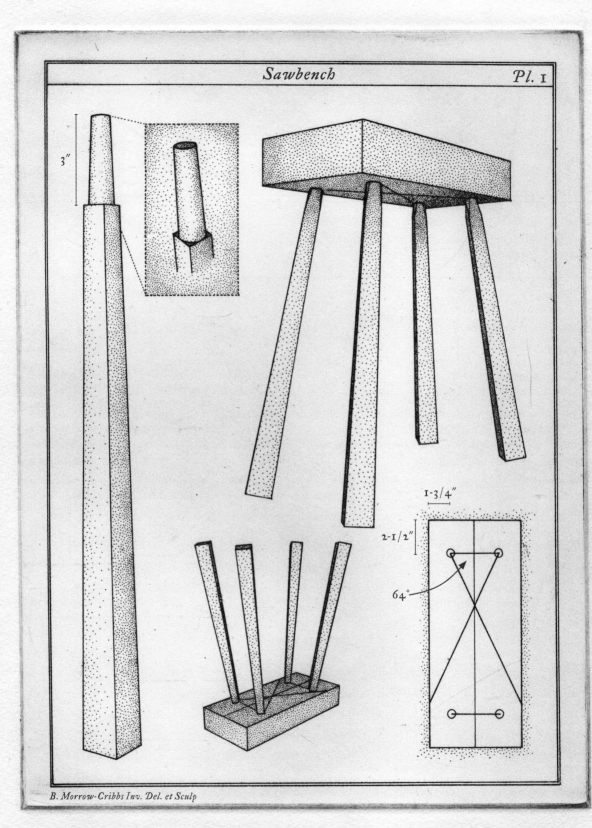

B. Morrow-Cribbs Inv. Del. et Sculp

CHAPTER 4

other builders.

Instead, I use the "resultant angle" – one angle that describes both the rake and splay – and "sightline" – a line where the leg appears to the eye to be dead vertical. You can calculate this angle with trigonometry, but there is a simpler way to think about compound leg angles for those of us who consider math a cruel mistress.

First you need to find the resultant angle and its sightline. You find this by locating the point at which a single leg appears to be perfectly vertical.

If I've lost you, try this: Sit on the floor with a chair in your house. (Make sure you are alone or are listening to Yes's 1973 "Tales from Topographic Oceans.") Rotate the chair until the leg closest to you looks to be perfectly 90°. Imagine that one of your eyes has a laser in it and can shoot a line through the leg and onto the seat. That laser line is what chairmakers call a "sightline" – an imaginary line through the leg and onto the seat. Put a single bevel gauge on that imaginary line and you can position a leg in space with a single setting on a bevel gauge. That setting is the "resultant angle."

Most plans for Windsor chairs include instructions for laying out the sightlines and the resultant angles for setting your bevel gauge. But what if you want to design your own chair? Or you want to build a table, desk or footstool using the same joinery?

So put away the scientific calculator and fetch some scrap pine, a wire clothes hanger and needlenose pliers. We're going to design and build a simple sawbench with five pieces of wood and compound angles. This model will give us all the information we need to build the sawbench.

Build a Model

When I design a piece of staked furniture, I make a simple half-scale model using scrap wood and bendable wire. This method helps me visualize how the parts will look when I walk around the finished object. The model also gives me all my resultant angles and sightlines without a single math equation.

I first learned this technique from Drew Langsner's "The Chairmaker's Workshop." I then adapted his method a bit to remove the math. Let's use it to design a sawbench.

Take a piece of 3/4" pine and cut it to half the size of the finished sawbench. The finished top will be 2-1/2" x 7-1/4" x 17", so make the top of your model 3/4" x 3-5/8" x 8-1/2". Next decide where you want

"Technique alone is never enough. You have to have passion. Technique alone is just an embroidered potholder."

— Raymond Chandler (1888-1959)

Leg layout. Here I've laid out the leg locations in this half-scale model of my sawbench.

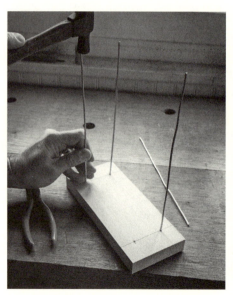

Guided by wire. The wire should be strong enough that you can tap it into its hole on the underside of the model.

Make the rake. Use the pliers at the base of the legs to bend them to 14° to match your bevel gauge.

the legs to be and lay out their locations on the model. Each of my legs is located 1-1/4" from the end of the model and 7/8" from the edge. A lot of this is "by eye" so don't worry too much.

Now snip four pieces of wire from a clothes hanger to 10" long. This wire will represent the legs of the sawbench. Drill a snug through-hole for each "leg" on your model. Put a little epoxy into the hole and tap the wire in.

Now comes the fun. Set your bevel gauge to 7° using a plastic protractor. Look at the model directly from the end of the board. Let's call this the front of the sawbench. Use needlenose pliers to bend the wire legs so they all splay out 7° from the top. Try not to manipulate the rake.

When they all match your bevel gauge, change the setting of the bevel gauge to 14°. This will be the rake. Look at the sawbench directly from its side and use your pliers to bend the legs to 14°. You might have to tweak things a bit so all the legs look the same.

Turn the model on its feet and look at the result. You will be surprised by how easy it is to spot angles that look wrong. Adjust the wires until they all look the same and the sawbench looks stable.

Find the Sightline & Resultant Angle

Turn the model back over. Place a square on the bench with the blade pointing to the ceiling. Rotate the model until one of the legs appears to be 90° in relation to the square. Place the handle of your bevel gauge against the long edge of the model and push the blade of the bevel gauge until it appears to line up with both the leg and the blade of your try square. (Hold your head still.)

Lock the bevel gauge. This is your sightline. Place the bevel gauge on the underside of the model. Butt it against one of the legs and draw a line. You have now marked the sightline. (By the way, it's about 64°.)

Now find the resultant angle. Unlock the bevel gauge and place the tool's handle on the sightline. Lean the blade until it matches the angle of the leg. Lock the gauge. That is your resultant angle – about 15°.

If your head hurts, don't worry. It's not a stroke – it's geometry. Once you perform this operation a single time, it will be tattooed to your brain. This chapter will explain how to lay out the resultant angle for your sawbench – you'll have nothing to calculate. But the act of marking out the sightlines will – I hope – make the concept clear and remove your fear of compound angles in chairs.

"We find industrial organisation ever screwing down and screwing down, we find the drive severer, the competition keener, we find industrial democracy ever closing in … the levelling and uniformity more necessary, more terrible. What becomes of the individual, of what weight is the little human soul upon this dark archangel's scale?"

— C.R. Ashbee (1863-1942)

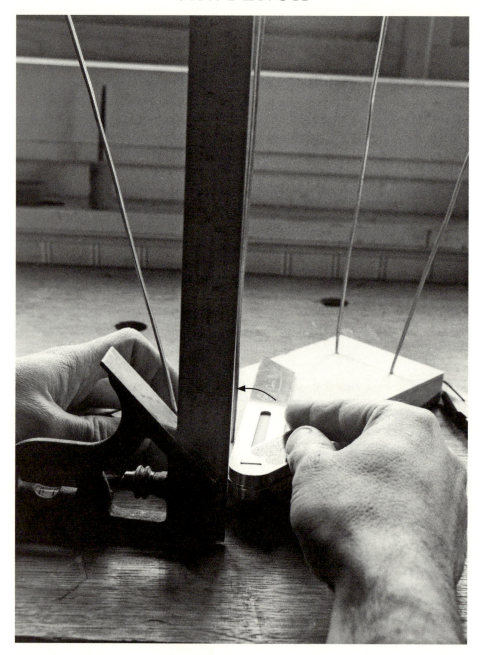

When the tools align. Rotate the sawbench until the leg looks vertical compared to your square. Adjust the bevel gauge until its blade aligns with the leg and square. In the photo I am pushing the blade toward the vertical line made by the leg.

CHAPTER 4

Mark the sightline. Use your bevel gauge to draw in your sightlines on the underside of the model. You are almost done. Unlock the bevel gauge.

The result. Put the handle of your bevel gauge on the sightline. Set the blade to match the leg. That's the resultant angle – you just did a good thing.

It's a dowel. A cylindrical tenon has all the hallmarks of dowel joinery. It is simple to make but weak in service. Chairs made using dowels are doomed from birth.

Sidebar: Two Kinds of Joinery

There are two common ways to fasten the legs to the top in a sawbench. One method is to turn or shave the top of the leg to a cylinder – like a dowel. Then you can drill a hole in the top. Glue the leg in the hole. Done.

The primary problem with this approach is the joint can fall apart because there is a lot of end grain in the joint and the glue fails. Just like in cheap store-bought chairs. This might take a few years or 100. But it will happen – usually on Thanksgiving Day for some reason.

The historical solution is to make both the tenon and the mortise cone-shaped. So the more you press down on the top, the tighter the joint becomes. Though it is theoretically possible to split the top, this rarely occurs. And it's even more rare for the leg to fall out. Why? The joint is also wedged from above to help keep the top fixed.

Chairs, stools and sawbenches made using this technique can survive hundreds of years of hard use. And the joint doesn't require a lot of expensive tools to execute.

CHAPTER 4

Lines of sight. Each sightline crosses through the centerpoint of its mortise. If the sightlines meet at the same place on your centerline, then your layout is likely correct.

How the Sawbench Works

So here's how this thing goes together. First you drill angled holes in the top to receive the legs and use a reamer to make the holes coneshaped. Then you shape the legs and create a cone-shaped tenon on the top using a lathe, a pocketknife or a special tool that's like a pencil sharpener for giants.

Then you glue and wedge the legs into the top. After the glue dries, you saw the ends of the legs so the sawbench is the right height and doesn't rock (much) on your shop floor.

If I make it sound too simple, that's because it is. When I teach people to make these sawbenches, the loudest sound during the class is one hand slapping a forehead.

About the Top & Legs

The top should be made from a species that is inexpensive, soft-ish and isn't easily rived; you don't want the top to split when you drive the legs into it. Elm would be the historical choice, but good luck finding that. Poplar or pine are readily available and suitable.

You want the top to be thick – about 2-1/2" to 3" is sufficient. A thick top gives you a lot of joinery surface for the conical mortise and tenon – and that's how you can get away without having any stretchers between the legs. The top should be about 7" to 9" wide x 17" long. But don't worry if your dimensions are a little bigger or smaller.

The legs should be stout, straight-grained stuff. Oak or ash are my favorite leg species. What's important about the legs is that you have little or no grain run-out, sometimes called "short grain." The strongest leg will have all the fibers arrow-straight through the entire leg. That's easily done when you rive your stock with a froe. But you can get close enough by selecting straight stuff at the lumberyard and correcting any grain run-out when you rip out the legs.

No matter how tall or short you are, the legs should start out at 1-3/4" square x 24" long.

Begin Work on the Top

Plane the top piece so it is "four square." That means the board's two broad faces should be parallel. The long edges should be square to the board's faces, and the ends should be square to both the edges and faces. It's fairly unusual to have to four-square a board in handwork – but for this project it makes life easier.

If the underside isn't flat or parallel to the top, then the leg angles won't be consistent. The result will be that your sawbench will resemble a drunken pig, with each leg going in a different direction.

With the board four-squared, layout of the joinery begins on the underside of the top. The first order of business is to draw a centerline on the face of the board along the board's length. The centerline will help point out any layout mistakes.

Next, lay out the locations of your legs. The centerpoint of each leg is

Proof of concept. This step might seem silly, but I do it every time I make a chair. It confirms that the leg will not be angled oddly and the seat will not be thrown into the burn pile.

2-1/2" from the ends of the top and 1-3/4" from the long edges. Set your bevel gauge to 64° or set the gauge directly from the model and skip the numbers altogether. Butt the bevel gauge against one end of your top and line it up with one of the centerpoints you just laid out. Draw a sightline through the centerpoint. Extend the sightline with a straightedge for clarity.

Set your bevel gauge to 15°, the resultant angle of the leg. Place the body of the bevel gauge on one of your sightlines and put the blade right over the place where you are going to bore a mortise. Pretend the blade

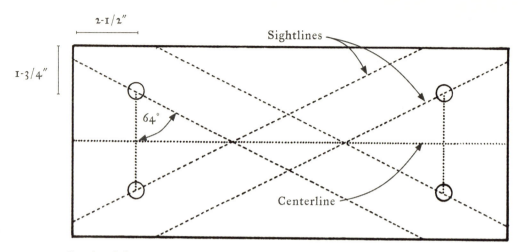

Sawbench layout.

of the bevel gauge is a leg.

This is the foundation of Windsor chairmaking. Draw sightlines and drill your mortises at an angle off the sightline.

Take your bevel gauge in hand and tighten the living crap out of it. You want to lock it at 15° because now you have to force some of this geometry into the wood.

Bore the Mortises: By Hand & Power

Before boring the mortises know this: Few chairs, stools or sawbenches ever end up with four legs at the exact angle intended by the maker. But the process is forgiving and our eyes are easily fooled. If the project looks good and doesn't collapse, then it's a success – no matter what oddball angles are involved.

When I bore the mortises in the legs I use a 5/8" bit that is powered by a brace, an electric drill or a drill press. All three methods work; use what you have on hand and suits your head.

When I bore the mortises with a brace or electric drill, I use an auger bit with a threaded lead screw. This bit allows me to start the bit right where I want it and also allows me to tip the bit to the correct angle (15° in this case) as the bit's spurs enter the wood.

To bore the correct angle, I put my bevel gauge on my sightline and

Chapter 4

The tricky side. When you bore by hand, it is easy to see if you are leaning to your left or your right. But determining if you are leaning too far forward or back is difficult. A spotter and bevel gauge can guide you.

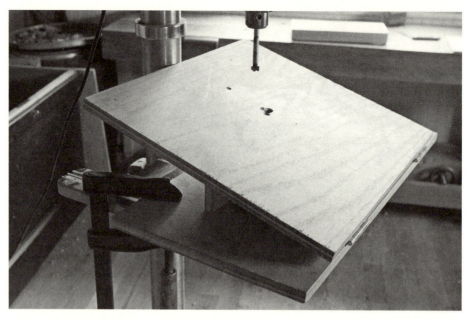

Skill? Who needs it? This simple jig negates all the skill I built up after a decade of making chairs. It's two pieces of plywood that are hinged at the front.

A scrap sets it. A scrap that is screwed (or clamped) between the two bits of plywood sets the angle, as shown here.

CHAPTER 4   59

The good eyeball. When I drill holes in tops or seats, I line up the sightline, drill bit and center post of the drill press by eye. No fussing. I am usually off by a half-degree or less. In chairmaking, that's gold. Trust your eye.

clamp or tape it in place so it doesn't get knocked around. Then I start the lead screw at the centerpoint of my mortise and tip the bit to the correct angle. If this is your first time, ask someone to spot you. Have them watch at 90° to your sightline so they can see if you are indeed boring at 15° off vertical.

After you bore 1" into the top, send the spotter away for a beer. You are committed to that particular angle, whatever it is. Bore the rest of that mortise.

If you have a drill press, you can make a simple jig that makes com-

> "Technical knowledge is harder to kill than any other kind, and is seldom subjected to religious, political, or military persecution."
>
> — *John Gloag (1896-1981), "A Social History of Furniture Design: From B.C. 1300 to A.D. 1960"*

pound angles ridiculously easy. I didn't invent this jig, and I'd be hard-pressed to say who did. I don't even know if the jig has a name. So I shall call it: Banjo.

The jig is made from two pieces of 3/4"-thick plywood that measure about 20" x 20" – enough to support a typical chair seat. Hinge the two pieces of plywood together at one edge so the two bits fold together flat. Clamp the bottom platform to the table of your drill press. Lift the top platform to the height required to hold the table at a 15° angle (your resultant angle) to the quill.

Tip: If you are having trouble setting the angle, insert a long screwdriver bit into the chuck. Then you can easily sight that against your bevel gauge.

Put a scrap between the two platforms to wedge the jig open at this setting. You can clamp or screw down the scrap so it won't move.

You are essentially done. Now you just have to know how to use the jig. What's important is that you align the sightline on the underside of your top so it lines up with the tip of your drill bit and the center of the cast iron pillar of your drill press. That's essentially all you need to know. You can screw fences down to the platform if you want to restrain the top. But a sharp eye and Kentucky windage is good enough.

Chuck a 5/8" Forstner bit in your drill press. I like a Forstner here because it works well at an angle and will enter the wood cleanly. A typical twist bit can chew up the top unnecessarily.

Set the depth stop and the quill speed of the machine (375 rpm for hardwoods; 1,600 rpm for softwoods). Drill the four holes for the legs. You are ready to ream.

Getting Reamed

The tapered, conical mortise and matching tenon are key to the long life of your sawbench. And no matter what sort of reamer you use, rest assured that its conical hole will be an improvement when compared to a straight, cylindrical hole.

So OK, time for a second wee dose of geometry. It's time to learn the term "included angle." This is a term used to describe an isosceles triangle, which is a good way to understand a reamer. The tip of the triangle (the vertex) has an angle from its two rays. The angle between the two rays is what we call the "included angle" of a reamer. (I like to think the included angle is the "inside" angle – the angle between the two rays.)

Reamers are described by their included angle. Commercial reamers

CHAPTER 4

Both work. A metallic reamer and a wooden reamer (with a cutter made from saw steel) both do the job. Debate the fine points if you will. Or build stuff.

Drill press tricks. One of the problems with using reamers in a drill press is the "throw" of the machine – how much vertical plunge you have. If your drill press doesn't have enough throw you can finish the job by propping your work up on battens, as shown here.

A smart dummy. Here I have shaved a dowel from another project to the shape of the tenon for this project. I can check and adjust my reaming using the dummy leg.

usually range from a 12° included angle down to a 6° included angle. Those six degrees of separation make a significant difference. Joints reamed with shallower angles – such as 6° – tend to hold better and split the work less. The reamers with steeper angles (12°) are less expensive and can be chucked into a drill press. I've made good chairs and benches with both kinds of angles, though I prefer the 6° reamers.

If you ream your holes using a drill press, life is simple. Chuck the reamer into the quill. Set the speed of the machine to its lowest setting. Keep the banjo jig in the same place as when you bored the pilot holes. Ream the holes. The reamer will find the center and pull the top into position – as long as you keep the sightline in the right position.

The only trick about reaming the mortises is to stop reaming when the section of the reamer that is 5/8" reaches the rim of your mortise that is pressed against the banjo jig. You need to set the drill press's depth stop and use dial calipers to confirm your setting.

Note that the resulting holes on the faces of the board are going to be oval-shaped. Don't worry about this because a wedge will fill small gaps between the hole and tenon.

Reaming by hand is a little trickier. My best advice is to take a 1-1/4"-diameter dowel that is about 12" long and make a tapered tenon on one end that matches the included angle of your reamer. This dummy leg will guide you as you ream.

Chuck the reamer in your brace or in your electric drill (my tool of choice these days for this operation) and place your bevel gauge on the sightline – a spotter can help you get into the correct position for reaming. Begin reaming the hole. After about 10 turns of the brace (or one good squeeze of the trigger of the electric drill), remove the reamer and push the dummy leg in the hole. Use your bevel gauge to figure out if you are on target or not.

If you are off in one direction (or two directions) then you need to lean on the pad of the brace in the direction that will correct the angle. When I correct a mortise, I make only two turns of the brace's handle then check my progress against my dummy leg.

Sometimes course corrections take two or three attempts. And sometimes they fail completely. Don't get frustrated.

Continue to ream the mortise until the 5/8" tip of the dummy leg reaches the rim of the mortise. Ream all four mortises this way. Small differences won't reduce the utility of the sawbench. Heck, large differences (5° or more) won't reduce the utility of the sawbench, though the odd angles might make the sawbench look like a fawn that is learning to stand up.

Easy octagons. To turn a square into an octagon, set your compass so it spans the space between one corner and the centerpoint of the square. Then, with the pin of the compass on the corner, scribe an arc. Repeat on the other three corners. Connect the endpoints of those arcs and you have an octagon.

With the four mortises reamed, clean up the top as you see fit. Bevel its underside if you like. You are done with the top and are ready to move to the legs.

Make the Legs

The legs can be as simple or as complex as you please. You can simply taper the legs from the floor up to the tenon then shape the conical tenon with whatever tools are handy, from a pocket knife to a lathe tool

CHAPTER 4

Taper the legs. Many pieces of staked furniture have legs that taper. You can taper yours with a jack plane and jointer plane.

to a dedicated tapered tenon cutter.

If you like turning, consider making the legs straight or tapered cylinders – those show up in a lot of early drawings.

The legs shown in this sawbench start as 1-3/4" octagons. Taper them with a jack plane so they are 1-1/2" octagons at the top of the leg. At the top of the leg mark out the tenon as 3" long and add about 3/8" as the area where you can shape the transition from octagon to round. This tenon length is more than you need, but it will allow you to use an inexpensive tapered tenon cutter.

Turn the tenon to 1-1/8" in diameter and shape the transition from octagon to round. You can do this on a lathe or you can shape it with a drawknife – even a coarse rasp if that's all you have. Then turn down the tip of the tenon to about 3/4" and rough in the shape of the conical tenon. It doesn't have to be perfect; that's the job of the tapered tenon cutter.

If you don't have a tenon cutter, you can shape the finished tenon entirely on the lathe. If you don't have a lathe, you can rough-shape the tenon with a drawknife and finish the job with the tenon cutter. If you

Two tenon cutters. While you can make your own tapered tenon cutter, it's faster to buy one. Here you can see a wooden version and metallic ones.

don't have either tool you can make do with a drawknife, spokeshave and scraper.

Take a little comfort from the fact that even imperfect conical joints can last for centuries.

Cut the Conical Tenon

Remove the leg from the lathe and use the 5/8" tapered tenon cutter to shave your tenon to size and shape. The cutter should bottom out on the area of the leg where it starts to change to an octagon.

A tenon cutter is a handy tool that works much like a pencil sharpener. Your tenon cutter should have the identical included angle as your reamer. If you use a vintage reamer, you might need to make your own tapered tenon cutter using scrap wood, a plane blade and geometry. There are plans available to make these tools, but I've always stuck to the commercial models to make my life simpler.

CHAPTER 4

The right kerf. In the top of each leg, saw a kerf that is perpendicular to the annular rings of the end grain. This will help keep the leg in place over the long haul.

If you buy a commercial tenon cutter, do yourself this favor as soon as you receive the tool: Get some straight-grained wood and shave a tenon with the tool's factory edge and factory settings. Put this tenon aside so you can easily return to this factory setting after you sharpen the tool's cutter. When you sharpen the cutter, place the sample tenon in the tool and push the cutter against the sample tenon. Lock the cutter in place.

The best way to use these tools is to use them as little as possible. Get your tenon close to size and shape with rough tools and use the tenon cutter to shave off the last bit to produce a perfect cone. Making a tapered tenon whole cloth from a square-cornered piece will wear the tenon cutter prematurely and will wear out your wrists after only a couple tenons.

Many beginners have trouble keeping the tenon centered in the tenon-cutter. The result is an off-centered tenon – that's unsightly but not fatal to the leg. Here's how I keep the tenon centered in the cutter: I hold the tool in my off hand and the leg in my dominant hand. And I keep my eye on the gap between the tool and the tenon as I turn the leg.

"I have cultivated my hysteria with joy and terror."

— Charles Baudelaire (1821-1867)

Grippy, not splitty. The wedge will be applied perpendicular to the grain of the top. If it were parallel, the top might split.

This grip lets you make small adjustments with each turn.

After you have made a few sawbenches or chairs you'll find it easy to create a finished tenon after only a rotation or two in the tenon cutter.

Again, if you are wearing out your wrists during this operation then you need to get your rough tenons closer to the finished size.

Assembly

With the tenon cut and mortise reamed you should show them to one another to make sure everything fits. You might need to do a little more reaming or a little more shaving to make the tenon seat.

A classic trick to train beginners in fitting tenons (especially handmade ones) is to color the mortise with pencil lead. Drive the tenon into the mortise. Pull it out. Use a card scraper to remove the lead-colored areas – those are the high spots. Then repeat until you have a good fit.

CHAPTER 4

Saw your own. Set your bevel gauge to 2° and mark down to a baseline. Flip the gauge over and mark down to the same point from the first mark. Keep flipping and marking.

Sawing practice. Wedges are a good way to warm up for dovetails. Half the wedges will fall out as you make these rip cuts. The remainder can be released by crosscutting the end off the board.

Once the tenon fits, you need to mark it so you put the wedge in the correct place. The wedge should be perpendicular to the annular rings of the tenon. Wood moves more along the annular rings than across them, so by pressing the wedge in this direction, it helps prevent the leg from shrinking and falling out in the dry months.

The second important detail is that the wedge should be applied perpendicular to the grain of the top. In other words, turn the wedge 90° to what you would do if you were trying to split the top like firewood.

If you happen to orient the wedge so it is parallel to the grain of the top, you might split the top when you drive the wedge.

If your tenons fit tight in their mortises, I recommend sawing a kerf in each tenon for its wedge that is about 1" deep before assembly. If the tenon is loose at the top, don't make a kerf. You can split the top of the tenon with a chisel after driving the leg home with glue.

So how should you make wedges? There are a few different methods – none is difficult. I make my wedges so they have a 4° included angle.

Band-saw wedges. This shop-made sled is angled at 2° to the blade. So by making a cut and flipping the stock to make a second cut, you make a wedge with a 4° included angle.

These slender wedges enter easily and wedge tightly.

First, and obvious I hope, is that the grain of the wedge should run from its fine tip to its blunt end.

To cut a wedge by hand, start with some stout wood – I like oak – that is 3/4" thick x 6" wide x 8" long. Set your bevel gauge to 2°. Mark a 2° line along the 1" length of the blank. Flip the gauge (or put it on the opposite end of the board) and mark a second 2° line that touches the point of your first line. Flip the gauge over and over to mark a long row of wedges. Saw them out using a dovetail saw and a bench vise.

If you have a band saw, you can do the same thing but without any layout. Begin with a blank of oak that is 3/4" thick x 6" wide x 1" long. Set your band saw's miter gauge to 2°. Saw one end of the blank. Roll the blank 180° forward. Make a second cut, which will create a wedge. Roll again and cut. Roll and cut.

You can make hundreds of wedges in less than an hour this way. So stock up when you can.

CHAPTER 4

Important marks. Number each tenon and mortise. Rotate the tenon so the annular rings of the leg's end grain are parallel to the top's grain. Then mark the tenon and top.

Assemble the Sawbench

First decide if you want to use glue. You can make your bench knockdown by skipping the glue and just using wedges. If you have tight-fitting joints, you can even skip the wedges.

If you are using glue, place the top of the sawbench face-down on the bench and support it from below with a couple scraps. Put each leg in its dry mortise and make a registration mark so you can position the leg so the annular rings and wedge are oriented properly. The marks will make the glue-up less stressful.

Paint glue on one tenon and its mortise. When applying glue I think of it as sugar glaze on a donut. You want a wet surface, but not runny, gloppy drips. Drive in the leg with a mallet. If you are using hide glue the leg should slip easily into position. If you are using yellow glue, the tenon might swell before you can get it in its mortise.

Either way, I recommend you whack the end of the leg with a mallet. Hard. When the leg stops moving, turn the top over to see if the tenon has filled its mortise. If not, hit the leg again and see if you can get the

Level the playing field. Level the top of the sawbench by sneaking wedges under the feet until the sawbench is level from the front and the side.

tenon to seat.

    Glue one leg at a time. After all four legs are in, turn the sawbench on its feet and get the wedges. Paint a wedge with glue and knock it into its kerf. If you didn't kerf the tenons, first split the tenon with a chisel driven by a mallet.

    Just like when seating the legs, stop tapping the wedges when they stop moving and they have deformed the tenon enough to fill its mortise. Hitting the wedges beyond that point is dangerous. You can split the wedge or, worse, crack the top.

    I like to wipe excess glue off each joint so I can see if the tenon and its wedge are tight. Then I leave the sawbench alone for a few hours so the glue can cure.

    To level each joint, I usually saw the tenon and wedge with a flush-cut saw. Then I clean up the entire top with a sharp plane. Unlike a chair, this is easy work because the top is flat, not saddled.

CHAPTER 4

This high. The length of the tape indicates the final height of the sawbench. The combination square below records the amount of wood that needs to be removed from the legs.

Mark around. This block-and-pencil method simultaneously levels the sawbench and marks the final length of each leg.

Leveling the Feet

Like many things in building chairs and staked furniture, leveling the feet seems difficult and mysterious until you do it once. After that it's so obvious you wonder why you didn't think of it.

There are multiple ways to do it, and several of them are covered in this book. You can choose the method that suits the project and the tools you own, and the one that makes sense to your head. So you'll see different variations on this procedure throughout the book. Most times, I use this method because it works for all projects – tables, chairs, stools and so on. And it's the first technique I learned, so I'm fond of it.

To level the feet and simultaneously cut them to their finished length, you need the following:

1. A spirit level
2. Small wedges and blocks of wood to prop up the feet
3. A level worksurface, such as a table or workbench
4. A tape measure
5. A mechanical pencil
6. A combination square
7. A crosscut saw

Go to your level worksurface, place the sawbench on it and level the top of the sawbench by wedging the four feet. Now decide how tall you want your sawbench – the typical measurement is from the floor to the bottom of your kneecap. For this example, let's say it's 20".

Lock your tape measure at that setting (20" in this example). Set the body of the tape measure on the top of the sawbench and let the tape dangle straight down. Set your combination square on your level surface to measure the distance between the worksurface and the tab of the measuring tape.

Write down that measurement. Let's say it's 3". Now measure the thickness of your mechanical pencil's body and divide that in half. My pencil is 3/8" thick, so one-half of that is 3/16".

With those numbers you can make a block of wood that serves as a platform for your pencil that will allow you to mark the final length of your legs. First, a tiny bit of easy math. Take your measurement from your combination square (3") and subtract half the thickness of your pencil (3/16") to get the height of your platform (2-13/16").

Cut a piece of scrap that length to make your platform. Place the platform on your worksurface and lay your mechanical pencil on top. Tape it on top of the platform if you like.

Now you can use this tool to draw a line all the way around the four legs. These lines represent a new imaginary floor that is perfectly level. Crosscut your four legs to finished length.

This procedure usually gets you close to perfect, if not bang-on. Before I try to correct any errors I take a rasp and chamfer the feet – a 1/8" x 1/8" chamfer is good. About half the time this chamfer removes the offending material. If chamfering doesn't fix the problem, it prepares your feet for the next step and prevents them from splintering.

This next trick I learned from chairmaker Peter Galbert. Place a block plane or bench plane (set for a fine cut) upside down in a bench vise so the sole of the handplane is coplanar to the workbench top.

Place your sawbench on your level surface and determine which of

"Furniture which is strictly useful, should be of good quality; strength and durability being generally the chief points to be regarded... it is therefore little affected by fashion, whereas the style of drawing room furniture is almost as changeable as fashion in female dress."

— Mrs. William Parkes
"Domestic Duties"
(London, 1825)

CHAPTER 4

Foot protection. Chamfer the feet with a rasp or plane. This will protect the legs from splintering when they are dragged across the floor.

Fine-tune the feet. Clamp a block plane in a bench vise so its sole is coplanar to the benchtop. Pull one of the long legs across the cutter.

the two legs stay in contact with the worksurface when it rocks back and forth. Mark those two legs. Run those feet over the mouth of the handplane a few times. Then check your work on the level worksurface.

Repeat until the sawbench sits level and does not rock.

Ease all the edges of your sawbench with a block plane or fine sandpaper.

Most sawbenches are left unfinished – until they are used beneath a project during finishing, that is. If you really want to add a finish to the sawbench, I'd recommend paint, boiled linseed oil or some sort of wipe-on varnish. You can make your own wipe-on finish by mixing equal parts varnish, mineral spirits and boiled linseed oil.

While this chapter describes making one sawbench, that's like teaching you how to make one sock or one shoe. You need two sawbenches to saw your stock with handsaws. So build them in pairs. Or make one, learn from your mistakes and make a second one that's better.

The first leg vise. One knee presses the work down. The other restrains the work from rotating.

Ripping. This is an effective way to rip, but it does make my back sore.

CHAPTER 4

Sidebar: Sawbenches in the Shop

Once you own a pair of sawbenches you will wonder how you worked without them. Even if you don't do much work with handsaws, sawbenches are handy platforms for projects in progress, stacking parts and sitting on while you work.

But most people use them for handsaw work. Here are some tips on sawing with them.

If your sawbenches are different heights (even slightly) then work on the tall one and use the shorter one to support your work. If you work on the shorter one, your saw will constantly get pinched in its kerf.

When crosscutting on a sawbench, your legs are the clamps. Bend your off leg and rest it on top of the work on the sawbench. Pull your dominant leg up to contact the work (if possible) so the work presses against your leg.

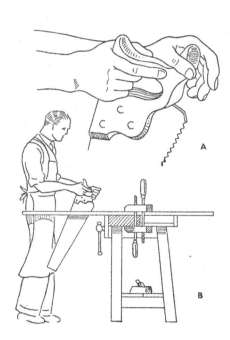

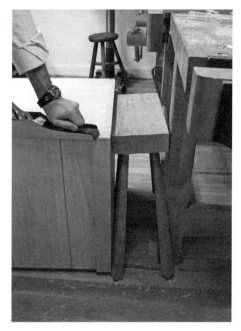

Overhand rip. I prefer to rip at the bench with the work secured like this or with it parallel to the benchtop – with the waste hanging off the front edge.

A good stand-off. Here my sawbench allows me to plane a carcase component without the plane ramming into the workbench.

Now you can saw the piece and it will remain stable. Your off leg supplies the downward pressure. Your dominant leg prevents the work from sliding laterally as you saw toward yourself.

I'm not a fan of ripping on sawbenches. I prefer to rip at the bench. If you do need to make long rips on the sawbench, I find it best to have three sawbenches: one to work on that is between a second that is infeed support and a third that is outfeed support.

One style of French ripping has the worker sitting on the work on the sawbench. Note that the saw's teeth are pointed away from the operator.

I use my sawbenches for many other operations. One of my favorites: I place an assembled carcase on two sawbenches and brace the carcase against the workbench. I can then easily plane the carcase to level its dovetail joints or whatever is sticking up. Or, if that doesn't quite work, the sawbench can be a spacer between the carcase and the bench.

Sidebar: Charles H. Hayward on Tapered Octagonal Legs

A minor problem that has to be faced sometimes is that of making tapered legs of octagonal section. There are two ways of doing it. One is to work the taper in the square first and follow by taking off the corners to form the octagon, and this is probably the better. The other is to plane the octagon shape first, and taper afterwards.

Square tapering first: Fig. 1. Having planed the wood square and cut off the ends true, the octagonal shapes are marked at the ends. At the top diagonals are drawn and a circle scratched in with dividers using the intersection as centre. Tangents at 45° are put in as shown at (A), Fig. 1.

At the bottom end the extent of the taper is gauged in all round, and diagonals drawn. A circle is again drawn the size of which is bounded by the gauge lines. Tangents are again drawn at where the diagonals cut the circle.

Square tapering follows, and it is a help if the bottom gauge lines are

STAKED SAWBENCH

NO.	PART	SIZES (INCHES)		
		T	W	L
1	Top	2-1/2	7-1/4	17
4	Legs	1-3/4	1-3/4	24

CHAPTER 4

Fig. 1. Square tapering. Various stages in the square tapering method.

Fig. 2. Octagonal tapering. Using this method the octagon is planed before tapering.

returned lightly on the surfaces as a guide. It is advisable to taper the opposite side first. The appearance of the work at this stage is shown at (B), where it will be seen that the ends of the tangents are marked on the surface. This enables the lines of the octagon to be drawn in if need be with pencil and straightedge. Some may feel this to be unnecessary since it is only a matter now of planing down to the lines at both ends, using a panel or trying plane. Any disparity in the width of the faces is obvious when the planing is completed and is corrected by a shaving where necessary. However, in a long leg it may be desirable to draw in guide lines.

Alternative method. In Fig. 2 is the second method of planing the octagonal shape first. Having planed the wood square the octagonal section is marked out on both ends. At the thin end the smaller octagonal outline is marked in the way already described. This is shown at (A), Fig. 2. Those who find it a help can draw in parallel pencil lines as at (A) to enable the octagonal shape to be planed (B).

It is now a case of planing the taper on each facet down to the lines marked at the end. This method is more suitable for short legs since one can rely more on the length of the plane to make each side straight, planing ceasing when the surface is down to the line.

— *Charles Hayward, from* The Woodworker, *October 1966*

EXTRUDE THIS
CHAPTER 5

More interesting than robotic flatness.

There is a three-step process for how people – woodworkers or not – approach a typical table.

1. They run their hands over the top to feel how smooth the finish is.
2. They run their fingers on the underside of the tabletop, right at the front, to see if it is also smooth.
3. If there is a drawer, they pull it out to see if it opens smoothly, and to look for dovetails – the mark of quality mid-priced factory furniture.

What annoys me about this ritual – and I've witnessed it 100 times – is not the people who look for dovetails. Heck, I want dovetails, too. Instead, what bugs the bejebus out of me is how people are looking for plastic textures and plastic drawer motion in a piece of handmade wooden furniture.

We have been ruined by plastic and its inhumane smoothness. I've watched people on a train rub their smartphones like they were rosary beads or worry stones. I've seen people pull drawers out of a dresser and feel the underside.

The message is that "smooth" equals "quality."

That is so wrong.

I refuse to equate quality with smoothness in a universal manner. The "show surfaces" of a piece should be smooth, though they don't have to feel like a piece of melamine or Corian. Subtle ripples left by a smoothing plane are far more interesting than robotic flatness.

Secondary surfaces that can be touched – think the underside of a tabletop, the insides of drawers or the underside of shelves – can have a different and entirely wonderful texture.

When I dress these surfaces, I flatten them by traversing them with my jack plane, which has a significantly curved iron (an 8" to 10" radius, if you must know). This iron leaves scallops – what were called "dawks" in the 17th century – that are as interesting as a honeycomb and as delightful to touch as handmade paper.

That is what old furniture – real handmade furniture – feels like. I refuse to call it "sloppy" or "indifferent." It's correct and it adds to the experience of the curious observer.

But what about the surfaces that will almost never be touched? Historically, these surfaces were left with an even rougher texture than dawks left by a builder's handplane. I've seen cabinet backs that had ugly reciprocating-saw marks left from the mill – even bark. To be honest, parts with saw marks and bark look to me more like firewood than furniture.

What should we do with these surfaces?

Here's my approach: When these parts come out of a modern machine, they are covered in marks left from the jointer and the thickness planer. The boards are usually free of tear-out, bark and the nastiness you'll see on the backs of historical pieces.

Should I rough these up with an adze and hatchet to imitate the look of the old pieces? Or perhaps just leave the machine marks?

Personally, I find machine marks ugly in all cases. I don't ever want to see them. So I remove them with my jack plane or a coarsely set jointer plane. The result is that all the surfaces are touched with a plane of some sort – jack, jointer or smooth.

Those, I have decided, are the three textures I want to leave behind.

And none feel like my iPhone.

> "1. Never encourage the manufacture of any article not strictly necessary, in the production of which Invention has no share.
>
> 2. Never demand exact finish for its own sake, but only for a practical or noble end.
>
> 3. Never encourage copying or imitation of any kind, except for the preserving of great works."
>
> — *John Ruskin, "The Stones of Venice" (1854)*

CHAPTER 5

Typical insides. This is what high-style furniture looks like on the inside. Unfinished. Tear-out. Knots. This is a late 18th-century North Carolina piece.

KINDA CREEPIE
CHAPTER 6

Creepy: One more leg than the typical Irish version.

It turns out that the simplest project in this book – a low stool – was the most difficult to design.

My search for a good stool design began when I read an ethnographic study of Ireland that discussed the "creepie" – usually a low, three-legged stool that allowed the sitter to "creep" toward the fire. It had three legs to give it sound footing on uneven floors. And it was low – very low – to keep the sitter's head below the cloud of smoke that filled the home's rafters.

So when I made my first and rough outline of this book, the creepie was one of its most important projects. And during the last six or seven years I've made several stabs at designing a creepie that was good enough to publish.

After 20 or so stabs, I came to a startling conclusion. First, ouch. Twenty stabs hurts. Also, designing a creepie is folly. These rude stools aren't supposed to be "designed."

They are three legs and a plank – parts that somehow seem like they belong together. The drilling angles are what they are (e.g. irregular). It's a spontaneous form – not something you can define with CAD or a drafting table.

If you are after a true creepie, put down this book and head out to the woods with a saw and a hatchet. Get a plank that is big enough for your butt. Get three sticks that look like legs. Join them. And *fin*.

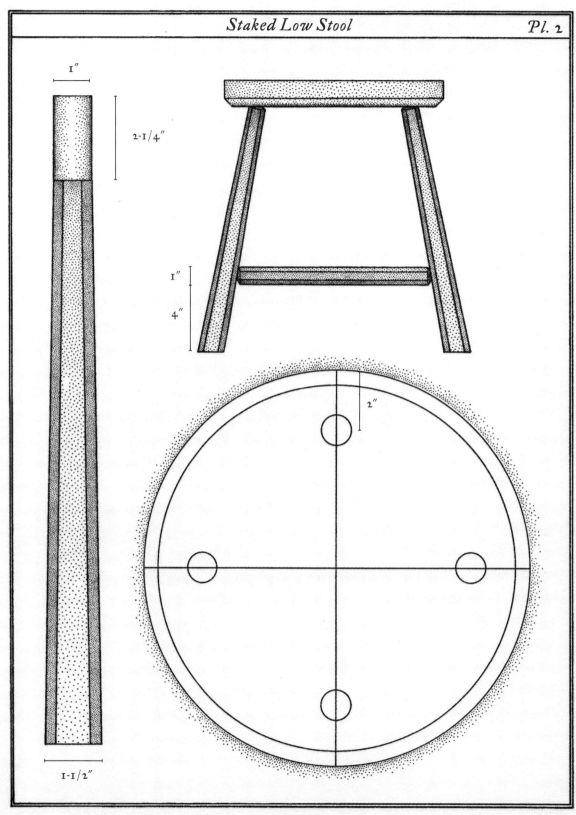

CHAPTER 6

An organic creep. Real creepies (such as this) have a casualness about them that cannot (or should not) be replicated with plans and precise measurements.

For the rest of us, here's a simple stool design that represents a lot of false starts, research and prototyping. It's not perfect, but it is a nice, stout stool. The stool is based on 18th-century low stools from American homes. This stool is also an excellent introduction into building the seat and undercarriage of a full-blown chair.

This stool has a pine seat and hardwood legs – ash in this case. The seat is 13" in diameter and the legs hold the seat about 16" off the ground – a good height for a low stool. The H-stretcher is a bit of overkill. But I think you should include it. It will teach you how to add stretchers to any of the chairs in this book – or from other people's books. So let's go.

Around & around. Here I'm marking out the diameter of the seat. Note the two holes in the corners of the blank. These are test mortises that will allow me to test the fit of the tenons on the legs. Waste not, blah blah, blah.

Make the Seat

The seat is a softwood that is about 1-1/2" to 1-5/8" thick. You can glue up the seat from two bits of wood (that's what I did) and put the seam in the dead center of the seat. Keep the leg joints away from this seam; you don't want the legs levering the seat apart. (Yes, a long-grain-to-long-grain joint is stronger than the wood itself in a perfect world. But that is not where we live.)

With the seat blank glued up, use a compass or trammel points to lay out the 13"-diameter seat.

Cut the seat to shape. Then cut a 1/2" x 1/2" bevel on its underside. This bevel lightens the look (and the weight) of the stool. You can do this on the band saw or do it with a block plane or spokeshave.

Now you can mark out the location of the joints. Here's the easy way. On the underside of the seat, draw a line through the centerpoint of the circle. Make this line parallel or perpendicular to the glue seam in the

CHAPTER 6

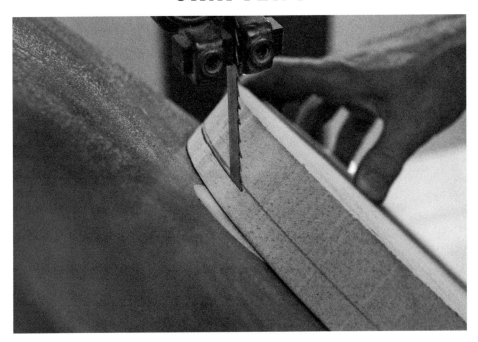

Around again. After cutting the seat round, tilt the saw's table to 45° to cut the bevel on the underside of the seat. Mark the 1/2" bevel on the seat's edge and follow that with your saw's blade.

"I've heard that all my life, a chairmaker never has a thing to set on."

— Chester Cornett as quoted in "Craftsman of the Cumberlands" (University of Kentucky Press) by Michael Owen Jones

seat (if you have a seam).

Place a protractor on your pencil line and mark the seat at 45° on both the left and right sides of 90°. Connect the marks with the centerpoint and you will have a perfect "X" on the underside.

Now take a ruler and mark out the location of the four leg mortises 1-1/2" in from the edge of the seat's bevel. (It's all shown in the photo on the next page if you look closely.)

Make the Legs

The legs are 1-1/2" x 1-1/2" x 17" and are made from a dead-straight hardwood such as oak, maple, ash or hickory. Knock off the edges until the legs are octagons. Then taper the legs so they taper to 1" at the top.

For this project, I decided to use cylindrical tenons. While I prefer

Good layout. There are 100 ways to do this. Place the protractor on your line and mark the seat at 45° on both sides of the protractor. Connect these marks to the centerpoint. And done. Perfect.

tapered tenons, cylindrical tenons are far more common in the historical record and are easier to make, especially if you own a lathe.

The tenons for this stool are 1" in diameter and 2-1/4" long. Turning them on the lathe is straightforward. If you want your tenons to be dead-on accurate, I recommend you purchase a bedan tool with a sizing attachment. A bedan tool is basically a wide parting tool with its sides relieved (like a traditional mortise chisel) to allow it to maneuver in the cut without binding. The sizing tool is an attachment that clamps to the tool and allows you to set the diameter of the cut.

To use the bedan tool and sizing attachment, first drill a test mortise and gauge the exact diameter of the bit that will drill your mortises. Set a dial caliper to that measurement (lock it) and use the caliper to set the bedan tool and its sizing attachment.

CHAPTER 6

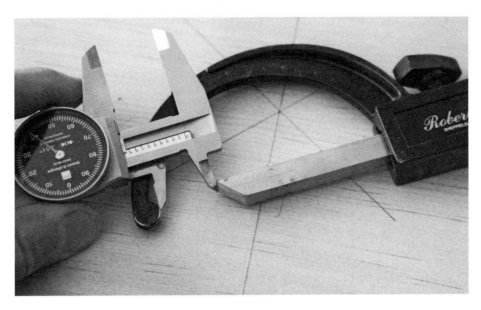

How this works. The bedan tool's sizing attachment is set to .940" – the diameter of the bit for the leg mortises. Slide the sizing tool toward the cutting edge until it matches this measurement. Then lock the position of the sizing attachment and make a test tenon. Really. Test tenon. Don't ignore me.

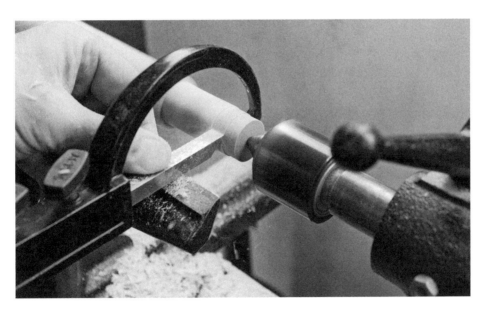

Perfect tenons. The sizing tool lets you cut tenons within .001". The tooling works just like any standard parting tool.

Test each tenon. After I cut each tenon, I check it in the test mortise (made with scraps from the seat). This is a backstop because I don't trust my bedan sizing tool, though it has yet to let me down.

Bore the Mortises

The leg mortises are bored at an 21° resultant angle. The sightline is 0° and runs directly into the centerpoint of the seat. Set a sliding bevel to 21° and tape it to the sightline. Clamp a backing board below the seat to reduce (but probably not eliminate) any splintering.

With this stool, I'm using a 24 mm bit from WoodOwl that is supposed to leave a clean exit hole without splintering. It does a pretty good job, though no bit is perfect (hence my backing board). These particular bits work best in an electric drill.

Drill the four mortises. Then put the legs into their mortises and have a gander at how accurate you were.

Rotate the legs in their mortises and orient them so their attractive surfaces face out. Then meaningfully mark the legs and the seat so you can get the legs back into this ideal arrangement.

Now it's time to bore the mortises for the side stretchers. These are positioned about 4" to 4-1/2" up from the floor. Here's how to mark

CHAPTER 6

The tape helps. The vibrations from boring can make your sliding bevel move. And even a little bit of movement makes a big difference in the leg angles. So spring for the tape.

them out. First, level the stool like you are preparing to cut the legs to length. Shim the feet until the seat is level all around. Then cut a 4x4 block of wood to 4-1/2" long and place it on the bench. Fetch the half-pencil (it's a pencil planed to half its thickness). Mark the location of the mortises for the side stretchers on the legs.

To bore the mortises, flip the chair upside down so the seat is on the benchtop. Place a couple sticks between the seat and benchtop to let the tenons poke through the seat. Then take an awl and mark the centerpoint of each mortise on each leg. I do this by eye. Measuring always seems to make it worse.

Chuck a 5/8" Forstner bit into a cordless drill. I drill the 7/8"-deep mortises in the legs entirely freehand, using the seat and the marks on the legs as a guide. Rotate the leg in its mortise so you can get the drill and the bit in position in line with the leg. The drill and bit should be aligned with the mortise on the opposite leg. The photo shows how this works.

Right about here. Putting the stretchers at this height makes the stool look like a chair that has been shrunk just a bit (which is a pretty accurate assessment of the design).

CHAPTER 6

On the tip of disaster. After you do this a few times, you'll gladly bore these mortises without guidance from others. Until you get this confidence, have a spotter tell you if you need to raise or lower the drill to keep the bit in line with both mortise locations.

Tiny test tenons. These thin offcuts determine the final length of the stretcher. Pinch them together and mark across the offcuts. Remove the pieces and reassemble them to determine the final stretcher length.

Stretchers. The side stretchers are installed. And the medial stretcher is laid on top. Now we're ready to drill the mortises for the medial stretcher.

Boring again. These mortises are only 5/8" deep. Put some fresh tape on your bit before boring these joints. This is not where you want to make a fatal error.

CHAPTER 6

If you lack confidence because this is your first rodeo, have a spotter give you some directions. They should be able to tell you if your drill bit is in line with both mortise locations in the legs. Drill the blind mortises, stopping before the bit explodes out the backside.

Make the Stretchers

The stretchers are 1" x 1" material that has been planed octagonal. After preparing the overlong stock for the stretchers, you need to determine how long they should be for your stool. To do this, fetch two skinny scraps. Pinch them together and press the ends into the bottoms of the mortises. Make a pencil mark across the two scraps. Remove them from the mortises. Reassemble them with the marks aligned. Measure the overall length, and that's the finished length of the stretcher.

Do this for both stretchers. Mine were slightly different lengths. If you are cutting the tenons on the lathe, then add 2" to the calculated length to give you some room to work without running your tools into the headstock and tailstock of the machine. (I wrote this sentence to remind myself to do this next time.)

Cut the 5/8"-diameter tenons on the side stretchers using the same techniques outlined for the legs. Yup to the bedan tool and the sizing attachment. After turning the tenons, saw the stretchers to their final length and install them in their mortises.

The medial stretcher is easy. Mark the centerpoint on each side stretcher. Use the same 5/8" Forstner bit to drill a 5/8"-deep mortise in each side stretcher. Once again, I drill these freehand. Keep the bit 90° to the stretcher and parallel to one of the facets of the octagonal stretcher.

You know what to do next. Get the skinny scraps and use them to determine the finished length of the medial stretcher. Cut the stretcher 2" overlong. Turn the tenons on the ends with the bedan tool. Cut the medial stretcher to finished size and fit everything. If the stool doesn't explode, you are ready to glue it up.

Assembly

Before you disassemble the dry-fit stool, mark where the wedges should go in the legs' tenons. I use a Sharpie for this to avoid confusion. Disassemble all the parts and mark them up so you can assemble them in the same orientation with glue in the equation.

The great leveler. This inexpensive saw made its way into our shop via an unknown path. I didn't purchase it. No one sent it to me. It just was there one day. So we stoned off the set of its teeth and use it as a huge (and fast) flush-cutting saw. If you are visited by the saw fairy (as I was) this is a good thing to do.

Kerf the legs to receive wedges. Use a band saw or a handsaw for this. You want the kerf to be of significant thickness. Make some 1"-wide wedges for the legs.

Right before assembly, clean up all the tool marks left on the legs, stretchers and seat with planes and spokeshaves. This is quick work with sharp tools.

Here is the sequence for assembly. Learn this and you'll be ready for a full-on chair in your future.

Glue the medial stretcher to the side stretchers. Twist the parts until the assembly sits flat.

Put glue in the mortises in the legs. Wipe off any excess and put the stretchers' tenons into the legs in the mortises. This will be an ungainly thing, like a baby goat. Rotate the legs until the assembly is stable. Set it on the bench.

CHAPTER 6

Paint the interior of the mortises in the seat with glue. Do not skimp or get in a hurry.

Take a deep breath.

Navigate the legs into their mortises. This might require some grabbing and bending. That's OK as long as the seat doesn't split. The goal is to get the tip of each tenon into its mortise.

Tap the legs down, working around the stool's four legs until the legs are seated. Small taps are better than big ones.

Flip the assembled stool over. Paint the wedges with glue and drive them in with a hammer.

Let the glue dry overnight. The next morning, saw the tenons flush to the seat. There are (at least) 50 ways to level your tenons. When your seat is flat and not saddled, the fastest way is with a Japanese ryoba saw. We took a hardware-store saw and stoned the sides of its teeth with a diamond plate to remove the set of the teeth. It now barely scratches the seat in use.

After sawing off the tenons, plane the seat to remove any toolmarks.

Level the Feet

As shown in other sections of this book, there are lots of ways to level the feet. Picking one method depends on how your head works. Here's how I did it for this stool. I first leveled the seat using wedges underneath the four legs.

Then I determined the final seat height (16") and made a block of wood to guide a pencil. The height of the block represented the amount of leg I needed to saw off to achieve the final seat height. In this case, the

STAKED LOW STOOL

NO.	PART	SIZES (INCHES)		
		T	W	L
1	Seat	1-1/2	13 dia.	
4	Legs*	1-1/2	1-1/2	18
2	Side stretchers*	1	1	14
1	Medial stretcher*	1	1	14

* Parts are oversized for fitting

The half-pencil and a block of wood helps you mark out the correct length of the legs.

block was about 1" high. I placed this block on the benchtop and used a half-pencil.

Then I sawed off the legs to their finished lengths. I then chamfered the feet to prevent the feet from splintering out when the stool is dragged across a floor.

And then you are done with construction. Finishing these stools can be as simple as a coat of linseed oil and wax. Or you can dive into milk paint, soap finishes or the Wild World of Wiping Varnishes. Do your best work – you don't want to be accused of polishing a turd. (And you thought you'd get away without a single stool joke.)

STAKED HIGH STOOL

CHAPTER 7

They cost $8 to make. Wait, am I a liar? No.

High stools – 22" to 30" off the floor – were uncommon in the United States until we repealed Prohibition in 1933. Pre-Prohibition saloons eschewed barstools – you just stood at the bar and did your drinking like you were in an episode of "Gunsmoke."

After the repeal of Prohibition, state governments tried to make the now-legal saloons less saloon-like. And requiring barstools was one of their tactics.

Somehow, I became enamored with barstools as a kid in the 1970s. Many of my friends had modern homes with high countertops and barstools. Sitting at these high countertops made me feel bigger and somehow more dangerous. Like Chip Paris might break a Coke bottle on the Formica bar and try to stab me because I was hogging the aerosol margarine.

Stab wounds notwithstanding, I've always had a soft spot for high stools such as these. Because of their height, you can do dramatic things with the rake and splay of the legs and the position of the stretchers. And because of the expansive buttocks of the American public, you have a wide array of things you can do with the seat, too.

Before we build one, let's talk about their design in general.

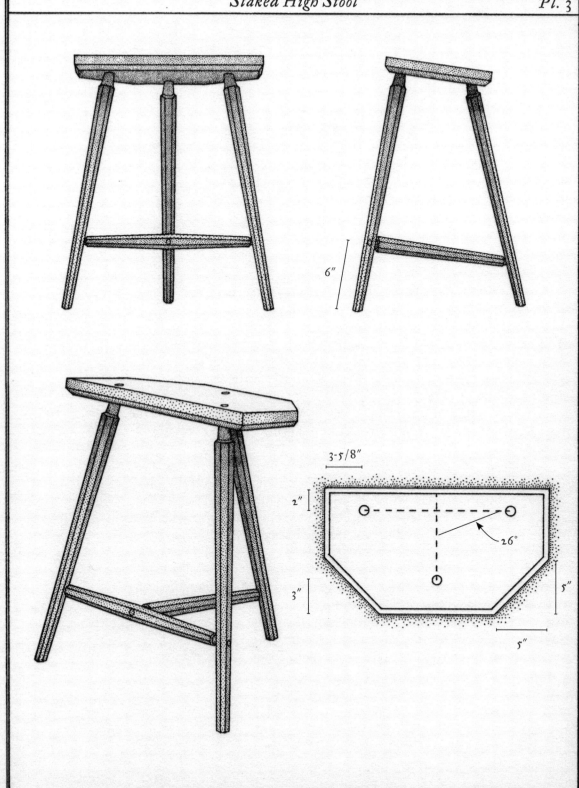

CHAPTER 7

Stools by the Numbers

Unlike chairs, barstools can be at a wide variety of heights – I've climbed into 36"-high stools and ones that were 12" lower. How can this crazy variance in height possibly work? By the creation of an artificial floor. Good, solid stools have stretchers (or a place to put your feet) that are located about 17" below the seat. This stretcher or footrest prevents your legs from dangling down and depriving your feet of blood.

You can raise this "floor" to bring the knees up a bit and make the stool ideal for supporting a guitar, for example. Raise the artificial floor too high, however, and your knees will ram into a typical bar.

The second thing to consider is the depth and width of the seat. If you wish to torture the sitter, make it small – like a 12"-diameter circle. People will not linger on your stools, and a new crop of drunks will churn through the bar within the hour.

I'm not that cruel. This stool is 11" deep x 20" wide. The shallow seat depth keeps your thighs from becoming petrified by cutting off the blood to your legs. The generous width is for a couple reasons. One, as a buttless man, I envy the larger cabooses of the world. Two, the additional width allows you grab the seat, adjust your position and jump off.

Finally, a bit on the pitch of the seat. Many stools have seats that are parallel to the floor. This is fine. You can even tilt it forward a bit if you like the look. I pitch mine back a wee bit because it looks better to my eye and doesn't seem to hurt the comfort of the stool.

But I encourage you to experiment with these stools. It's easy to do because they cost about $8 to make and you can knock out one in a day. Wait, am I a liar? No.

Raw Materials

I use Southern yellow pine to make these stools. I can fabricate two stools from a clear 8'-long 2x12. These 2x12s cost about $10 each at the home center. Add some glue, wedges and finish and you get to the hefty $8 price tag.

Note: Don't have Southern yellow pine in your area? I offer two suggestions. One: Use whatever construction lumber is available – hemlock, hem-fir, fir, Scots pine or the like. Ask for the stuff they use for joists or rafters in house construction. Two: Move your household. Cheap yellow pine is the best.

To the line. Tapering legs with a sharp jack plane is simple. Work to the lines marked on the feet and try to keep the facets consistent around the leg.

Processing the Stock

Rip the legs and stretchers from the straightest material you can find. If you are using dimensional stock, you'll probably end up with 1-3/8"-square stock. After ripping the legs and stretchers to size, use your band saw, table saw or jack plane to make these parts octagonal.

Then taper the legs. The top of the legs should be 1-3/8" x 1-3/8". The feet should be 1-1/8" x 1-1/8". I create this taper using a jack plane at the bench. First, I mark the desired shape on the feet. Then I use a cradle to hold the leg as I plane down to those lines.

The top of the legs needs to be a tapered tenon that is about 3-1/8" long and is 5/8" diameter at the tip. You can make this tenon in a variety of ways. I rough out the shape on the lathe (though a drawknife is equally effective). Then I use a 5/8" Veritas Tapered Tenon Cutter to finish the job. It's like sharpening a big pencil.

The seat can be any shape you or your bottom pleases. The seat shown here is six-sided. For this seat, begin with the size indicated in the cut-

CHAPTER 7

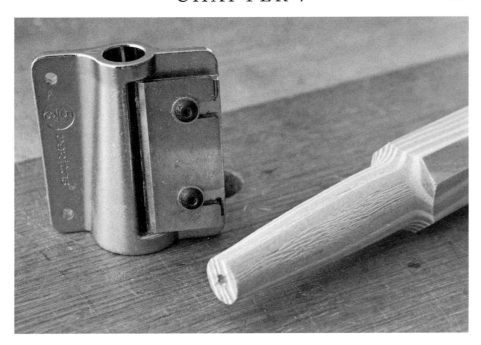

Pointed. The tenons are tapered using this commercial tenon cutter. You can make your own, but these tools are so reasonably priced that I don't see the point.

ting list. Then clip the rear corners at 45° starting 5" from each end of the seat. Then bevel the underside of the seat with a jack plane. The bevel is 1/2" x 1/2".

Lay Out & Cut the Mortises

Use the construction drawings to lay out the location of the three mortises on the underside of the seat. Then draw in the baseline, the centerline and the sightlines. Set your sliding bevel to 13° (the resultant angle) and tape the tool on a sightline for the front mortises. Drill a 5/8" hole through the seat. Keep the bit in line with the sightline and tilted to match the blade of your sliding bevel. Do the same operation for the other front mortise.

Then ream the front mortises with the matching Veritas tapered reamer (I use the company's large standard reamer). Check your angle by inserting a dowel into the joint that you have pointed with the tapered

Quick joinery. Tapered mortises and tenons are not tricky to make as long as you have a reamer and tenon cutter that have matching included angles.

tenon cutter. Adjust your reaming if need be. After reaming both front mortises, work on the rear mortise.

Set the sliding bevel to 22°, your resultant angle for the rear leg. Tape the bevel down to the centerline (which is also your sightline in this case). Drill then ream the rear mortise.

Drive the legs into their mortises. Now is a good time to designate which leg goes where. Mark the legs so you can get them back into position. Now turn the stool over and mark where the wedges should go in the tops of the tapered tenons. Remember to orient the wedge so it is 90° to the grain of the seat so the wedge doesn't split the seat.

Remove the legs. Use a tenon saw to cut kerfs in the tops of the tenons for the wedges. Reassemble the stool.

Stretchers, the Easy Way

I avoid complex setups whenever possible. And I'll always choose learning a skill over a making a jig. In this case, I'm going to show you how to drill the joints for the stretchers without any angle calculations.

CHAPTER 7

109

Mark the mortise. Use an awl to prick the location where the centerpoint of your mortise should go. The rubber band here is merely to show you where the stretcher will go.

It requires a little confidence with a cordless drill, but most woodworkers pick up this skill in a flash because they already have a ton of experience with a cordless drill.

Before we get to the fun part (drilling), we need to make the stretchers. The stretchers are 6" up from the floor. Use a ruler or block of wood to mark the locations of the mortises on the three legs. Now measure the length of the front stretcher inside the two front legs, then add 1-3/4" at either end for the tenons that will pass through the legs. For example: If you have 16" between the legs, the final stretcher will be 19-1/2" long.

Cut your front stretcher to length and plane it to an octagon. Then turn the 5/8" x 1-3/4" tenons on the ends of the front stretcher. You can instead use a straight tenon cutter, but you'll need to taper the ends of the stretcher first for the tenon cutter to work.

After you finish the tenons, compress them just a bit with some non-scratch pliers (an alternative is to wrap tape around the jaws of your regular pliers to prevent the teeth from marring the wood).

Now comes the fun part. Get a 5/8" spade bit with a long shaft. These are available at any hardware store. Reduce its diameter by about .010"

Hot dogging. Keeping the drill level and in line isn't as hard as you might suspect. Note that I have rotated the leg a bit so the inner flat face of the leg faces me.

The backup plug. The 5/8" dowel prevents the spade bit from wrecking the mortise as it drills from the outside of the leg.

CHAPTER 7

A crutch. If you aren't confident in your drilling you can cut a block of wood to the exact height required to keep your drill level. This works as long as you can clamp the block firmly in place.

by filing or grinding its edges at the grinder. This will make an undersized mortise and a tighter joint in the end.

Drilling the mortises in the legs is straightforward. Rotate the leg a bit toward you so you can drill straight through the leg. Drill through the inside face of the leg. Keep the drill level and aligned with the mortise location in the other leg (you can have a friend sight you during this until you gain confidence). When the centerpoint of the spade pokes through the other side, stop drilling.

Now finish the hole from the outside face of the leg. To make this operation more accurate, place a 5/8" dowel into the mortise to prevent the spade bit from shattering its way into the mortise. (This is a method I learned from Welsh chairmaker Christopher Williams.)

Disassemble the stool and insert the stretcher into its mortises. You might need to compress the tenons a bit more. (Don't worry, they'll expand when the hot glue hits them.)

Mark the centerpoint of the front stretcher and drill the 5/8" mortise

The joint. Here's the through-tenon after drilling. Not bad for freehand work.

through the front stretcher using the same methods listed above.

Remove the front legs and front stretcher. Put the back leg in place. Drill its mortise with the 5/8" spade.

Now assemble the stool and measure the distance between the inside face of the back leg and the inside face of the front stretcher. Add 1-3/4" to both ends for the tenons. Cut the tenons. Compress them with your pliers. And assemble your stool.

Mark the ends of all the tenons for wedges. Then disassemble the stool and cut kerfs for the wedges in the ends of all the tenons.

Shape the Stretchers

You can leave the stretchers the full 1-3/8" thickness if you like. They look a little clunky, but they will be strong. I prefer to taper the stretchers. For the front stretcher I taper both ends, leaving the middle at full thickness. For the back stretcher I taper it from front to back. The front is full thickness and the back is tapered.

CHAPTER 7

Worth the work. The tapered stretchers look much better than straight ones. I've also turned them, which looks pretty good, too.

I do this with a jack plane and a cradle – the same one I used to taper the legs.

Assembly

I use liquid hide glue that I've heated up to make it easy to apply. Assemble the undercarriage first. Paint glue on the mortises and tenons and pull everything together. Then paint glue on the mortises and tenons for the seat.

Drive the legs into the seat with a heavy mallet (I prefer a small sledge here). Keep striking the leg until it stops moving. Pull the legs toward each other to ensure they are butted up against the tenon shoulders of the stretchers. Clean up the gluey mess with a wet toothbrush.

Now wedge all the joints with stout oak wedges. If the joints have closed up during assembly, use a 5/8" chisel to open them up and deform the top of the tenon. This will allow the wedge to get into the tenon. Paint glue on the wedges and knock them in with a hammer. Keep strik-

Wedged. Here you can see how the wedge is 90° to the grain of the stretcher. Had I oriented it parallel to the grain, the stretcher would have been a goner.

ing the wedges until they stop moving. The sound will also change when the wedges are seated.

Let the glue dry overnight. Then trim the tenons flush with a saw, chisel and plane.

Finishing

These stools look great with a wiping varnish (equal parts boiled linseed oil, satin varnish and paint thinner). Wipe on thin coats and stop when it looks good.

You also can use "shou sugi ban," a charred finish popular in Japanese architecture for making building materials fire- and bug-resistant. You char the wood with a propane torch, brush off the soot then apply a finish of linseed oil and beeswax.

If you are going to burn your stool, char the parts before assembly and protect the tenons with tape and the mortises with wet rags. Then, after assembly, touch up the unburned places with a handheld torch.

CHAPTER 7

Propane weed burners are cheap tools – about $35 to $50 is typical. They attach to a propane tank such as one that fuels your gas grill. And they work like a flamethrower. The wood doesn't stand a chance.

I rested my project parts on cinderblocks and blasted them with the propane-fueled flame. Keep a squirt bottle of water (and a fire extinguisher) on hand to douse any flare-ups.

After charring the parts, use a stiff-bristled brush to scour the wood. This removes the excess soot so it won't end up on your hands and clothes when you use the stool. Add any topcoat finish over the wood – I used Allbäck Linseed Oil Wax.

STAKED HIGH STOOL

NO.	PART	SIZES (INCHES)		
		T	W	L
1	Seat	1-3/8	11	20
3	Legs	1-3/8	1-3/8	25
1	Front stretcher	1-3/8	1-3/8	21
1	Rear stretcher	1-3/8	1-3/8	16

Photo by Narayan Nayar.

DRINKING TABLE
CHAPTER 8

More meat for your mortises.

Three-legged tables are a common sight in English pubs and in paintings from the Middle Ages. While most examples of drinking tables – sometimes called cricket tables – that I've inspected were made using square mortise-and-tenon joinery, the early ones were clearly staked.

The other curious thing about the artwork from the Middle Ages is that many times these tables are shown outdoors with trees in the background. That caused me to wonder: Did these tables break down so that the round top could be rolled to the party and assembled?

It would make some sense and there is precedent: Early trestle tables (they're later on in the book) broke down quickly into pieces to make them easy to move.

So this particular table knocks down. The legs are friction-fit into the mortises. The wood-on-wood friction, angled legs and gravity keep them from falling out when you pick up the assembled table to move it. But it's also a simple thing to twist each leg and pull it out.

And if three legs isn't enough, stay tuned for one with six legs.

How the Table Goes Together

There are two circular tops that are face-glued together – one that's 1" thick and one that's 1-3/8" thick but a smaller diameter. The smaller top thickens the areas around the joints to add meat around the tenon.

DRINKING TABLE

Photo by Narayan Nayar.

CHAPTER 8

One-board top. Though there are four boards in this glue-up, they all were cut from the same long plank to ensure the top will be consistent in color and grain.

The tenons and mortises for this project are not conical, simply because I couldn't find a reamer big enough for the 2"-diameter mortises. While I prefer a conical joint in all cases, I think these cylindrical joints will be fine because they are so big.

Like many staked pieces, the legs are tapered octagons. These legs taper smaller toward the tip of the foot. Other early pieces had the taper reversed – the foot starts thick at the floor and tapers up to the tenon.

Begin With the Thin Top

To make the top look its best, I recommend you try to get all the pieces for the tabletop cut from one long board. That strategy will ensure consistent color and grain, creating a 1" x 40"-diameter top that does not look jarring.

Joint the edges and glue up the top. When the glue is dry, get your

120 DRINKING TABLE

"Warning: If you are reading this then this warning is for you. Every word you read of this useless fine print is another second off your life. Don't you have other things to do? Is your life so empty that you honestly can't think of a better way to spend these moments? Or are you so impressed with authority that you give respect and credence to all that claim it? Do you read everything you're supposed to read? Do you think everything you're supposed to think? Buy what you're told to want? Get out of your apartment. Meet a member of the opposite sex. Stop the excessive shopping and masturbation. Quit your job. Start a fight. Prove you're alive. If you don't claim your humanity you will become a statistic. You have been warned."

— Tyler Durden, "Fight Club"

Three is not enough. Some early tables are shown with as many as six legs. This one, an adaptation of a Middle Ages painting, shows a typical monkey party gone bad.

CHAPTER 8

Shaved round. A sharp spokeshave makes short work of the sawblade marks. The standard shave with a flat bottom will work fine.

trammel points and set them to 20" – the radius of the top. Mark the radius, cut the top (I used a band saw) and clean it up with a spokeshave.

Flatten the top and the underside of the top using a jointer plane. Save the final finish planing of the tabletop's surface until right before assembly – parts can get beat up in the shop during construction.

Now the Thick Subtop

The subtop gives you more meat for your mortises. And because it is smaller in diameter than the top, the overall table won't look like an enormous poker chip with three toothpicks for legs.

The edge of the subtop is beveled. It's a simple detail, but it makes the whole table visually lighter and reflects the angle of the staked legs.

Just like the top, you'll need to glue up boards into a panel then cut them round. But unlike the top, the boards for the subtop don't have to

Drinking Table

Pl. 4

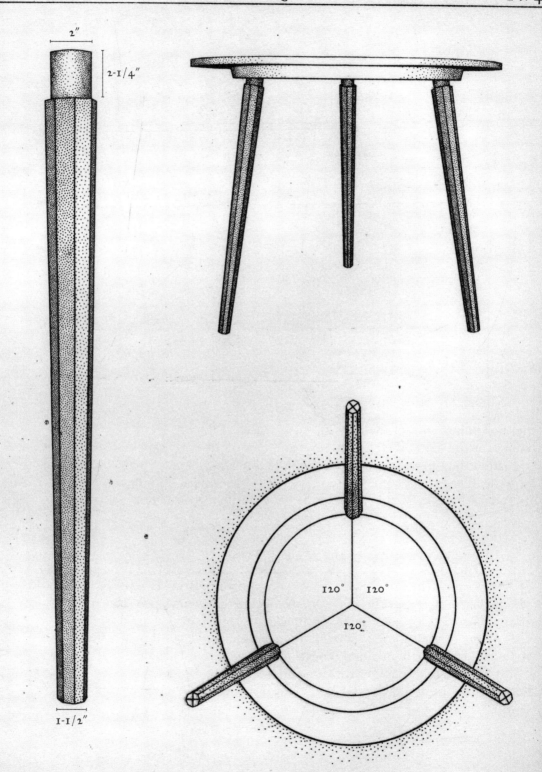

B. Morrow-Cribbs Inv. Del. et Sculp

CHAPTER 8

Set to bevel. Tilt the table to 14° and confirm the setting with a bevel square. The exact angle is unimportant, but a consistent bevel is.

match one another for grain or color because they're not highly visible.

The edge of the subtop is cut at a 14° bevel. I made the cut on a band saw by tilting the table 14°. You'll want to lay out the circle's shape on both faces of the subtop so you can work to both lines with a spokeshave to get a consistent bevel.

The layout is easy. Using trammels, scribe the finished diameter –

Scribe the circle for the joinery. With the trammels set to a 12-5/8" radius, scribe a line for the joinery all the way around the smaller circle on the subtop.

30-1/2" – on one face of the subtop. The radius is 15-1/4". Flip the subtop over and lay out a second circle that is 1-1/4" smaller in diameter. The radius of the second circle is 14-5/8". The difference in diameter between the two circles creates an edge that is 14°.

Now you can cut the bevel on the edge of the subtop by following the circumference of the larger circle with the sawblade of the band saw.

Clean up the sawn edge with a spokeshave, working to the lines left by the trammel points on both faces of the subtop.

Lay Out the Mortises

The mortises are cut on a drill press with a 2"-diameter Forstner bit. To make the parts a lot easier to handle by yourself, it's best to bore the mortises all the way through the subtop first. Then glue the subtop and top together. Finally, deepen the three mortises with the Forstner bit

CHAPTER 8

Walk the trammels. Select the location of one of the legs. Walk the trammels around the circle, making a prick at each point where the trammels intersect the circle. Select every other prick and you have your three joint locations.

in a drill. The mortises in the subtop will act like a doweling jig.

To lay out the locations of the mortises, fetch your trammel points and open your mind for a bit of geometry insertion. Set the trammels so they scribe a radius that is 2" smaller than the small diameter of the subtop (12-5/8" in my instance).

Do not change the setting of the trammels.

Now decide where one of the legs will go on this circle. It's fairly arbitrary, but I don't want a mortise to intersect a glue joint. Once you decide where the first leg will go, mark that position on the circle with an awl.

Now for the geometry lesson. We need to take our first point on the circle and lay out an equilateral triangle inside the circle to get the other two mortise locations. Lucky for us, the radius of a circle equals one-sixth its circumference.

Take your trammels and walk around the circumference of the circle, making a prick at six points on the circle and ending up where you start-

Create sightlines. Use a straightedge to join the center of the circle to the three mortise locations. These are your sightlines for boring the mortises.

ed. Circle every other prick on the circle and join the points. You have created an equilateral triangle and laid out the joinery for the table.

To complete the layout, use a straightedge to join the mortise locations with the centerpoint of your circle. These lines are the all-important sightlines for boring the mortises.

Bore the Mortises

Set the banjo drill press jig (see Chapter 4 – I told you not to skip it) so it slopes to 12° compared to the quill of the machine. Design note: I also made prototypes with 14° legs that looked really good. I settled on 12° because 12 matches my mental age.

Now line up the sightline on the subtop so it is – via eyeball accuracy – in line with both the spur of the 2"-diameter Forstner bit and the iron post of your drill press. Clamp the subtop to the banjo jig and bore the mortise all the way through the subtop.

CHAPTER 8

Boring perfection. The banjo jig makes this operation laughably easy. Stop boring when chips from the jig's table start coming out of the hole.

If you take it slow, you'll avoid the rim of the Forstner grabbing the rim of your mortise and ripping out a chunk.

Unclamp the subtop and repeat this process for the other mortises.

To finish up the subtop, plane away the layout lines and any scarring from the Forstner bit. I used a jack plane with an iron ground to a 10" radius. I planed with the grain, which created a nicely furrowed texture.

Scraps for stops. Clamp the scraps from cutting your top to your bench and use those as stops to restrain the subtop while planing it.

CHAPTER 8

Three cauls. Rough scraps that are cantilevered off the subtop are all you need to get the pressure where you want it. Clamp the ends of the cauls and you'll press the two pieces together just fine.

Join the Top & Subtop

The top and subtop are merely face-glued to each other. The only difficult part of this operation is getting clamp pressure in the right place – we're going to use flexible wooden cauls (a.k.a. scrap) to do the job.

The first order of business is to scribe the shape of the subtop on the underside of the top so you can position the subtop in the middle of top. Set your trammels to a 15-1/4" radius and scribe this circle.

Paint a thin layer of hide glue on the subtop and flip it over onto the underside of the top. Important note: You want the grain of the subtop and the top to be dead parallel. This will ensure the two pieces will expand and contract sympathetically without cracking up your glue joints.

Gluing the top and subtop together is easy with six clamps and three scraps that are about 36" long. These scraps act as cauls to press the subtop against the top. Array the scraps across the subtop and clamp the

Deeper for strength. To deepen the mortises into the top, insert the Forstner into the existing hole and run your drill up to full speed before pushing the bit into the top. Take it slow and the results will be crisp.

scraps down. You don't need massive amounts of pressure, just enough to keep the pieces together while the glue cures.

After the glue dries, deepen the mortises by chucking your Forstner bit in an electric drill and running it into the mortise in the subtop. The overall depth of the mortise should be about 2". Measure from the long surface of the joint – you'll know what I mean when you get there. Any deeper than that and you'll bore through the top.

Make Legs

The three legs for this table are made just like the octagonal legs for the previous projects, except that the tenon is a cylinder, not a cone.

The legs taper from 2-1/2" at the tenon shoulder to 1-1/2" at the floor. Cut each leg to a rough octagon then plane the eight faces so they taper to 1-1/2".

I cut the tenon on the lathe – it's 2" in diameter and 2-1/4" long. If you don't have a lathe, you can cut the tenon with a spokeshave and refine the cylinder with a scraper. Chamfer the top edge of each tenon to make it easier to insert it into its mortise.

Finish the tenons with #120-grit sandpaper. Here's how: Insert the tenon into the mortise. When it sticks, pull it out and use the sandpaper to remove the burnished high marks. Repeat until the tenon seats all the way and can be removed by judicious twisting.

Finish

As this table is mahogany, it demands a little color. I applied two coats of garnet shellac then rubbed on some black wax to fill the pores of the wood.

DRINKING TABLE

NO.	PART	T	W	L
			SIZES (INCHES)	
1	Top	1	40 dia.	
1	Subtop	1-3/8	30-1/2 dia.	
3	Legs	2-1/2	2-1/2	30

DRINKING TABLE

CHAPTER 8

A Different Drinking Table

Some of the early drinking tables I encountered had six (!) legs and a single thick top. And the legs were square and reverse-tapered: thick at the floor and thin at the tenon.

Paintings of these tables offer no instructions for how to use them, so we must be creative and make some (perhaps incorrect) assumptions. My following thoughts are guesses. I'll leave it to scholars of the Middle Ages to set the record straight from original Latin or Arabic sources.

Why six legs? While the table at left has six legs, other drinking tables are shown with anywhere between three and six legs. Six legs seem ungainly, but when you set the table on an uneven floor, at least three legs – sometimes four – find the ground, and the table is stable.

On soft ground, all six legs press into the soil, presenting a remarkably solid tabletop.

Can you sit at a six-legged table? Yes. Try sitting at the table with one of the wooden legs between your meat legs. Though I have yet to find a painting that shows this seating arrangement, it could provide advantages to those wishing to protect their reproductive organs during benders.

Is the table easy to move? With the legs fixed into the top, the table is awkward to move, especially for one person. I propose, with zero evidence, that these tables could have been knocked down. The legs and top might have been separate. One person rolled the top to the party's location. A second person carried the legs. When you arrived, you drove the legs in place with a mallet (or tankard) and flipped the table over.

I made one of these to see how it looked and worked.

Here are some specs:

The top is 2-1/2"-thick x 38"-diameter oak. In our area, it's easy to find 12/4 white oak (*Quercus alba*) that has been surfaced to 2-1/2" thick for less than $3 a board foot. This stock is used to make fireplace mantles. Tulip poplar (*Liriodendron tulipifera*) is also readily available in thicknesses up to 4". It's more expensive than the oak (yes, that's odd), but thick pieces look right and are actually easier to deal with in a shop with basic tools.

The six legs are red oak: 1-3/4" x 2-5/8" x 30". The legs taper to 1-1/4" square up at the tenon. The tenon is a tapered cone that begins at 1-1/16" in diameter and tapers to 5/8" over 3". The legs are laid out on the underside of the top in the same manner as the other drinking table. The only difference is that you have six legs instead of three.

"Given the teeming riches of the whole earth to play with, brought to us by the modern enterprise of science and commerce, we tend to leave neglected the possibilities of our own hands and brains. It is so easy not to use them when so much is done for us. But the more we develop our own powers of doing and creating, of training our hands and our minds, the more sturdily do we set our faces against being mere ciphers and not men.

"We may not have a success that can be measured in terms of money, but we shall find our own fulfillment in terms of living."

— The Woodworker

Check insurance. Clamp the key across the split and trace around it with a knife. Note the split is difficult to see here, but it crosses the key at its narrowest point.

The sightline is the line from the mortise location to the centerpoint of the top. The resultant angle is a mere 5°.

The mortises are created with a 5/8"-diameter auger bit and a tapered reamer. The tenons are finished with a tapered tenon cutter. You can wedge and glue the legs in place, or skip the adhesive and make the table knock down for travel.

As I finished up the top I decided to add a butterfly key to help keep a check in the top in place.

Sidebar: Stabilize a Split with a Wooden Key

Most repairs to furniture during the construction process are a drag because I am kicking myself for making an error in the first place. But that's not so when adding wooden keys to a slab tabletop.

Thick wood such as this oak tends to split. And left unchecked, the

CHAPTER 8

Room to chop. Bore out some waste to make the chopping easier. The holes also act as depth stops.

split can continue to open during the seasonal expansion and contraction cycle. The traditional fix is a wooden key that looks like two dovetails kissing. Or a butterfly. Or a unicorn sparring with its sacred mate.

While I am sure someone has written rules and regulations regarding wooden keys, I have yet to read and obey them. I make mine so they have the same slope as my dovetails, and they are thick enough to reinforce the slab.

How thick? I'm patching a split in some 10/4 oak in this example. My key is about 1/2" thick. Depending on how I feel, I might put a key on the underside as well.

Note that there are less traditional ways to keep a split in check. Try countertop connectors – sometimes called "dog bones" in the trade – or

Clean the floor. The bottom of the mortise is where the patch gets its strength. So get it mostly flat. I always leave a couple low spots for excess glue, however.

pocket-hole screws that span the split. These metallic fixes have the advantage of being adjustable. I know, I know; fetch your torch and pitchforks.

Saw out the key from a stout wood. I used a scrap of bog oak for this repair. Clean up the sawblade marks with a chisel and ensure all the key's edges are 90° to the faces.

Clamp the key across the work with the narrow neck right over the split. Then trace the shape of the key using a marking knife or a sharp pencil. Remove the key.

Root out the waste. I like to bore a couple holes with an auger to get the process started. Then I chop out the rest of the waste with a chisel. Stay away from the knife lines until the end. Resharpen your chisel and pare to the knife lines. This mortise took about 15 minutes to bore and chop.

Check the walls of the mortise with a small square. They should be 90° or slightly, slightly undercut. Clean up the bottom of the mortise

CHAPTER 8

Finished. As you can see, the fit isn't perfect. One knife line got a little rounded over. And a tiny speck of grain popped out. The slab can shift around when you insert the key. However, after some planing, some finish and a little black wax, it will look seamless.

with a router plane if your chiseling left it rough.

Then put some glue in the mortise and tap the key in. Plane it flush. It shouldn't require clamping (but clamp it if it does).

I try to keep the process simple. There are lots of variants on this procedure – you can bevel the edge of the key to create a cork effect, but you better practice that first before jumping in.

FURNITURE IN THE WATER

CHAPTER 9

There is no 'Book of Cletus.'

Up into my 30s, I wrote songs as much as I wrote newspaper or magazine stories, and I was always bewildered about where melody came from. How, after so many generations of births and deaths, could we still manufacture new melodies?

The answer is, of course, that we can't.

Growing up in Arkansas in the 1970s, it was impossible to escape traditional music. You'd hear it at every church picnic, at the gas station and while eating at the Irish pub/barbecue restaurant. It was even piped into the town elevator.

Fingerpicking was like the fluoride in the water. Banjos hummed like the mosquitos in your ear.

I didn't think much of it all until I encountered the alt.country band Uncle Tupelo in the 1990s. One of the bonus tracks on the CD "No Depression" was "John Hardy." And the first time I heard the song I instantly began singing all the words.

John Hardy was a desperate little man
He carried two guns every day
He shot a man down on the West Virginia line
They saw John Hardy getting away

It was the closest thing I've ever had to a repressed memory bubbling to the surface. I grabbed the CD case and saw the song was credited to Lead Belly. That was weird. It wasn't a Lead Belly song I'd ever heard. After some digging, I found the source of where I'd learned the song: the Carter Family.

Then, like every aspiring songwriter, I soon found that the Carter Family was the source code for an astonishing mountain of American rock, folk, pop, blues and bluegrass. That statement sounds like hyperbole, but it's not.

True story: While on tour with her husband, Johnny Cash, June Carter once demonstrated this deep truth by switching on the radio in their tour bus. About every third song, June began singing the Carter Family version over the version playing through the radio. Different lyrics. Different instrumentation. Same song.

This small songwriting revelation (which nearly every American songwriter has) turned out to be as important to my furniture making as it was to my love of music. And so, if you'll indulge me a bit, learning a little about Sara, Maybelle and A.P. Carter can help you understand vernacular furniture and how to design it.

Bristol, 1927

Many musical historians and musicians peg the beginning of country music to a series of recording sessions in Bristol, Tenn., in the summer of 1927. Ralph Peer of the Victor Talking Machine Co. toured through several Southern cities equipped with new recording technology and a desire to capture examples of "old time" or hillbilly music.

He attracted local artists with newspaper advertisements and the opportunity to get paid for their work. While in Bristol (a town that bleeds over into Virginia), he snared his biggest catch, the Carter Family. Led by A.P. Carter, the group was comprised of three people named Carter: A.P., who arranged the songs and occasionally sang; his wife, Sara, who played autoharp and had an enchanting and powerful voice; and Maybelle, who played guitar (plus other instruments), sang and was Sara's cousin.

The Carter Family recorded six songs with Peer over two days during that first recording session. The three were paid and they returned to their Virginia homes. After the royalty checks began coming in, A.P. sought to record more songs (the Carter Family eventually recorded more than 250 songs, according to the documentary "The Winding

Stream"). And this is where things get interesting.

The songs that the Carter Family brought to record were a combination of traditional tunes, original songs the three had written, plus songs that A.P. had "collected" and then adapted – changing the words, adding a beat here or there, tidying it up.

So that's why you'll see a song such as "John Hardy" attributed to three or four (or a dozen) people. These were songs that were transmitted from person to person and that changed based on who was singing them, when and where. The songs didn't belong to one person. They belonged to the whole culture.

These melodies are deeply embedded into the American psyche – especially among Southerners – and it can be shocking (and sometimes uncomfortable) to have the curtain pulled away.

Listen to the Carter Family song "Wayworn Traveler," sometimes titled "Palms of Victory." (You can find it on the contemporary album "Carter Family: Storms are on the Ocean.") The song is commonly regarded as a hymn attributed to a New York reverend from 1836.

Bob Dylan rewrote the song as "Paths of Victory" in the early 1960s. Then he rewrote it again as "The Times They Are a Changin'."

In my mind, there is nothing wrong or shameful about this process of evolution. Each artist adds or subtracts something from the original to suit the time or place. And the work rises or falls based on the talent of the writer or singer.

By the end of his life, A.P. Carter had traveled thousands of miles all over the South to collect the songs that he, Sara and Maybelle would then hone, record and perform. Their true genius was in acting as one of the most incredible funnels and filters of American song culture. (Also, Maybelle Carter happened to invent the concept of lead guitar with her "Carter scratch" style of playing. She was a pioneering badass.)

For me, this way of looking at traditional music has profound implications when applied to vernacular furniture.

The Vernacular Pattern

As I mentioned at the beginning of this book, the high furniture styles tend to be transmitted via pattern books – basically big catalogs of ornate or expensive works that are connected to a big name such as Chippendale, Hepplewhite, Stickley or Maloof. That's why we have schools of furniture that are connected to famous names. And, as a bonus, there's a book to consult that lays out the boundaries of the

"I try to keep in mind that if I dropped dead tomorrow, all of my acrylic workplace awards would be in the trash the next day, and my job would be posted in the paper before my obituary."

— *Bernie Klinder, a consultant for a large technology company,* The New York Times, *Jan. 26, 2019*

CHAPTER 9

style. Chippendale has its somewhat Chinese details and distinctive feet. Stickley has a particular joint and a particular material (quartersawn white oak). Maloof has a language of curves and joinery that is easily understood.

High-style music is similar. We have the works of Mozart, Bach, Brahms and the Beatles to endlessly parse and parlay. There is (usually) a definitive body of work. And it's fairly straightforward to say when a particular piece of work is either inside or outside of a particular style.

Vernacular music and furniture do not work that way. There is no "Book of Cletus" when it comes to backstools. No detailed drawings to tell us if a certain detail is proper or inadmissible. So the only thing we can do is study the furniture record, which mutates across time and state lines and is always incomplete. We'll never see it all.

But if you see enough of it, then the form's design elements become like a melody you've heard your entire life. You know what details and proportions create harmony. And what's a wrong note. If you sing it enough times you probably will change the pitch to suit your vocal range. Or change a curve to better suit your spokeshave and skills. And when you encounter a new version of the form that you've never seen before, it can cause you to shift your work again in response.

The boundaries of what's acceptable and what's not are softer and more nebulous. But they are there.

Again, I like to think of vernacular furniture design as a shared melody. If your work is appealing, then others will sing along. In their hands and on their lips, your melody will endure and change over time. If, on the other hand, your work fails to resonate with others, then it dies alone at the curb, never to be sung again.

What Does This Mean to a Designer?

If you want to build in vernacular styles, I think you need to explore the forms for yourself. Building pieces from this book or other books on vernacular furniture is a start. But it's like singing songs from a Pete Seeger songbook that you bought at the mall. That might be where it starts, but that's definitely not how it ends.

Like A.P. Carter, you need to get in your car and drive to the next town to see what is happening there. And then adapt what you find to your needs.

As I build these forms over and over they change. You might not notice it from one chair to another, but every piece is a little different.

Sometimes it's because the material demands it. Right now I'm building a series of four armchairs in white oak, and the seat material is thicker than usual. I could spend some extra time planing it down, or I could slightly increase the thickness of the legs to look harmonious with the seat. Or increase the bevel on the seat to look harmonious with thinner legs. Either change might push my next set of chairs in that direction.

John Brown, the famous Welsh chairmaker, noted this sort of evolution in his columns for *Good Woodworking* magazine. After making seats using thick material for years, he was once backed into a situation where he had to use some thinner stock for the seat. It became a turning point for his work, and his chairs became lighter from that day forward. But they still looked unquestionably like Welsh stick chairs.

The change might be due to a mistake. The rake and splay of the front legs of my chairs changed when one day I set my bevel gauge to the wrong resultant angle – a full 6° off. But the result was pleasing, so that's now the angle I use every day.

Other times, changes come because I've seen a beautiful old piece or a new piece by a fellow woodworker I admire. There might be something about it – a curve, an angle, an overall pose – that pushes my work in a different direction. I might not even realize I'm absorbing it at first.

And when I feel guilty for it, I again remember A.P. Carter. Collecting those songs preserved them from extinction and ensured their place in our nation's memory. Likewise, the only way to ensure vernacular furniture survives against the onslaught of manufactured flat-pack pieces is to build the stuff again and again. To allow it to change with the needs of the maker and the tools and materials at hand.

I also think it's healthy to reject dogma and allow techniques to change as well. Like when Dylan went electric at the Newport Folk Festival in 1965.

Vernacular stuff doesn't have to be built out of riven green wood (just like folk music doesn't require an acoustic guitar). It can be built out of what you have on hand. If that's riven green wood, use that. If it's poplar and oak from the home center, use that. The same goes for tools. Vernacular furniture generally requires a smaller tool kit than the high-style stuff, but almost anything can be in that kit. My first piece was built using a jigsaw, drill and block plane. Nothing more. Use what you got. Today I use a band saw, bench planes and lots of other tools. And the tool kit neither diminishes nor improves my work.

There are fewer limits than you think.

In fact, many times we think of "tradition" as a thing that reduces the scope of our work. I would argue that idea is false. Traditional music and traditional furniture – when disconnected from the high styles – offer immense freedom for you as a maker and a composer.

There is a vast supply of forms and melodies all around you, ready to be collected, changed, rebuilt and adored. Look for them and listen. They are the mundane objects that escape attention – the background music stitched into your heart.

And they are beautiful.

Photo by Narayan Nayar.

Photo by Narayan Nayar.

WORKTABLE
CHAPTER 10

This table should seem familiar.

If you boil down the idea of a table to what is functionally important, you end up with legs and a top.

However, few table designs have only these parts. Tables, like chairs, take heaps of abuse and need additional parts and joinery to ensure they don't end up spread-eagle on the floor like a squashed cockroach.

So legs are reinforced with aprons, stretchers or both. The top is secured to the joined base with all manner of sly and lightweight joinery, from nails or pocket screws to sliding table buttons.

In the end you have what's like a modern bridge. It's a flat surface that, through the genius of the joinery engineering below, can support immense weight.

Early table forms are also engineering miracles. But their genius is in the robust joinery directly between the tabletop and the legs. It's a simpler solution, but it can look odd to modern eyes. Early tables and workbenches were built more like modern Windsor chairs: To remain stable, the legs were pounded into thick planks used for the tabletop.

To work, the tabletop has to be quite thick – 3" or so. Or it has to be thick in the areas where the legs join the top. So one early solution was to use a thin top, which conserves material and reduces weight, and to beef up the top only where the legs intersect it.

You could strengthen the joinery with a batten in a sliding dovetail (what I've done here), or by splitting a log lengthwise and nailing the flat

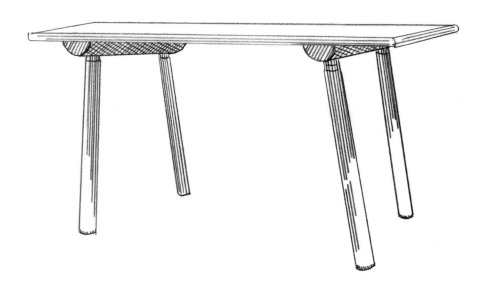

Pre-Lincoln logs. This Scandinavian table uses split logs as a way to beef up the joinery area between the legs and the tabletop.

> "You can have art in your daily life if you want it, but you don't. You prefer fountain-pens and motor cars."
>
> — Eric Gill (1882-1940), the creator of the Gill Sans typeface, as quoted in "Country Craftsmen" by Freda Derrick (1945)

face to the underside of the tabletop. Then bore your legs into the log – bark included.

European chairs, backstools and stools have used this sort of joinery for hundreds of years and many German and Moravian forms still do.

This worktable is adapted from several design sources. The basic form appears in the Middle Ages in the "Tacuinum Sanitatis," a guide to health for lay people that was published in Europe during the 13th to 15th centuries, but also had its roots in 11th-century Arabic culture.

The book shows scenes of everyday life, everything from farming and making pasta to copulation and drunken brawls. Scattered throughout all the different versions of the "Tacuinum Sanitatis" are pieces of everyday furniture. One of the most common forms is a four-legged table with a square tabletop that is being used for some sort of work. Between the legs and the top are (usually) additional pieces of wood, which I call battens. These thicken up the joint between the legs and the top.

Sometimes the staked leg is shown passing through both the batten and tabletop. Other times the leg's mortise stops in the batten.

CHAPTER 10

No battens. This image from the "Tacuinum Sanitatis" shows a worktable without battens between the top and legs.

The genesis of my version of this worktable was actually a Moravian stool that I copied years ago from the collection at Old Salem in North Carolina. That remarkable stool led me to look for examples of furniture that used the same technology on a bigger scale.

Thanks to researcher and woodworker Richard Byrne I found an 18th-century Scandinavian worktable that used the same basic format: a

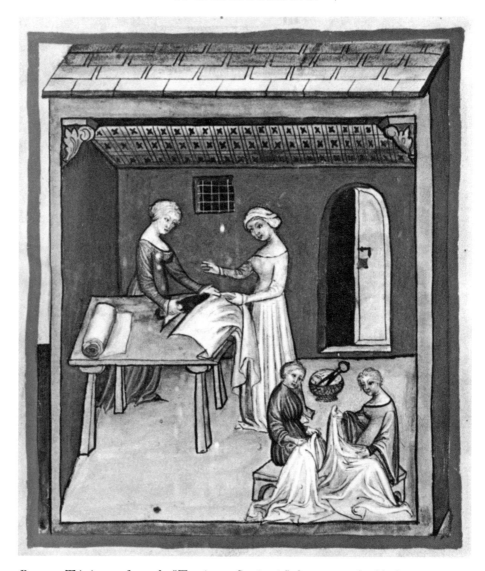

Battens. This image from the "Tacuinum Sanitatis" shows a worktable for cutting linen that does have battens (perhaps logs) between the top and legs.

thin-ish top, thick battens attached via sliding dovetails and four staked legs. Additional research turned up many more examples.

So I built a version with a 32"-square tabletop and massive 3-1/4"-thick legs. Visually, the legs overwhelmed the piece, even though they tapered and much of the bulk was hidden below the top. Plus, I wasn't happy with the square shape of the top. Its shape just wasn't useful for the work in our home.

But I was happy with the rake and splay of the legs and the battens. So I took photos of the first version, drew changes to the undercarriage and made the top a useful rectangle for a workstation – 24" x 52". A small drawer – an obvious addition – completed my design.

Construction Overview

This worktable is unlike some other staked pieces in this book in several ways. The biggest difference is that the mortises and tenons are cylindrical, not tapered cones. My biggest tapered reamer is only 1-1/8" in diameter, and I really wanted to use 2"-diameter tenons to strengthen the leg joints.

There are lots of surviving examples of staked pieces that use cylindrical joints, so I am certain this table will survive.

The other significant difference on this table (and the first Drinking Table) is that the mortises don't penetrate the tabletop. They are blind. This is another detail I've observed in paintings and in the Scandinavian table mentioned above. This construction method allows the top to move with the seasons and reduces the chance of the top splitting.

Aside from those differences, this table should seem familiar. The angled legs are staked into the thick battens then back-wedged. The thick battens are let into the top with sliding dovetails – an easy joint to cut with hand tools. The drawer is a nailed-together box. Though we haven't yet covered nails, you can skip ahead to the next section if you would like to get a preview of how they work.

I built this table from maple. The prototype was made from poplar and pine. But just about any species will do.

Begin with the Top

With many tables, making the top is the last task – the cherry on top of all the work below. With this table, however, you need to make the top first because everything below flows from and is joined to it.

The top can be almost any typical thickness, from 3/4" to 1-1/4", depending on the stock on hand. The tops shown in these photos are

Staked Worktable

Pl. 5

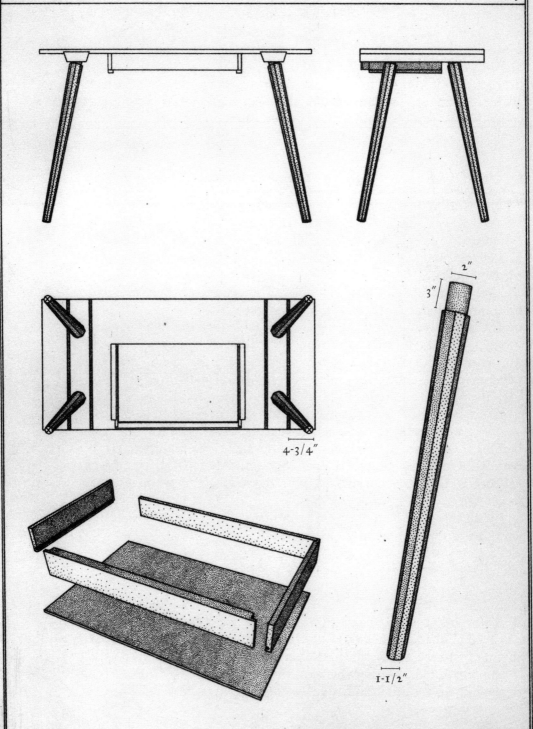

B. Morrow-Cribbs Inv. Del. et Sculp

CHAPTER 10

Saw & square. Squaring up a tabletop with hand tools is far easier than trying to set up a small machine to do the job. Try handsawing and planing the ends square. You'll be surprised by how easy it is.

between 3/4" and 7/8" thick. Glue up the pieces necessary to make the square or rectangle you desire and cut it to width and length. The ends of your top need to be dead square to the long edges to make it easy to lay out and cut the sliding dovetails for the battens.

With the ends squared, cut the two battens (1-7/8" x 5") to length and plane the angle of the sliding dovetail on the long edges. I used 16° because that's a common angle I've seen on the Moravian pieces that I like most. A few degrees one way or another won't matter.

Monster Dovetails

The battens are the templates to make the 3/8"-deep dovetail sockets in the underside of the tabletop. The long edges of the battens act as a guide for your saw to create the walls of the socket. You just have to

Square helps. Because the ends of the tabletop are square, you can use a combination square as shown to lay out one wall of the sliding dovetail socket.

shift the battens to the correct place before you saw.

Begin by laying out the location of the sliding dovetail wall that is closest to the ends of the tabletop. You can use a combination square to position the batten 4-3/4" from each end. This dimension is somewhat arbitrary and can be altered if you like.

With the batten in the right spot, clamp it to the tabletop and fetch a saw. You can use a tenon saw or a handsaw to cut this joint. The most important consideration is that the handle doesn't ram into the batten when you work. And that depends on the hang of the handle and the thickness of your batten. Don't worry if you end up using a ripping saw for this crosscutting operation.

Cut one wall with each batten. Then remove the clamps from the battens. To lay out the other wall of the sliding dovetail, you could measure the width of the dovetail and the slope of the batten. But you would likely make an error. There is an easier method, of course: Use a template.

Where do you get a template? From the battens themselves. Crosscut off a thin sliver of each batten. You can then show this piece of scrap

CHAPTER 10

One wall. The best saw in my shop for this operation was a large tenon saw that was filed rip. It chewed up the underside of the tabletop a bit, but I got over it.

Measuring is the enemy. Rather than measure the width of the batten and its slope, use an offcut of the batten itself as a pattern for the dovetail socket.

The chiseler. Most of the waste removal is done with the chisel held bevel-down. This orientation of the tool allows you to control how aggressively the tool cuts. If you use the chisel bevel-up, it will dive into the work too quickly.

to the tabletop and lay out exactly where the other wall for the sliding dovetail should be cut.

With the other wall of the socket laid out, you can clamp the battens back to the underside of the top. Make sure they are positioned inside the waste of the dovetail socket. How far inside the waste? The thickness of the toothline of your saw (including the set of the teeth).

Saw the other wall of the socket and remove the battens.

Waste Removal

Removing all the waste between the walls of the dovetail socket might seem a daunting task, but it's pretty quick if you use the right tools. Remove most of the waste with a chisel and a mallet. The chisel can rip out huge chunks of wood when working across the grain like this.

Remove as much waste as you can with the chisel. Then smooth the

CHAPTER 10

Router it flat. A full-size router plane is just big enough for this operation. If your dovetail socket is too wide, attach a thin and wide temporary sole to the router plane with double-sided tape.

bottom of the socket with a full-size router plane. It should take only a few passes with this tool to level the entire floor of the socket.

If things are taking too long, go back to the chiseling.

Fit the Battens

Sliding dovetails give many power-tool woodworkers fits. They machine the socket and the male portion to absolute precision. When they put the two parts together, the joint seizes up after they drive it in about one-fourth of the way. There is just too much friction.

If you have a sharp handplane, this is easy to fix. The trick is to hollow the middle of the male portion of the joint (in this case, the batten) by planing out the middle. You can do this by taking stopped shavings on the middle of the batten. The shaving should start about 3" from one end and stop about 3" away from the other end.

Test-fit. With the long edges of the batten planed a little hollow, the sliding dovetail should go together with only light mallet taps. If it seizes up, remove the batten and plane out the middle a little more.

Boring mortises. Here my batten is clamped to the jig's platform, which is 16° off horizontal. The sightline is drawn on the batten – I've extended it off the edges of the batten to make it easier to line things up on the jig.

Removing the middle by four or five shavings prevents the joint from tightening up until it is driven all the way home. Also, a little paraffin in the middle of the joint (there's no glue there) will help things slide home.

Once the battens fit, remove them and set the tabletop aside. It's time to bore the mortises in the battens.

Angled Mortises

The goal with the mortises is to bore them in a spot so that the feet don't stick out from the shadow of the tabletop. The feet are, in plan view, right at the corners of the tabletop.

Previous chapters show you how to lay this out without numbers or

CHAPTER 10

Turn or chisel. The 3"-long x 2"-diameter tenons can be turned on the lathe or pared out with a chisel.

measuring. So read those. Or follow the simple plans here.

Use the drawings to mark the location of the mortises on each batten (they are centered on the width of the batten and 6" from the finished length of the batten). Prick that location with an awl. Then draw a 45° sightline through each prick.

Because this mortise is 2" in diameter, you'll need to use a drill press, a 2" Forstner bit and an angled platform that holds the batten at 16° off the horizontal surface of the machine's table.

I made a platform (I call it the "banjo jig") from sheet goods and scraps. It clamps to the table of the drill press. Once the jig is clamped to the table and the Forstner bit is chucked into the machine you can line things up.

The sightline you drew on the batten should point from the centerpoint of the Forstner to the center of the iron pillar of the drill press. Once the sightline lines up with those two points, clamp the batten.

Then bore a through-hole in the batten. Repeat the process for the other three mortises.

Don't assemble anything yet. It's time to make the tenons on the legs.

"The world is filled with people who are no longer needed – and who try to make slaves of all of us –

And they have their music and we have ours –

Theirs, the wasted songs of a superstitious nightmare."

— Woody Guthrie (1912-1967), from the liner notes of "Mermaid Avenue" by Billy Bragg and Wilco

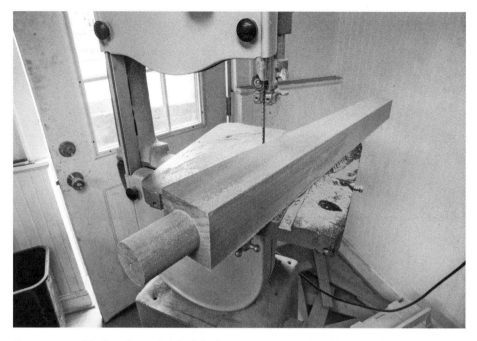

Long tapers. The band saw is ideal for long rips such as this. Lay out the tapers on one face. Make that rip. Then lay out the tapers on the adjacent faces and rip those.

Big Leg Tenons

The legs are big tapered octagons with a 2"-diameter x 3"-long tenon on one end. After making these legs using several different methods, here is the way I prefer to do it:

1. Turn the tenon on one end.
2. Cut the tapers on four faces with a band saw.
3. Create the octagonal shape with a jack plane.
4. Clean up the faces with a smoothing plane.

The easy way to create the tenons on the ends of the legs is with a lathe. I first made a sample mortise in a piece of stock then turned each tenon until it fit snug in the sample mortise.

If you don't have a lathe, lay out the diameter of the tenon using a compass. Cut the tenon shoulder with a crosscut saw or electric saw. Then pare the tenon to shape with a chisel. Fit the tenon to the sample

CHAPTER 10

Work to lines. Here you can see the lines that demarcate the tapered octagons. Once you have layout lines such as this, it's easy to plane nice octagons.

Blind wedges. Glue and wedge the legs into the battens. This locks the legs in place and allows the top to move with the seasons.

mortise to ensure you get a snug fit.

    The legs taper on all faces to 1-1/2" at the foot. Lay out the tapers on two faces of each leg. Cut them on the band saw. Then lay out the tapers on the adjacent two faces and cut those. Smooth the sawn surfaces with a jointer plane (the ideal choice) or any smaller plane if that's what you have.

CHAPTER 10

Make Octagons

Once you have the legs tapered on four faces, you need to turn them into octagons by jack planing the four corners of the tapered legs.

First comes some layout. Measure the width of each face at the shoulder up by the round tenon. Let's say it's 2-5/8", which is what it should be according to the cutting list. Divide that width into four using dividers. Do the same at the foot – divide each face into four units.

Then use a straightedge to connect the points at the shoulder and the foot to create guidelines for keeping the taper consistent while you plane the leg to an octagonal shape.

You need to remove more material at the bottom of the leg than the top. So start planing up by the bottom. Take a short stroke. Then take a longer stroke. Continue to take longer strokes until you plane all the way from the foot to the tenon. Work to your lines.

Assemble the Legs & Battens

The legs and battens are glued and wedged together. Then each assembly is knocked home into its dovetail socket. That means that the inside of the joint doesn't have to be pretty – just strong.

The first task is to knock each leg into its mortise and make a mark on the tenon and the batten to indicate where the legs should go. Then mark the tenon so you can slice a kerf into the tenon for a wedge.

The wedge should be 2" wide with a thin point (consider a 4° included angle). Blunt or thick wedges will bounce out of the kerf, especially with the lubricating effect of hide glue.

To join the legs and battens, paint each mortise and tenon with glue, drive the legs home and wedge each tenon. After the glue dries, saw and plane the joint flush. With all four legs glued, you are ready to drive the battens into the sliding dovetails.

Final Base Assembly

Little glue is necessary to finish the table. First drive the leg assemblies into their sockets from what is the back edge of the tabletop. Right before the batten reaches the front edge of the tabletop – about 1" – stop knocking the batten.

Paint the socket with glue and knock the batten until it is flush to the

Ready for glue. Only the front 1" of the joint should get glue. This drives all the wood movement in the tabletop to the back edge.

front of the tabletop. Put a clamp across the joint for good measure.

Next up is to assess how tight your joints are. The table should be a little flexible because of the thin tabletop. But if the battens move in their sockets, you can secure them with pocket screws or nails. The fasteners will allow the top to move with the seasons and will be unseen below the tabletop. If you use screws you will need to ream out the clearance hole in the tabletop to let the wood move. Nails will just bend.

Finishing Up

Level the feet using the same methods illustrated throughout the book. The optional drawer is somewhat of a compromise in my mind.

CHAPTER 10

I'd typically dovetail this drawer together, but my goal with this book was to stick to simpler joints.

So the drawer is assembled with rabbets, glue and nails. The drawer front is rabbeted on its ends – 1/2" x 3/4". That gives plenty of space for glue and nails. The drawer sides are rabbeted at the back – 1/2" x 1/4".

You'll also need to plow a groove in the sides and drawer front to hold the drawer bottom. That groove is 1/4" x 1/4", located 1/4" up from the bottom edge of the drawer sides and front.

Glue and nail the drawer front and sides together with 4*d* headed nails, such as clouts or roseheads. Fasten the drawer back between the drawer sides with 4*d* brads and set them 1/32".

The drawer bottom is rabbeted on three edges so it has a 1/4" x 1/4" tongue on those three edges. It should slide into the grooves in the drawer. A single nail through the bottom and into the drawer back holds the bottom in place.

After you assemble the drawer, you can build the drawer guides and runners. When the runners and guides are complete, they create an "L" shape that the drawer rides on.

Make the runners and guides to fit your drawer – don't follow the cutting list. The guides should be 1/16" wider than the height of your drawer. Screw them to the underside of the tabletop. Then attach the runners with glue and screws. Fine-tune the drawer's fit, if necessary, by planing down the drawer sides.

"But when it comes to saying exactly why a design is good it generally becomes a matter of falling back on instinct – which is admitting that we don't know."

— The Woodworker, *January 1955*

WORKTABLE

NO.	PART	T	W	L
1	Top	13/16	24	52
2	Battens	1-7/8	5	25*
4	Legs	2-5/8	2-5/8	31-1/2*
1	Drawer front	1	3	24
2	Drawer sides	1/2	3	15-1/4
1	Drawer back	1/2	2-1/2	23-1/2
1	Drawer bottom	1/2	14-3/4	23-1/2
2	Drawer guides	3/4	3-1/16	14
2	Drawer runners	1/2	1	14

* Overlong; trim to final length

STAKED BED

CHAPTER 11

Like a confident insect.

To be clear, I've not seen a staked bed like this in the furniture record. That doesn't mean it's a new form – I don't think there is such an animal. But this bed is not a copy or an interpretation of any other piece I know of.

Instead, it's like my waterbed from Arkansas hooked up with the worktable in the previous chapter and had a baby. It's essentially a platform bed (for a twin mattress) with staked legs.

Despite my defensive caveats above, the bed works well. It can be assembled and knocked down in about 10 minutes with a 9/16" socket wrench. It offers a platform that you can place any mattress upon – from a Tempur-Pedic memory foam thing to an air mattress. And it is quick to build. I made this bed in only a few days in the shop.

You might notice that this bed is made from mahogany. That was not my intent; I'd originally meant to build it from yellow pine from my home center. But after scouring the racks there, I came up empty-handed. So I went to my local lumberyard to get some maple. No dice. As a result, I cracked into my supply of mahogany, which I had earmarked for some campaign-style pieces.

You can use any species you like for this project. Unlike the chairs and backstools in this book, this bed is overbuilt so you could make it from questionable 2x4 pine. One additional design note: You can easily raise this bed by 3" to 4" without changing its stability.

STAKED BED

"'Leave me to my repose,' is the motto of the sleeping and the dead."

— William Hazlitt (1778-1830), literary critic

Construction Overview

The bed sits on six tapered octagonal legs that are mortised into two burly battens that measure 2-3/8" x 4" x 78". The bed's 10 platform pieces are bolted to the battens using 3/8" x 16 x 3-1/2"-long cap screws with washers. To secure the screws, I nailed 24 "weld nuts" to the underside of the battens, which are threaded to receive the 3/8" x 16 cap screws. The net result of all this effort is that you will be able to assemble and disassemble the bed with a single ratchet in just a few minutes.

Begin with the Big Battens

The long battens are the backbone of this bed, and they are the most difficult pieces to mill because they are 78" long. I managed to flatten the battens and plane them to finished size with the tools in my shop. But when it came to cutting them to finished length, I was stuck.

So I clamped the two battens together and crosscut them simultaneously with a circular saw. I don't think I hit the 78" mark exactly, but both battens ended up the same length because they were cut at the same time.

I tapered the long edges of the battens to lighten their weight and

CHAPTER 11

Accurate sawing. This can be done with a handsaw or a circular saw. If you cut the battens with a circular saw, clamp the two battens together then clamp a fence to the work to guide the saw.

their look. The taper begins 1/2" from the top of each batten and ends when the batten is 3" wide at its bottom edge. (In other words, plane a 1-7/8" x 1/2" bevel on each long edge.) After marking out the bevels I planed them down with a jack plane and cleaned up the coarse work with a jointer plane.

Before boring all the bolt holes and angled mortises in the battens, it's a good idea to make the six legs.

Tapered Legs

The tapered octagonal legs on this bed are much like the other tapered legs in this book. The legs begin as 2-1/2" x 2-1/2" x 9-1/4" blanks. The top 2-1/4" of the leg becomes a 1-1/2"-diameter cylindrical tenon. The remainder of the leg becomes an octagon that tapers to 1-3/8" at the floor.

Staked Bed

Pl. 6

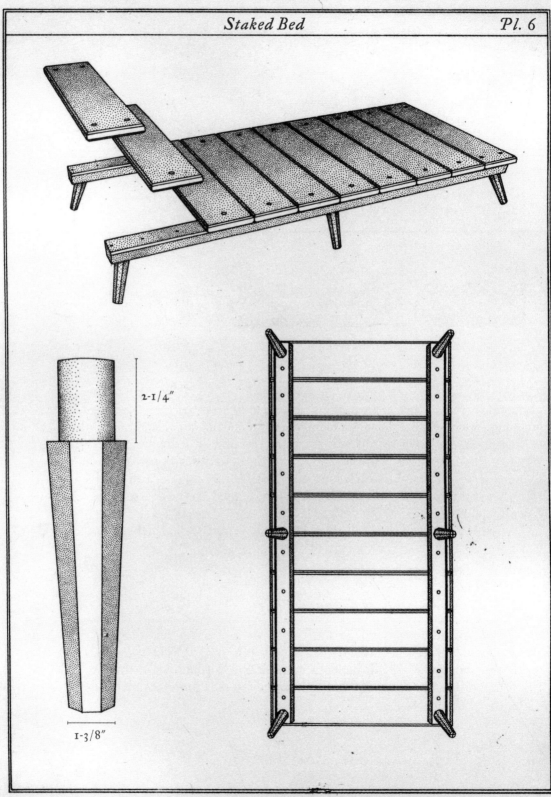

2-1/4"

1-3/8"

B. Morrow-Cribbs Inv. Del. et Sculp

CHAPTER 11 173

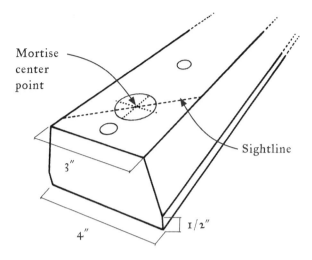

Underside of batten.

You can make the tenons on the lathe or create them by sawing and chiseling the tops of the legs to shape. After making the tenons, transform the remainder of the leg into a tapered octagon with a jack plane. Finish up the leg with a smoothing plane to remove the rough marks left by the jack plane.

Bore the Mortises

The mortises for the six legs are made easily on a drill press with the "banjo jig." The goal is to get all six legs looking like they have a consistent stance, like a confident insect. To make this happen, you need to use one set of angles for the four legs at the corners and a second set of angles for the two legs in the middle of the battens.

Let's talk about the four legs at the ends of the battens. Lay out the location of these mortises. They are 2" from each end of the battens and are centered on their width.

The sightline for these mortises is 45°; that's easy to mark out. Draw a 45° line through the center point of the mortise. Now set the banjo jig on the drill press so the table is 24.7° to the quill of the machine. That is the resultant angle.

Turn the tenon. The cylindrical tenons for this bed are 1-1/2" in diameter and 2-1/4" long. The little cove I turned at each tenon shoulder is 100-percent decorative.

Taper the legs. This simple bench fixture allows you to transform each leg into an octagon, then taper it with a handplane.

CHAPTER 11

The easy mortise. The mortises for the middle legs have a 90° sightline and an 18° resultant angle. The mortises should be about 2-1/4" deep.

Boring these mortises is tricky by yourself. You'll need to either recruit a helper (marriage is awesome) or rig up some sort of whack-doodle bockety platform to hold one end of the batten as you bore it. I recommend the marriage option. Bore the four mortises into the two battens. They should be about 2-1/4" deep.

The mortises for the middle legs are easier. The sightline is 90° across the batten. Set the banjo jig so it's 18° to the quill of the drill press. Bore the mortises to the same depth as the mortises at the corners of the battens.

Make the Slats

The 10 slats that create the platform for the bed are simple to make. They are all 1-1/4" x 8" x 39". The two slats at the head and foot of the bed each receive four bolts (and washers) to help square the bed frame. The remaining eight slats each receive only two bolts and washers.

All of the holes and counterbores on the slats are identical and are 3" from the ends of the 10 slats. On the two end slats, the holes are 1-5/8"

Counterbore first. The 7/8"-diameter counterbore holds the washer and head of the cap screw. Bore the counterbores first. Then follow up with the 31/64" through-holes.

from the long edges. On the other eight slats, the holes are centered on the width of the slat. First drill 7/8"-diameter x 5/16"-deep counterbores on the top face of each slat. Then drill 31/64" through-holes for the bolts in the center of each counterbore.

This hole diameter seems fussy, I know, but it is designed to hold the weld nut precisely. After you drill all the holes in all 10 slats, bevel the top and bottom edges of the slats. I cut a 1/4" x 1/4" bevel on all the edges.

Bolt Holes in the Battens

I used the holes in the slats to lay out the matching holes in the battens. While you could lay out everything using math, I think it's better to match one part to another to ensure theory and practice match up.

The slats at the head and foot of the bed overhang the end of the battens by 1". Clamp the end slats to one batten and use a try square to get them positioned perfectly on the batten. Then use a brad-point bit to transfer the position of the holes in the slats to the batten below. Don't

CHAPTER 11

Mark, don't measure. Position the slats on one batten as they will go when everything is assembled. Then use the 31/64" drill bit to transfer the location of the holes from the slats to the batten below.

unclamp anything yet.

Place the remainder of the slats on the batten. These slats should fit between the clamped battens with no space between them. You might need to plane the slats' long edges to make this happen.

After laying out all the hole locations on one batten, transfer those hole locations to the second batten. Clamp the two battens together and use a square to make sure the holes match up on both battens.

Drill all the 31/64" through-holes in both battens.

Clean-up & Weld Nuts

Dress the battens with a long plane so they are straight and smooth. Then nail the weld nuts to the underside of the battens. The collar of each weld nut should slip into each through-hole in the batten. I used vintage 2d brads to secure the weld nuts. But just about anything will do – from a headed wire nail to a small screw.

One to one. After marking the layout on one batten, clamp the batten to its mate. Transfer the location of the holes to the second batten.

Beat down. Small headed nails hold the weld nuts in place. If you don't like nails, consider using small screws to do the job.

CHAPTER 11

Twist again. Paint the mortise and tenon with liquid hide glue then twist the leg into its mortise. Whack it with a mallet to get it to seat fully.

Glue the Legs

The six legs stay put thanks to hide glue. If you have a snug fit between your mortises and tenons, that should be enough to keep things tight because you don't pick up a bed as many times as you pick up a chair.

To get a snug fit, twist each leg into its mortise. If it sticks before seat-

> "Looking around at contemporary furniture, one is more and more conscious of how little there is of really pleasant, comfortable attractive design for the ordinary men and women who want just that in their home and can feel no enthusiasm for freakishness or oddity or the bleakness of peg-legs and the like in the furniture they have to live with.
>
> "And how utterly bleak those peg-legs will look when the novelty and newness have worn off and only the barren, unimaginative ugliness remains."
>
> — The Woodworker, August 1954

Flat-footed. Clamp a mechanical pencil so it marks the exact length of the legs. Shift the entire jig around to mark all the facets on the legs.

The pencil represents the floor

ing fully, pull it out and remove the high spots (they will be burnished) with #120-grit sandpaper. Then try again.

Once all the tenons fit, squeeze liquid hide glue into each mortise and paint the walls of the mortise with the glue. Any excess glue should be transferred to the tenon with an acid brush or stick.

Then twist the tenon into its mortise and rotate it until it looks the way you want it to look. Move onto the next mortise and tenon.

Let the glue cure overnight. Now it's time to cut the legs so they all sit flat on the floor.

CHAPTER 11

Trim the legs. A carcase saw makes short work of trimming the legs to their final length. Simply follow the pencil lines you marked on the legs.

Make Flat Feet

The lucky thing about this bed is that it's easy to level the feet using your workbench. Set one of the battens on your workbench with the feet pointing toward the ceiling.

Now fetch a handscrew, a thin scrap of wood, a mechanical pencil and a small F-style clamp. You are going to make a quick jig to level the feet.

The handscrew sits flat on the bench. It holds the thin scrap. The mechanical pencil is clamped to the thin scrap at the exact point where you want the floor to intersect the legs of your bed.

Mark all six legs using the jig then cut the legs to their final length using a carcase saw. Clamp the legs to your benchtop and make the cuts by following the lines you marked.

Finish & Assembly

I finished all the parts while the bed was disassembled. I used lacquer, but any finish is fine. Why no color, like on the mahogany drinking table? The mattress covers the bed, so you don't see the wood. The surfaces of beds don't take much abuse. It's really all a joinery game when building a bed that will last.

Assembling the bed is simple. Thread the cap screws and washers through the holes in the slats. Secure them to the weld nuts in the battens with a ratchet. Don't over-tighten the cap screws – leave that task to some future pinhead.

With the platform assembled, throw a mattress on top. Done.

STAKED BED (TWIN SIZE)

NO.	PART	T	W	L
2	Battens	2-3/8	4	78
10	Slats	1-1/4	8	39
6	Legs	2-1/2	2-1/2	9-1/4*

*Overlong; trim to sit flat on the floor.

24 Steel weld nuts, 3/8" x 16 thread
24 Cap screws, 3/8" x 16, 3-1/2" long
24 Steel flat washers, 3/8"

Common mattress sizes in North America:
Twin: 39" x 74"
Full: 54" x 74"
Queen: 60" x 80" (I recommend a third batten in the center for this size)
King: 76" x 80" (I recommend a third batten in the center for this size)

CHAPTER 11

Photo by Narayan Nayar.

Photo by Narayan Nayar.

TRESTLE TABLES
CHAPTER 12

Autopsies, butchering animals & fine dining.

It might seem far-fetched to make a dining table, desk or worktable using staked-foot technology, but the people of the 14th century didn't think so.

Any survey of Western paintings from the Middle Ages will turn up a fair number of these tables, which were used for circumcisions, autopsies, butchering animals and fine dining. When used for the bloody stuff, the tables are shown uncovered. When used for eating, they are decked out with a tablecloth.

Many furniture historians consider this staked table as the ancestor to what we now call a "trestle table," a lightweight and sometimes-knockdown table that shows up in the 16th century. (One of the earliest images of a "modern" trestle table is in Albrecht Durer's "St. Jerome in His Study," circa 1514.)

There are several forms of this staked table out there. This particular form has a removable top and two trestles, sometimes called "trussles" or "dormans." The trestles typically had three legs that were staked into a thick and narrow plank, much like a tall sawbench.

Usually the end of the trestles with the single leg is where you would sit, giving you more leg room side-to-side. The end where there are two legs is where you were served food and drink, offering more stability.

Sometimes the pair of legs were joined by a stretcher. The stretcher could be as simple as a round spindle or as elaborate as a pierced and

TRESTLE TABLES

"With industry there is no coping. More and more it is establishing its own claims, which we are forced to recognize.

"But men who have fighting souls will keep intact their freedom to do and be, and there is no better way than the craftsman's for safeguarding those things."

— The Woodworker, January 1962

shaped flat panel. Sometimes this flat panel was tenoned into the legs. Sometimes it was obviously nailed to the legs.

Speaking of the legs, they typically were tapered octagons, tapered squares or simple round-ish shapes. The joinery between the legs and the plank was typically covered up by the tabletop, but we know from some surviving examples and a few paintings that these joints could be round or square.

The other variable with the legs is the angle between the leg pair. This typically ranged between 15° and 30°, which offered a trade-off between legroom (15°) and stability (30°).

The top itself was almost always unremarkable – a plank of wood lain across the trestles.

This type of table was easy to move or dismantle, which was necessary for a household based in a great hall or a single room. And the tables were useful for garden parties. Paintings show these tables used outdoors for working, drinking wine or the occasional alcohol-soaked brawl.

The two tables in this chapter are similar. They use the same layout for the leg mortises (though their sightlines and resultant angles are different). And the tabletop is the same for both. The first, "standard," table has a single round stretcher between the front legs; the second, Mughal, table has a flat, decorative panel, as shown in the drawing at left.

I did add one detail to both tables that is period-incorrect: wooden-thread screws that hold the trestles and top together. This complication can be skipped if you want to go old school for your next Renaissance fair.

Let's start by building the trestle table with a simple turned spindle between the octagonal legs.

About Those Legs

The legs can be any tough, straight-grained wood that you can get in 8/4 thicknesses. While shopping for 8/4 red oak, I saw this hard maple that was creamy white, arrow-straight and about the same price.

Saw the legs to 1-1/2" square and about 30" long. Then plane them to octagons that taper to 1-1/4" at the top. Rough in the 3"-long tenons at the top of the legs using a drawknife or a lathe. Then use a 5/8" tapered tenon cutter to shave them to their final dimension.

With the legs complete, you can design the plank they'll be staked into and determine the sightlines and resultant angles for boring and reaming the leg joints.

Trestle Table

Pl. 7

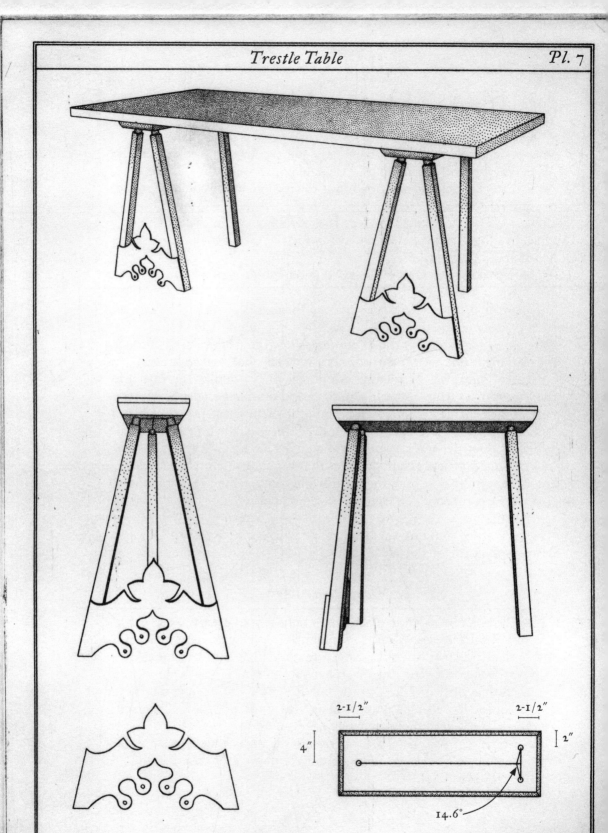

B. Morrow-Cribbs Inv. Del. et Sculp

CHAPTER 12

Lots of legs. I always make a couple extra legs for chairs and other staked furniture projects because one leg usually gets spoiled (and then becomes a smaller part in the project).

Skinny-legged Models

The top planks of the trestles should be thick, 7" to 10" wide and slightly shorter than the width of the tabletop. My top planks were 1-3/4" x 8" x 29". Once I knew the size of the top plank, I could make a half-scale wire model from some 3/4" construction plywood and wire from clothes hangers.

By eye, determine where the legs should go. I recommend keeping their centers about 2-1/2" from the ends and 2" from the edges. Any less and the legs could split the top plank during assembly (or during an outbreak of kickboxing in your living room). For my trestles, all the legs are 2-1/2" in from the ends of the top planks.

The goal here is to make each trestle stable but to keep the legs from wandering too far out and snagging a human foot. So the pair of legs at one end have a rake of 4° and a splay of 8°. The single leg at the opposite end has a rake of 4° and no splay (0°).

This arrangement will give you a good balance for a dining table. If

Real wireframe models. Alter the rake and splay with needlenose pliers that are guided by a bevel gauge. Too much rake or splay here will create a tripping hazard.

CHAPTER 12

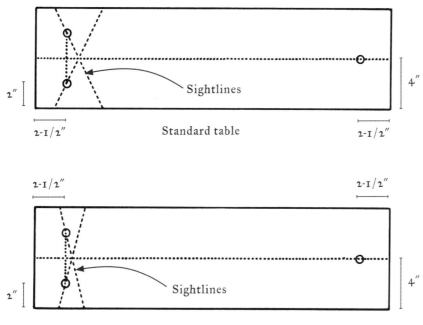

Mortise layout, both tables.

you are making a table that is designed more for work than eating, consider a more dramatic splay of 12° to 15°.

If you use my angles, your sightline will be 26.5° and your resultant will be 9° for the pair of legs at the front of the plank. The lone third leg has a sightline of 0° and a resultant of 4°. Lay out all your mortise locations and sightlines on the underside of your top planks then add any desired decorative shape to the planks.

Many of the planks in paintings have a rough, roundish shape – like they were a log split lengthwise through the middle. You can create that shape with a jack plane. Instead, I planed a bevel on all four edges of each plank. My bevel is 1/2" wide and 1-1/4" tall.

Joinery

The joinery for this table is exactly the same as many other staked pieces in this book. Bore a 5/8"-diameter hole then ream it. The only complexity in this project is that the lone third leg uses a different

A clean exit. When boring the mortise with the auger bit, bore until you can feel its lead screw poke through the top of the plank. Then flip the plank over and bore the exit hole. Here I'm using the bevel gauge to guide me.

Ream in pairs. Here I'm reaming two legs to make sure they lean at the same angle. By reaming each hole bit by bit, you end up with trestles that look identical.

CHAPTER 12

First turn. Make your stretchers before boring the mortises to receive them. This will allow you to position the stretchers on the legs so they will do the most good.

bevel-gauge setting than the pair at the other end of each plank.

When reaming the mortises for this table, I recommend putting the two planks side by side on your workbench and reaming each bit by bit, testing both and reaming again until all the legs look symmetrical. The exact angle of the legs isn't as important as the fact that all the legs should appear to have the same splay.

Marking mortises. The scrap is a platform for the pencil. Mark the mortise locations on both legs and mark at least three flat faces of each octagonal leg.

The Tricky Stretcher

"Crappy work I do twice, good work I do three times."

— Paul Fussell (1924-2012)

Many of the old trestle bases have a stretcher between the pair of legs at one end. If you try to calculate the compound angle for this joint you will quickly lose your taste for staked-leg furniture and, perhaps, life itself.

Luckily, there is a way to bore the mortises that doesn't require any geometry or math. All you need is a stick to guide you.

Before diving into the joinery for the stretcher, turn or shave some stretchers to final shape. My stretchers are 3/4" x 3/4" x 9-1/2" and terminate in 1/2"-diameter tenons that are 1-1/2" long.

With the stretchers turned, knock your legs hard into the top planks. Find an ideal location for your stretchers. You want them to penetrate the legs about 1" and be able to slightly spread the legs out to lock things in place.

If you used my angles, the stretcher should be about 18" down from the top plank. But where the stretcher is located exactly doesn't change how you bore the mortises that receive it.

Begin the process by cutting a scrap to a length that roughly equals the distance from the stretcher to the top plank. You are going to put

CHAPTER 12

Hot-doggin'. Line up the shaft of the bit extension with the lines you marked on the leg near the drill. That is all the accuracy you need to drill this mortise.

No glue. This joinery is solid enough that you could get away without using glue and wedges. You could knock these trestles down to five parts each if you wanted.

a pencil on top of this scrap so its point is exactly where you want the mortise to be. My scrap ended up 17-13/16" long.

Turn the dry-fit trestles upside down on your bench. Place your scrap on your top plank. Place the pencil on top of the scrap. Mark the mortise locations on both legs on at least three faces of each octagonal leg. Note that you cannot simply measure up from the tenon of each leg and be certain the stretcher will be parallel to the floor. If either leg is at a slightly different angle, then your stretcher will be cock-eyed.

To bore the mortises, you'll need a 1/2" spade bit, a bit extension and a drill. (Why a spade bit? It has a long center spur, which allows you some more room to steer in this application. Also, you can grind down the sides of the spade bit to make your mortise undersized if need be.) Chuck the bit and extension together and mark the dead center of the mortise on one of the flat faces of one of the legs.

Place a piece of tape on the spade bit that's 15/16" from the spurs that cut the circumference of the hole. That will be the depth of the mortise.

Place the lead point of the spade bit on the center point of the leg where the mortise will go. Rotate the leg a tad in the mortise so you are entering that face perpendicularly. Trust yourself a bit on this.

Line up the shaft of the bit extension with the marks for the mortise on the opposite leg.

Run the drill up to full speed without plunging into the leg. Once the bit is running at full speed, plunge slowly into the leg. Repeat the same procedure for the mortise in the opposite leg. Yes, it really is that easy.

After cutting the mortises in the legs, dry-fit the trestles. Drive a stretcher into one leg and put that leg loosely into its mortise in the top plank. Put the other leg in its mortise and thread the other end of the stretcher into its mortise. Use a mallet to drive both legs home.

Remove the legs and kerf the tenon of each about 1" deep to receive wedges. You want the kerf to be perpendicular to the grain of the top plank, just like with all the other staked pieces in this book.

The last task before assembly is to bore an optional 1-1/4" through-hole centered in the top plank for the wooden-thread screw to join the tabletop and each trestle.

Assembly

I glued the legs to the top planks and back-wedged them to create a permanent joint. Here's how I did it to minimize clean-up.

I used liquid hide glue, which cleans easily with water (even when

"But now, perhaps just because peace is not going according to plan, certainly not in the way that we, the ordinary citizens, had imagined it, there are opportunities which will give us the thrill of vital living if we care to seize them, the difference being that these opportunities do not come unsought.

"We have to find them."

— The Woodworker, December 1947

Drive it. Knock the legs into the plank until you hear a dull thud and the legs stop moving. If you hit the leg again after that point you risk splitting the top plank.

cured) and offers lots of assembly time. Begin by painting the inside of the mortises in the legs with glue. Drive the stretcher into one leg with a mallet.

Now brush glue into the tapered mortises in the planks. Place one leg loosely into its mortise. Place the other leg loosely into the mortise and thread the stretcher into its mating mortise. Drive the legs into the top plank with a mallet.

Pause. Use warm water and a toothbrush to clean any glue squeeze-out. Then glue the third leg in place and clean up any excess glue.

Flip the assembled trestle over and wedge the tenons. Clean up any excess glue and leave the assemblies overnight. Then trim the tenons flush to the top planks and plane the top surfaces of the planks flat.

The Tabletop

I made my tabletop from three 8'-long yellow pine 2x12s from a home center. The tabletop is supposed to be covered in a tablecloth, so the planks don't have to be pristine if you plan to cover them.

When gluing up the top, it can be tricky to keep the seams aligned

CHAPTER 12   201

Back-wedging. I use oak wedges with a 4° included angle to back-wedge the tenons in their mortises. Paint glue on the wedges and drive them in with a hammer. When the wedges stop moving into the joint, stop hammering them.

along the entire length of the tabletop. If you have some way of aligning the boards – biscuits, splines or tongue-and-groove – this extra bit of joinery can save you lots of time when flattening the top.

Glue up the top boards and let them sit overnight.

Because of end checks, splits and other nastiness in the boards, my top ended up 7' long. By the time I dressed all the edges true, the top ended up about 30" wide, which is plenty wide for your next dinner party or autopsy. Saw the tabletop to its finished length.

Before planing up the tabletop, it's best to make the screws and tap the top. The tapping process can chew up the tabletop, so you want to plane away any ugliness after tapping.

Wooden Screws

I made my wooden screws from leftover octagonal leg stock that didn't work for one reason or another. I cut a 7"-long section for each wooden screw. A 3"-long octagonal section serves as the handle; the remainder is turned down to be threaded.

Feel the difference. I use a slow-setting liquid hide glue when making big tabletops. The extra assembly time allows me to shift the boards around as I apply clamp pressure.

CHAPTER 12

Totally screwed. The wood threader cuts nice threads if the tool is well-lubricated. You can use tallow or wax. Another way to get clean threads is to soak the shafts in boiled linseed oil for a couple days before threading. No, it won't gunk up the cutter.

I used a metric wood-threading kit that makes 28mm wooden screws (that's about 1-1/8" in diameter). After some experimentation, I turned the shaft of the screws to 1.10", which fit nicely into the threader. If you don't own decimal calipers, that number is a hair shy of 1-3/32".

Then you can tap the tabletop. The holes should be 12" from each end and be centered on the width of the tabletop. This 12" distance looks right and is a fairly typical spacing for the trestles.

To tap the top, you first need to drill a 23mm hole through the top. This hole needs to be plumb, so use a try square to guide you.

With the holes bored in the tabletop, you can tap each hole. The German tap I used was aggressive. In the sample joints I made using the tap, it chewed up the rim of the hole. The solution was to slightly bevel the entry and exit holes with a half-round rasp.

Most of the beveling and nastiness in the wake of the tap will be planed away, but it's always best to minimize the ugliness by making the chamfer. Tap the hole. I didn't have a tap handle, so I grasped the tap with locking pliers. This works fine if you take care to ensure the tap is cutting perpendicular.

After tapping the holes, run the threads in to ensure everything

Round & square. Take your time when boring this hole. Check your drill from both axes to ensure it is boring perfectly perpendicular to the tabletop.

screws in smoothly. The threaded handles pass through the underside of the top plank and thread into the top. The threaded section should be far too long at this point; you'll cut it flush to the tabletop after you plane it flat and smooth.

Plane the Top

Begin by planing the underside of the top with a jack plane. Traversing the top with a jack will create a wooly surface and allow you to remove material quickly. After getting the underside flat (check your work with winding sticks), stop. The rough surface on the underside is actually an advantage so the top won't slide around on the trestles.

Flip the top over and plane the show surface of the tabletop. If your joints are out of alignment by 1/32" or more, you'll want to dress the top flat with a jack first. If all your planks are nicely aligned, start planing with a small smoothing plane. The goal here is to get the surface looking clean and flat. Absolute flatness is not the goal.

Remove any tool marks on the ends and long edges of the top.

CHAPTER 12

Tap that. When tapping metal or wood, it is good practice to advance the tap a turn then reverse its rotation for half a turn to break the chip. Some taps require this more than other taps, but it never hurts to advance and then retreat a tad.

Another Way to Make a Top

If you don't want to make a thick top, you can make a thin one from 3/4" home-center pine and use battens across the width to keep the top flat. The trick is to use clenched nails to lock the piece together yet allow wood movement.

Glue up the tabletop – this one is 30-1/2" x 81-1/4" – and make 3"-wide battens (3/4" x 3" x 29") from the scraps left from the tabletop construction. Plane a 1/4" x 1/4" bevel on four edges of each batten. Arrange all the table parts upside down on your bench and clamp the battens to

Position the trestles. I put the battens on the outside of the trestles to prevent sitters from kicking the trestles out from under the tabletop.

Samples. If you don't know this particular nail like a brother, make test joints and clench the nails to make sure things will work. Repeat the test. Then you can drill the pilots for real. I used eight nails in each batten.

CHAPTER 12

A good start. A pair of pliers allows you to bend the tip of the nail in the desired direction. Note that large works requires longer clench nails, as in this example.

the top so they are 8" from the ends.

Flip the top over. Then lay out a line on the tabletop for the pilot holes for the 20d (4") clinch rosehead nails. Before you drill the pilot holes in the top, make some sample joints. These nails can split a squirrel from his nut.

Drive the nails through the top and the battens. Remove the clamps.

To clench the nails you'll need to put the top of the tabletop on any piece of iron or steel. I used the top of my table saw.

The traditional way to clench a nail such as this is to hammer the nail's tip and bend it back into the work – across the grain like a giant staple.

Not all nails, however, will bend to your will. So it helps to persuade them by bending the top 5/8" of the nail into a hook shape. Then beat it.

To keep this thin top in place on the trestles I opted for another likely

Finish the deed. Then drive the tip of the nail back into the work – making sure the tip goes across the grain.

historically-inaccurate-so-sue-me technique. I glued pegs in holes in the underside of the top. These pegs drop into blind 1-1/4"-diameter holes in the trestles. The pegs are located on the top so that they gently press the trestles against the battens under the top.

Layout is easy. Position the trestles upside down on the top and push them against the battens. Clamp them in place. Drill a 1-1/4"-diameter hole through the trestle and into the top – penetrate the top only about 3/8" or 1/2".

Now shape a 1-1/4"-diameter peg. It should be about 1-3/4" long.

CHAPTER 12

For alignment. A peg between the top and trestle makes the table more stable. Yet it's still easy to knock down.

The part that fits in the hole in the tabletop should fit tight. The rest of the pegs should be slightly tapered so all the pieces will go together. You can taper the peg on the lathe or with a shop knife.

I glued the pegs in place with epoxy – this joint doesn't offer a lot of long-grain-to-long-grain strength for traditional wood glues.

A peg & its hole. You can see there's a slight taper on the peg, which allows the top to slip on easily and slide into place.

Level the Trestles

You want the top planks of the trestles to be level and the same height from the floor. Find a level surface in your shop and place one of the trestles on it. Use small wedges to level the trestle so the top plank is level in all directions.

Now take a tape measure and determine how high the top plank should be off the floor. Mine needed to be 28-1/4" high so the tabletop would be 30" off the floor. Figure out how much leg needs to be removed – I needed to cut away 1". So I made a block, taped a pencil to it and marked all around the legs to remove 1".

After sawing the legs of the two trestles, compare them to one another on your flat surface. If the top planks don't line up, you'll need to adjust the legs. One of my trestles ended up about 1/16" taller than its mate. I used a marking gauge to capture this exact difference and gauged that dimension all around the feet of my too-tall trestle. Then I sawed those three legs again.

Use a rasp to bevel the corners of the feet so they don't splinter when someone drags them across the floor. Then you are ready for your finish.

CHAPTER 12

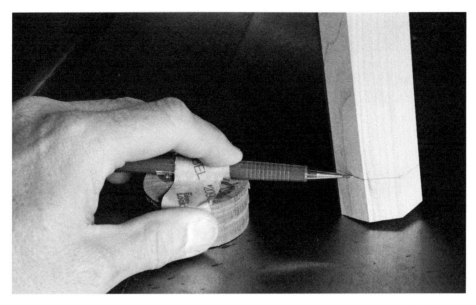

Mark the floor. The pencil point on this 1"-tall block represents the floor. Mark all around the three legs then saw away the waste.

Compound crazy. This angle is something odd. Your best bet is to make a shallow kerf on four faces of the octagonal leg before sawing the waste off. The shallow kerfs will guide the saw during the cut.

Finish

After studying paintings of these tables, my guess is they didn't do much to finish. Maybe some oil or wax. So finish your table in any manner you please.

I used a clear film finish – no pigment.

STANDARD TABLE

NO.	PART	SIZES (INCHES)		
		T	W	L
6	Legs	1-1/2	1-1/2	30
2	Top planks	1-3/4	8	29
2	Stretchers	3/4 dia.		9-1/2
1	Top	1-1/4	30	84
2	Threaded handles	1-1/2	1-1/2	7
Alternate Thin Top				
1	Top	3/4	31-1/2	81-1/4
2	Pegs	1-1/4 dia.		1-3/4
2	Battens	3/4	3	29

CHAPTER 12

"Magazines all too frequently lead to books and should be regarded by the prudent as the heavy petting of literature."

— *Fran Lebowitz (1950-)*

Photo by Narayan Nayar.

TRESTLE TABLES

Photo by Narayan Nayar.

CHAPTER 12

All downhill. If you use straight (or rived) stock for your legs, planing the tapers should be easy. Plane from the bottom of each leg to the top until the tops of the legs are 1-1/4" square.

Mughal Trestles

Some early trestle tables had decorative panels that joined the front two legs. Many times these panels had a Gothic flavor with lancet arches, but I became enamored with one that looks more Mughal – an empire on the Indian subcontinent with roots in the 16th century.

Except for the decorative panel, these trestles are actually simpler to build. The legs are tapered squares – not octagons. And the decorative panels are nailed to the legs.

Tapers on Tapers on Legs

The legs taper on all four faces so they are 1-5/8" square at the floor and 1-1/4" square at the top. This is easily done with a jack plane followed by a jointer plane. Mark out the finished dimension on the tops of the legs and jack plane the tapers. Clean up those tool marks with a jointer plane.

Instant, perfect tenon. The tapered tenon cutter makes a finicky operation easy. Hold the tenon cutter with one hand and the leg with the other. This particular grip allows you to eyeball the gap around the tenon to ensure it is centered on the leg.

Next is cutting the tapered conical tenon on top of the six legs. The tenon is made using a 5/8" tapered tenon cutter.

To prepare each leg for the tenon cutter, you need to rough in a taper on the top 3-1/2" of each leg to make it easier for the tenon cutter. You can rough in the tenon by whittling it, turning it or using a drawknife.

The goal is to create a 1-1/8" diameter at the base of the tenon that tapers to about 5/8" at the tip. I used a lathe, which is fast. After roughing in the tenon, shave it to final size with the tapered tenon cutter.

CHAPTER 12

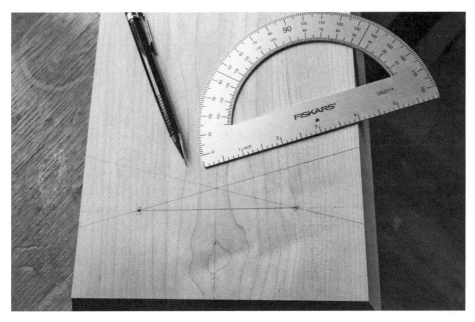

Mortise layout. You are looking at the mortise locations for the two front legs. Note the baseline that connects the two mortises and the sightlines that are 14.6° off the baseline.

Top Planks & Geometry

The top planks are the interface between the legs and the tabletop. While you can leave them as square-edged boards, old paintings typically show them with slightly curved edges. I used a jack plane to round over the long edges and ends of the top planks so the underside was 7" wide x 28" long.

To lay out the locations of the mortises, first strike a centerline on the underside of the top planks. The mortises for the two front legs are 2-1/2" from the ends of the top planks and 2" in from the edges. The mortise for the single third leg is centered on the underside and is 2-1/2" from the end.

After laying out the mortise locations, draw a baseline that connects the two mortise locations at the front of the top plank. Then use a protractor to strike a sightline from each mortise that is 14.6° off the baseline. (Study the photo above if you are scratching your head.) The sightline is the pencil line that your bevel square will sit on as you bore the mortise.

In line. Here I'm boring the rear leg. The centerline is the sightline. The bevel square is set for 4°.

Ream & verify. After every four rotations of the reamer, remove the tool from the mortise and insert the dummy leg. Make small adjustments to how you tilt the reamer to correct the angle.

Set a bevel square for 15.5° off of 90° and tape its handle to your sightline. Chuck a 5/8" auger bit into your brace. You are going to drill a hole through the top plank that is parallel to the blade of your bevel square.

Stand directly in line with the bevel square and put the tip of the auger on the mortise location. Tilt the brace to the same angle as the bevel square's blade and crank the brace until the spurs are buried about 1/4" into the work. Stop and check your angle. Crank the brace a few more times, adjusting the angle as necessary.

Once you are about 1" into the wood your angle is fairly locked. If you are off, don't fret; you can fix that when you ream the hole.

Crank until the lead screw pokes out the other side of the board. Flip the board over and finish the cut by boring from the other side.

CHAPTER 12

The single rear leg is simpler. The sightline is the centerline on the top plank. Change the angle of the bevel square to 4° off of 90° and tape it to the sightline for the rear leg. Bore the hole in the same manner as you did the front legs.

Ream the Mortises

Some scholars have guessed that the conical mortises on historical pieces might have been burned to shape. While I like fire as much as the next overgrown boy, the tapered reamer is more predictable.

Before you ream the mortises, use your tapered tenon cutter to make a dummy tenon on a 1" dowel. It's easier to confirm the angle of your reamer by checking it against a cylindrical dowel than against a tapered leg.

Set your bevel gauge to the same angle you used for boring the 5/8" holes and tape it to the sightline. Ream each hole in short bursts for better control. After four or five rotations of the reamer, remove the tool and place the dummy leg in the hole.

Ream the hole until the opening is 1-1/8" wide. You will be surprised how quickly this goes, so be cautious as you begin because it is easy to overshoot your mark. Ream all the mortises (don't forget to change the angle for the rear leg). Check your work by knocking the legs into their mortises and see if they line up like they should. If things are off a little, don't despair; there is still another chance to make things look right.

Assembly

The tenons are glued and wedged into the top planks. To make life easier, do these things before you slather on the glue:
• Trim the tops of the legs so they protrude only 1/8" above the top of the trestle top.
• Saw a 1-1/4"-deep kerf in the top of each tapered tenon. The kerf receives a wedge. The kerf should be perpendicular to the grain of the trestle top so that the wedge will not split the work.
• Make some hardwood wedges with a shallow included angle – about 4° is right.
• For each trestle, have two clamps and a flat board at the ready.
If you are going to add a flat decorative stretcher to the front legs, you

Clamped for success. The two clamps and flat board keep the front legs lined up during assembly.

CHAPTER 12

Upside down & backward. Here's another way to level the legs. This looks odd, but it works. Clamp a pencil to the drill press table. Show the legs to the pencil.

Cut vertical. I find that I can keep the coping saw's blade perfectly vertical if the work is horizontal and the blade is vertical. A traditional bird's mouth support platform can make this easier.

Rasp horizontal. When I clean up the sawblade marks with a rasp, it's easier for me if the work is clamped in a vise. Here I'm using a fine rasp.

CHAPTER 12

need to keep the front faces of the legs in the same plane when you glue up. That's what the clamps and flat board are for.

Paint glue in the mortises, drive the legs into their mortises. Then clamp the front two legs into the same plane using the clamps and flat board. Don't freak if this makes the legs a little cockeyed compared to the top plank; it (probably) will not be noticeable.

Drive the wedges into the kerfs in the tops of the tenons. After the glue dries, trim the tenons and wedges flush to the tops of the planks.

After assembly, cut the legs to their final length and get the top surfaces of the two trestles in the same plane. An easy way to do this is with the drill press. Yes, the drill press.

My drill press has a table that is infinitely adjustable for height. I clamped a pencil to the table and cranked it so the pencil tip was 28" from the floor. Then I turned the trestles upside down on the shop floor and rubbed the legs against the tip of the pencil. Simple.

Saw the legs to final length using a crosscut backsaw. Clean up the feet with a rasp or plane and chamfer their bottom edges.

The Bottom Stretcher

The decorative bottom stretcher is a bit of a head scratcher. Should the grain run vertical or horizontal? I settled on vertical, which I think will make for a stronger trestle and make the decorative details less likely to snap off. I also think it is the best solution to deal with the wood movement of the stretcher and the top planks during the long run.

Lay out the pattern on your stretcher panel and cut it to shape with a coping saw. Clean off the sawblade marks with a rasp.

The stretcher is both glued and nailed to the legs. I used 4*d* wrought-head nails from a blacksmith for authenticity. You can substitute rose-head nails if you are on a budget.

To attach the stretcher, glue it to the legs then trim away any overhang. Then lay out your pilot holes for the nails. Drill pilots and drive the nails in.

The Tabletop

The top is merely a plank, usually about 5' to 10' long according to examples in paintings. I made mine 7' long to fit the back of my truck so I could easily transport the table.

My top is three yellow pine 2x12s that are edge-glued. I left the un-

Decorative strength. The nails are as much for decoration as for strength. You can see them clearly in paintings of these tables from the Middle Ages.

derside rough from traversing it with my jack plane. I use this as a work surface as things are much less likely to slide around. On the other face, I planed and finished the top smooth so it could be used for dining by merely flipping the worksurface over. You can use the threaded handles to secure the top, pegs or just let gravity do its job.

We have no way to know how these pieces were finished. They could have been left bare, oiled, waxed or painted. Some of the paintings show the tables as dark, which could be the wood, a pigment or the result of the smoky interiors of homes in the Middle Ages. In other paintings these tables look like they have no finish or a clear finish.

I used a homemade oil/varnish blend that I wiped on. The oil gave it a little color; the varnish gave it a little protection against spills.

CHAPTER 12

227

Note: This line depends on the final angle of your legs. Cut it square and over-wide at first.

Stretcher pattern. Enlarge 150 percent.

MUGHAL TABLE

NO.	PART	SIZES (INCHES)		
		T	W	L
6	Legs	1-5/8	1-5/8	30
2	Top planks	1-3/4	8	29
2	Stretchers	1/2	20*	13-1/2*
1	Top	1-1/4	30	84
2	Threaded handles	1-1/2	1-1/2	7

*Oversized

SEEING RED

CHAPTER 13

Something glandular.

Sometimes I think my taste in furniture comes from the fact that I'm easily startled. I'll sometimes spit a mouth full of toothpaste onto the mirror when my wife appears behind me in the bathroom.

I don't want to be alarmed or injected with adrenaline when I look at a chair, table or a sideboard because of its car-like surface finish, carving, inlay or dizzying grain patterns.

Furniture should be as natural as your fingers. Your hands are logical, unadorned and familiar. Yet when you choose to examine them closely you will be amazed at every aspect of their mechanics and form.

So when I look at furniture, I mentally divide what I see into pieces that are "red" and those that are "green." This is all standard color theory stuff that you can learn about in an introductory psychology class.

Colors in the "warm" spectrum – red, orange and yellow – tend to excite us. Colors in the "cool" spectrum – blues and greens – tend to relax.

The first time I visited Winterthur Museum – Henry Francis du Pont's amazing collection of high-style furniture from the entire timeline of American history – I felt like I needed a stiff drink afterward. While there are some fine vernacular pieces in the collection, the entire experience left me wrung out and on edge. That was a red day.

Seeing one carving by Grinling Gibbons inspires awe. Seeing an entire room of his work induces nausea.

I don't mean to pick on Winterthur. It's one of the most fantastic

CHAPTER 13

"Progress consists, not in the increase of truth, but in freeing it from its wrappings. The truth is obtained like gold, not by letting it grow bigger, but by washing off from it everything that isn't gold."

— *Leo Tolstoy's Diaries (1985) edited and translated by R. F. Christian. London: Athlone Press, Vol 2, p. 512*

furniture collections on the planet. To be fair, I get the same unpleasant blood buzz in European castles and manor homes. There is only so much of the stuff I can endure.

Contrast that with my first visit to the Aiken-Rhett House in Charleston, S.C. The 1820 house is opulent in many ways, but much of that is muted by the fact that many rooms were empty of furnishings during my visit. For me, what's most remarkable about the house are the slave quarters and work areas on the building's ground floor. And the work yard shown on the previous spread.

The first time I walked in there, I didn't want to leave. While our tour guide encouraged us to climb the stairs to the "nice" portion of the house, I stayed put. The room and its furnishings were worn, logical, suited for use and – above all – oddly soothing.

I'm a white guy who was raised in the deep South in schools that were *de facto* segregated. (My high school mascot was a fat Confederate named "Johnny Reb.") I'm not supposed to feel comfortable in slave quarters. But I did.

My affection for "green" furniture was sometimes a hindrance in my career as an editor of a woodworking magazine. When you have a title like "editor" you get asked to judge other people's work at furniture shows and hand out blue ribbons for design and construction.

I'll be honest: If you want to win a ribbon at an American furniture show, it pays to have a piece that incorporates carving, marquetry, veneer and French polish. Figured wood helps, too. You want to grab the judges by the lapels and open all the ports on their glands.

Those pieces win the prizes almost every time. And perhaps it's the ornament that also makes people open their checkbooks to purchase them. But what happens when the adrenaline fades? When you have to live with a "red" piece in your house? To me it's like having a giant leering (if harmless) vampire in your living room. It's unsettling.

During furniture competitions, I always stick up for the pieces that I would want to live with. I like pieces that are well-made, well-finished and emphasize form over flash. But mostly I want to take them home – not show them to my wife's boss as proof of my good taste.

That approach will put you in the minority among the judges in a furniture competition.

Think about this when you fall in love with a piece of furniture in a magazine or book. It can be like a heavy crush on a Hollywood starlet. Something glandular. That's fine when looking at pictures. But turn the page for a minute and think: Would I want to live with that every day for the next 30 years?

CHAPTER 13

CHAIRS! CHAIRS!
ANOTHER INTRODUCTION

Chairs.

Years ago we had a huge party in our house before the start of a Woodworking in America event. I know it was a good party because the cops showed up a couple times.

The first time they showed up, they were responding to a report from a neighbor that possible terrorists were walking down Greenbriar Avenue. However, it turned out to be just woodworkers with long beards and black clothing.

The second time the cops showed up it was for noise. I missed this second encounter with the constabulary because I was trapped in my kitchen listening to two chairmakers who were stoned out of their gourds.

"What do you like to do outside of woodworking?" one guest asked the chairmakers.

"Chairs! All I think about is chairs," responded one high-as-a-kite chairmaker. Cue a long awkward silence. Then he said: "Chairs! Chairs!"

And then he said quietly, like pillow talk: "Chairs."

I don't do drugs, but that's exactly how I've felt since the late 1990s when I first picked up a copy of John Brown's "Welsh Stick Chairs." I love the sculptural aspect of chairs. The weird geometry. The fact that you have to ask – no, demand – that just a few sticks of wood do a damn difficult job.

And chairs have to look good if they are to survive.

Ash and elm stick chair, 1760-1840. Difficult to date and probably impossible to ascribe to a particular area. Chairs of this kind are normally quite plain, often with three legs, but can have shaped combs, turned uprights, and occasionally shaped back splats.

The chair that inspired my design, from a Shire pamphlet published in the U.K. on Welsh furniture by Richard Bebb titled "Welsh Country Furniture" (1994).

CHAPTER 14

After I read Brown's book, however, I was at a loss as to what to do next. I wanted to take a class in chairmaking, but I didn't want to learn to build a Windsor. (Note: There's nothing wrong with Windsor chairs as long as you fancy sundresses, parasols and lacy underwear.) I wanted to travel to Wales and camp out on John Brown's doorstep *á la* "Fight Club" until he taught me to make a chair. But I didn't have the money to fly to the U.K. Hell, I don't think I could then find Wales on a map.

Then – thanks to the vagaries of global currency – the Canadian dollar took a giant goose dump.

Suddenly I could afford to take a chair class in Canada. And Dave Fleming, a chairmaker in Cobden, Ontario, was willing to teach a class in making a Welsh stick chair.

I convinced a near-stranger named John Hoffman to take Fleming's class with me (John is now the co-owner of Lost Art Press, our publishing company). And I can honestly say that that single week in 2003 was the most mentally and physically exhausting five days I've ever endured. We were in the wilds of Canada. In March. With a crap ton of snow. And it was heaven.

On the day we saddled the elm seats I thought my fingers might break off. When we turned the spindles on the spring-pole lathe I was certain I was going to gouge out an eyeball. And on Friday night, the last day of the class, Dave worked with us until almost midnight to get our chairs assembled and ready for the trip south.

I came home from that class and built a second chair within a couple weeks. And since then, I've been building chairs every year. Many of them were horrible and were given away. A couple were chopped up for parts. And eventually I began to sell a few.

But despite my crazy passion for chairs, there are two reasons I've never felt like a true "chairmaker," the people who chop down a tree and transform it into a log.

One, I live in a dense urban environment. Getting forest logs is no small affair. And street trees are terrible for chairmaking because they grow in 10 different directions at once. Second, I've also spent most of my life making casework – I love cutting dovetails, sticking moulding and fitting drawers. Most people in the chairmaker's club just do chairmaking. (And marijuana, I hear.)

So I've mostly kept my mouth shut about how I make chairs. Compared to real chairmakers, my methods are odd. I try to use tools, woods and techniques typical to joiners and cabinetmakers instead of chairmaking. I don't use spoon bits. Heck, I just bought my first adze in June, and I rarely ever use a drawknife.

Plus I've always had a sneaking suspicion that my chairs suck.

When I wrote "The Anarchist's Design Book" in 2014, I decided to include some staked backstools and side chairs in the book. These greatly simplified proto-chairs were good baby steps for woodworkers who were interested in woodworking. And they allowed me to discuss some basic methods I use.

Then I turned 50 years old in 2018, and I said "screw it." I decided my chairs were good enough. And that's why you are reading this rambling story right now.

A lot of the methods you'll find in the following pages are cribbed from a variety of sources. Some are techniques I've picked up from reading every book I could find on making chairs. Some techniques are from taking classes. Some are from traditional woodworking practice. And a few I've developed on my own (which I take no credit for as they were certainly discovered centuries ago).

The same goes for the designs. The armchair and high stool are based on Welsh designs. The stool springs from a book by Richard Bebb titled "Welsh Furniture 1250-1950" (Saer Books). He shows a similar three-legged stool from his collection in that book. I took the idea and made radical changes to the geometry and shape of the components.

The armchair is based on many many historical Welsh chair forms. But the stinger of inspiration came from a Shire pamphlet on Welsh furniture (also written by Richard Bebb) where he showed a stick chair without an undercarriage that was ink written like lightning.

Of course I made a ton of changes to that chair. And I continue to make small changes to its design to this day.

I also insist on boring you by naming the people who influenced me deeply in chairmaking. At the top of the heap is John Brown. But not his chairs in "Welsh Stick Chairs." Those were his early chairs. I love his later chairs, which I've recently discovered were also the result of many years of hard labor by Christopher Williams, a Welsh chairmaker who worked with Brown for a decade. Together, they did incredible work.

Dave Fleming gave me my first good taste of the craft. Don Weber showed me how to do it with even fewer tools. And Peter Galbert, author of "Chairmaker's Notebook," pulled the curtain away on many advanced techniques. (I am eternally grateful that Pete doesn't build Welsh chairs because I'd probably have to hang up my brace.)

I hope that these written accounts of my techniques will inspire you

CHAPTER 14

One of many unusual chairs I've built through the years. This one in sycamore and maple.

to pick up the tools and give it a try. The first chair you build is the hardest. They get easier and easier until you end up in someone's kitchen in Kentucky with weed on your breath and the cops at the door.

But I'm getting ahead of myself.

NOTES ON CHAIR COMFORT

CHAPTER 15

Make friends when you make chairs.

Years ago, I stumbled into an old storefront in rural Virginia with some friends and encountered one of the thousands of rocking chairs that have been inspired by Sam Maloof. It was a dramatic example of the form with a huge sweeping back and long rockers. But most amazing was the seat itself.

It was a massive chunk of walnut that had been deeply scooped out – perhaps a 2"-deep saddle. And the pommel of the seat was tall – almost 2" high.

One of my friends said, "Do you know how come that's a lady's chair?" The rest of us shrugged.

"Because that seat 'lifts and separates.'"

Underwear jokes aside, the guy was right. Sitting in the chair felt like I was being prepped for a medical exam that few people enjoy. The seat looked gorgeous, but you don't sit on a seat with your eyeballs. So, you have to think hard about the human rump (and other body parts) when designing a chair.

Chair design is a topic that can fill an entire book. We don't have the space for that here, so I'm going to write about how I design the

You don't need much. A shallow saddle provides enough contact so it doesn't feel like you are sitting on a board. Yet it doesn't constrict movement or blood flow.

all-wood chairs that I build. Some of my guidelines might seem at odds with modern rules for chairs, but that's because my chairs aren't entirely modern. I take many cues from ancient chairs.

Start with the Saddle

One of the most important principles in chair comfort is that "sitting" and "sitting still" are not the same thing. And we rarely sit still.

> *One of the major difficulties in the design of seating is that sitting is…viewed as a static activity while, in actuality, it is a rather dynamic one.*
> — *"Human Dimension & Interior Space," by Julius Panero and Martin Zelnik*

This is the problem with deeply saddled seats. We sit in them and they feel amazing at first – they support and cradle the bottom in a pleasant way. The only problem is that we can't often sit still. Here's why. In a typical chair, the sitter's weight is confined to about four square inches of buttocks. The pressure on that small area requires us to shift our weight, even just a little, to remain comfortable.

But a deeply saddled seat doesn't allow us to move much, if at all. So, these sorts of seats become agonizing in short order.

I have yet to see an ancient chair that is sculpted as dramatically as our modern Jell-O moulds with legs. I'm sure they are out there, but they've never been the dominant form. Instead, many old chairs had shallow saddling (maybe 1/4" to 1/2") or even no saddle whatsoever. A shallow saddle gives you some curve but also allows you to reposition yourself with ease. (Oh, and they are easier to make.)

I also suspect that many all-wood chairs would be draped with an animal skin or a small cushion. I've put sheepskins on all my chairs and can attest that even the minor cushioning they provide makes a world of difference in the department of butt comfort. (You'll see this cushion concept again when I sneak it into a discussion of seat height.)

For some reason, some modern chairmakers are masochists and seek to make a chair as comfortable as a La-Z-Boy recliner via the magic of curvy valleys. This strict attitude reminds me of people who insist that a single scrap of sandpaper in a shop is an abomination. Lighten up, Francis, and go fetch a cushion.

Seat Height

How far is the front of the chair from the floor? The typical modern chair height is 18". Sorry to say, I think that is too high to be a general rule.

Tall seats are punishing for shorter sitters. If their feet cannot rest flat on the floor, the front edge of the seat will constrict blood flow in the thighs and produce agony.

Slightly shorter seats, however, are just fine for tall sitters. Their feet can still sit on the floor and their thighs hover above the seat – allowing blood flow. The only downside to a tall person sitting in a shorter chair is the short chair is a little more difficult to dismount.

(Side note: This is true for a table's height as well. Standard table height is 30". A high table is a pain for a shorter people. But a slightly shorter table – 29" or even 28" – is no problem for a tall sitter.)

CHAIR COMFORT

22"

8" to 9"

16-3/4" to 17"

So, if 18" is too high as an overall rule, what should the height be? The answer is not cut and dried with a custom chair. Here are the questions I ask to calculate the seat height:

1. What is the sitter's "popliteal height?" Some people call this "stool height." It's the distance from the bottom of the foot to the bottom of the thigh of a seated person. It ranges from 14" to 19-3/8" in the general population.

2. What sort of footwear will the sitter use? Work boots, 3"-high heels and moccasins all can change the equation.

3. What is the chair to be used for? If it's for dining or keyboarding, it should be a little higher so it is easy to mount and dismount. If it is for relaxing, it should be lower. How low? Seats can be as low as 12"-13" for lounging. Low seats allow you to stretch your legs – a luxury. Low chairs are harder to get out of – but that's the point.

4. Will there be a cushion or other seat cover? Cushions can add 2" or more to the seat height, so you should subtract that when making the chair's frame.

You might be wondering how to determine the seat height for the general populace instead of for a particular person. When I need to do that, I typically use 16-3/4" or 17" for a dining/working chair. And 15" to 16" for a lounging chair. These are on the low side, but they aren't radically low. Tall people will hardly notice. Short people definitely will, and they'll be grateful.

Seat Depth

A typical seat depth for one of my chairs is 16". Once you get deeper than 17", you risk cutting off the sitter's blood flow behind the knees. Surprisingly, shallow seats work well. I have made seats as shallow as 12" and they sit just fine (unless you have an epic backside or the seat is too high. Having both is a disastrous combination). A shallow and low seat also prevents the blood in your thighs from being constricted.

In general, I don't mess with the seat depth too much. If it's between 14" and 16" I know it will work in most cases. This slight flexibility allows me to build using narrower boards. If I have to glue up my seat from two 7"-wide boards, I'll do that and call the 14"-deep seat done. I won't glue on an additional 2"-wide strip of wood to get to the magic 16" depth.

We're not done with the seat quite yet. But to understand the last bit of seat data, we need to first understand the armrest/armbow.

"In the usual way of thinking, you have ideas, and then you learn technical skill so you can express them. In reality it's often the reverse: skill gives you ideas. The hand guides the brain nearly as much as the brain guides the hand."

— *"The Lost Carving" (Penguin) by David Esterly*

Three fingers. Here I've elevated the front legs of the chair until the seat is three fingers out of level. This tilt slides the body back toward the tall sticks and armbow.

Armrest Height

Biometric data suggests the top of the armrest should be about 7" to 10" from the seat, depending on the sitter. I usually shoot for 8" to 9" (or less). People have asked for 10" – this height makes some people shrug their shoulders, and you can feel it in the neck after a while. My rule of thumb is 8" for shorter people and 9" for taller ones.

Backrest & Seat Tilt

The small of the back – sometimes called the "lumbar" region – is where I do a lot of work to make a chair comfortable. If you build a chair that supports the lumbar spine, you will make friends – as well as chairs. The lumbar is about 7" to 9" above the seat. This is why I keep my armbows at 8" as much as I can and add a "doubler" above it (and sometimes below it) to increase the thickness of the armbow so I can support the lumbar.

Chairs that lack lumbar support are fatiguing to me. I squirm to push my lower back against the chair's back, but my shoulders and buttocks prevent it. I guess this is why we have lumbar pillows. Nothing wrong with a pillow.

One of the oft-overlooked aspects of chair design – the seat's tilt – can help the lumbar region get to its destination, which is the armbow in my chairs or a lower slat in ladderback chairs.

Most chairs tilt a little toward the back. A seat that is flat to the floor can feel like you are being thrust forward and out of the seat. Adding some additional tilt can encourage the sitter to slide backward and put their lumbar directly on the armbow.

But how much tilt? I like Welsh chairmaker John Brown's method of using his fingers and a spirit level. Put a level on the seat's pommel so it runs from the front to the back of the chair. Raise the spirit level at the rear of the seat until it indicates it is level. If you can get one finger (plus a little more) under the level at the back, that's a chair that's for dining or other proper things – keyboarding etc. Two fingers and you have a chair that is good for lounging. Three fingers – alcohol consumption.

You can cut the legs down to get the tilt you want (this is a technique shown multiple times in this book).

Back Angle

For me this is where the rules get blurry and surprisingly flexible. Most modern chairs have the chair's back tilted back about 5° to 7° or so. That's fine. But adding a couple degrees can also encourage the body to touch the chair's armbow and doubler.

So, I tend to tilt the back about 9° backward, but I will tilt it a little more at times. And I will continue to play with different angles as there are some discoveries to be made. Recently I built a copy of an Irish chair that had its back tilted at 25°. That's about three times as much as normal. As I built the chair I imagined that sitting in it would be like visiting the dentist. I was wrong.

It wasn't as different as expected. This chair – called a Gibson, hedge or famine chair – was historically used as a kitchen table chair. Even though it looked more like a chair for sunbathing. Your eyes and expectations can deceive you. So don't believe them, this book or your vicar. Work it out yourself.

Sit back. The back on this Irish Gibson chair tilts back at 25°. Yet, it doesn't feel like a deck chair. It feels quite normal.

Crest Rail Height

How high should the crest (aka headrest or comb) be? That depends. For customers who want to be able to pass out in their chairs I want to have a high comb to cradle the head during unconsciousness after reading a good novel. So, I measure to the base of the skull. I think these chairs look too tall, but some customers like them.

What I prefer is to have a crest that supports the shoulder blades without the crest digging into them. This is about 22" above the seat.

But this location can be tricky depending on how beefy the sitter is. Broad-shouldered sitters can feel the ends of a significantly curved crest rail push into their shoulders. Thinner sitters of the same height cannot.

The easy way out is to simply raise the crest rail a couple inches, however this dramatically affects the way the chair looks. I prefer a compact chair. Another way out is to make the crest rail so it doesn't have as pronounced a curve. My crest rail typically has a 10" radius. That's tight, but it keeps the back sticks from being bent during assembly because the curve of the crest, armbow and seat all match. (Study the drawings in the chapter on the armchair's templates and you'll understand what I mean here.) The crest can be curved less, such as a 14" or 16" radius (which is OK). Or it can be flat (which fixes one problem but causes another by reducing support for the curve of the shoulder blades).

Here's the good news on the crest rail: You can do it at the end of the construction process and experiment with different crest rails – different curves and stick spacing. Dry-fit a prototype crest rail and see how it feels to your back. Make some changes and see how they feel.

Nuclear Sheep

When I talk about chair comfort with other chairmakers, it's inevitable that someone will say: Ah heck, just put a cushion on it and call it done.

Me, I like sheepskins – a traditional Welsh chair covering. They don't add much bulk to the seat, and they won't make the seat too high. But they do add some cushioning and warmth. (And they give me an excuse to go to IKEA without a disguise.)

So do your best to make your chairs comfortable. But know that it's never a bad idea to become a man (or a woman) of the cloth.

STAKED BACKSTOOL

CHAPTER 16

An unstable past.

Somewhere between the stool and the chair is an intermediate form of staked furniture that has been largely discarded and forgotten: the backstool. This simple seat is exactly as its name suggests: a stool with a simple backrest, no arms.

The base of a backstool can have three, four or five legs, and the back can be almost anything: spindles, sticks, roots or a solid plank of wood.

This form shows up frequently in the Western world, and is still built in some European countries where it features a backrest that's a solid plank that's typically carved, pierced or shaped.

After looking at a lot of backstools, I suspect that some started as stools with a back added later. Likewise, I suspect that a lot of five-legged backstools started life as simple three-legged stools. Later owners added a back and a couple legs for stability.

The three-legged form of backstool is ideal for uneven or dirt floors, though it looks wrong at first to modern eyes, like a Zap Xebra three-wheeled car. Though we know intellectually that a three-legged stool is stable, adding a backrest to it throws our eyes off.

Even Victor Chinnery, the dean of English furniture, wrote the following warning about backstools in "Oak Furniture: The British Tradi-

Stool sample. A collection of backstools at the Swiss National Museum (photo by Mark Firley).

tion" (Antique Collectors Club, 1979):

> *Three feet will stand with greater stability on an irregular surface, but it nevertheless takes a certain amount of skill to sit comfortably in such a chair, since it is easily overbalanced.*

Judging from the number of extant three-legged backstools, that statement seemed like it was written with the eyes, not the buttocks. But the only way to test the statement was to build a three-legged critter and sit in it after a few beers. So I did – that's the prototype with a roundish seat you'll see in some photos in this chapter.

An unstable past. Many furniture writers claim the three-legged backstool is tippy. I think it's unlikely they ever sat in one.

Skipping to the End

As I designed this backstool, I followed the geometry I found in other three-legged backstools and chairs – usually the rear leg rakes backward significantly. So I was careful to replicate that feature when I made models of three-legged backstools before building one.

As my backstool came together I sat on it at every stage in construction. At first I expected to be tossed to the floor. That didn't happen. And when I had my first formal sit-down in the completed backstool, here's what I felt: stable.

My front legs were planted over the front legs of the backstool. My tailbone was on top of the back leg. I leaned back and my head hovered over the footprint of the rear leg. I cautiously creeped my cheeks left. Then right. I reached for my fourth beer.

And…nothing.

How does the backstool get its reputation as being tippy as a drunken uncle? Part of the instability is an optical illusion, but part of it is real. It just has little to do with sitting on the thing.

"I sit on a man's back, choking him, and making him carry me, and yet assure myself and others that I am very sorry for him and wish to ease his lot by any means possible, except getting off his back."

— Leo Tolstoy (1828-1910), "Writings on Civil Disobedience and Nonviolence" (1886)

Backstool   Pl. 8

B. Morrow-Cribbs Inv. Del. et Sculp

CHAPTER 16

We use chairs and stools for more than sitting. If you stand or kneel on this seat and the downward pressure is outside the triangle created by the three legs, you'll get a rude surprise. Or say you stand behind the chair and lean on the crest rail. If you lean on its center then nothing happens. If, however, you lean on one end of the crest rail, you might just kiss the floor.

If you aren't sold on the idea of a three-legged place to sit down, that's OK. It's simple work to make this backstool with four legs instead of three. But consider this: If you do have the guts to make the three-legged version, you'll never have to yell at your kids for tipping backward in their backstool.

Begin with the Seat

When making the seat board, you can orient the grain in either direction (front to back, or left to right). I've done it both ways. In theory, running the grain from front to back makes the chair stronger and makes some parts of the scooped-out section, called the saddle, easier to make.

But I've seen lots of old chairs with the grain running left to right that have survived a few hundred years. So it's a valid way to make a backstool or a chair and is the grain orientation I used in these backstools. We will be scooping out the seat with a jack plane, so either grain configuration is fine.

The photos of the construction process show two backstools being made, a prototype and a finished version. The only significant differences between the two are the shape of the seat, the curvature on the crest rail and the leg profile. The finished version – with its square-ish seat and deep crest rail – is the superior design, but feel free to adopt details from either in your backstool.

Just like with the sawbench, you want a thick plank for the seat of the backstool. I started with 3"-thick rough poplar that I planed down to about 2-1/2". I had to glue up three pieces of wood to get to the correct width. I think it's best to plan your seat joints so that the legs do not pass through these edge joints. In theory, this shouldn't matter – a good glue joint is as strong as the wood. But in practice….

Once you get the seat to finished size, lay out the position of the three legs on its underside. You can follow my leg layout in the illustration or make a half-scale model with wire like in the sawbench chapter and

Thickness by hand. By traversing the seat blank with a jack plane, you can quickly flatten it and get it to its finished thickness. Don't bother removing the furrows – called "dawks" – left by the jack.

tinker with the rake and splay.

The centers of the mortises for the two front legs are 2-1/2" from the front edge of the seat and 2-1/2" from each side of the seat. The rear leg is on the centerline of the seat; its center is 2-3/4" from the rear edge of the seat.

To lay out the sightlines for the front legs, first draw a line that connects those two mortise locations for the front legs. The sightline for each front leg is 21° off that line. The resultant angle is 13°. Lock your bevel gauge to 13° and tape it to the sightline. Bore a 5/8"-diameter mortise through the seat. Repeat for the other front leg.

The rear leg uses the centerline on the underside of the seat as its sightline. Its resultant angle is 23°. This provides a dramatic backward sweep to the rear leg and adds stability to the backstool. Lock your bevel gauge to 23°. Tape it to the centerline and bore a 5/8" mortise for the rear leg.

CHAPTER 16

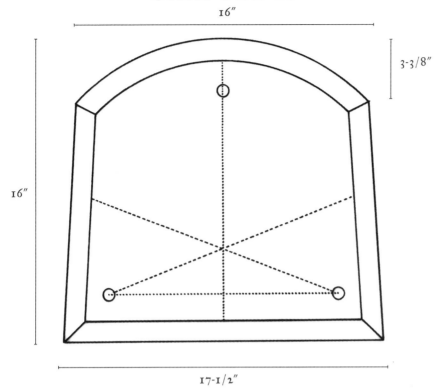

Underside of the seat.

Ream the Mortises

When I reamed these mortises, I used an electric drill instead of a brace or drill press. All three tools do a fine job, and you might develop a preference for one over the other. Most chairmakers do.

Keep reaming until the tool fills the small end of the 5/8" mortise, then stop. Be careful that you don't let the reamer spin uselessly in the mortise because that will burnish the interior of the mortise, which makes it difficult for the glue to do its job.

Shape the Seat

The seat can be almost any shape, including just leaving it as a rectangular plank. Some backstool seats even have the bark still on them. My prototype has a D-shaped seat, which you can mark with trammel

Eschew the banjo. I use the banjo drilling jig to teach others about resultant angles, but I find it faster and simpler to drill mortises with a brace and auger bit. Try it a couple times on some scrap and you might rethink that banjo solo.

Ream & confirm. Ream each mortise and check your progress as you go. I have a 3/4"-diameter dummy leg with a tapered tenon cut on one end that I use to check the angle of the leg and the progress of the reamer.

CHAPTER 16

Easy peeler. You can remove a shocking amount of material with a sharp drawknife. Use a slicing motion; move the knife laterally as you pull it toward you. You will quickly get a feel for the seat's grain direction, even if it's your first time with the tool.

points. (A stick, nail and pencil will also do.) The finished backstool has a trapezoid-ish shape with a curve at the back.

I sawed the seat to rough shape with a band saw and relieved the underside with a drawknife. I roughed in a 1-1/8" x 1-1/8" chamfer around the seat. Then I cleaned up the edges with a spokeshave and handplane.

Shave a Leg or Three

By this time, I was honestly a bit weary of working on the seat, so I took some time to shave the legs and cut the tapered tenons on their ends. The legs start out as 1-5/8"-square sticks that I turned into tapered octagons with a jack plane.

Then you can use them as is, or shave them round with a spokeshave and scraper.

No matter what profile I use, I want them to be 1-5/8" diameter at

A close shave. A flat-bottom spokeshave set to a fine cut will remove the tool marks left by the drawknife. Stop refining the surfaces when you are satisfied.

Make facets. This scraping tool, sometimes called a chair devil, works like a spokeshave to clean up the legs (left). A variety of leg profiles work, including the six-sided legs in the Swiss stool at right (photo by Mark Firley).

CHAPTER 16

Eyeball that gap. Hold the tenon cutter and leg like this to ensure the tenon will be centered on the leg. If you cannot see the gap between the tool and the leg then you cannot control it.

the foot and taper to 1-1/8" diameter at the top. (The 1-1/8" is the maximum diameter my tapered tenon cutter can receive.) I then rough in the shape of the conical tenon with either a drawknife or on the lathe.

The tenon should be about 3-1/2" long and 1-1/8" in diameter at its base.

Then cut the tenon to its final shape with a 5/8" tapered tenon cutter. Set the tool to take a light and consistent cut. If your tool is poorly set the tenon will not match its mortise, or its surface will be so rough there won't be much contact inside the joints.

Knock the legs into their mortises and give the stool a test-sit. Don't be worried if it feels odd to your bottom. The legs haven't been trimmed. Now it's time to transform the stool into a backstool.

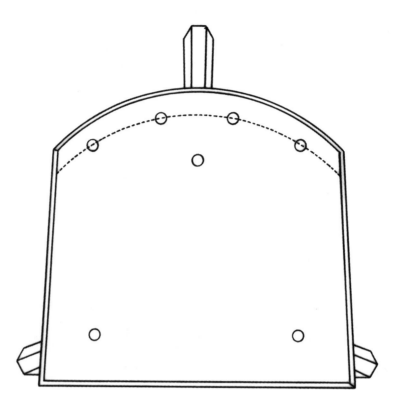

Spindle layout on the seat.

Lay Out the Spindles

This backstool has the simplest spindle layout possible, yet it works well when you put your back into it. The four 5/8"-diameter mortises for the spindles are centered on a line that is parallel to the curved back edge of the seat and 1-1/8" in from the back edge.

First draw the curved line on the seat – I aligned a pencil to the rule of a combination square set to 1-1/8" and kept the square's head in contact with the seat as I steered it around the curve. Then I transferred the centerline of the seat from the underside to the top of the seat.

Set a pair of dividers to 2". From the centerline, walk the dividers one step along your layout line for the mortises. That's the location of the first spindle. Take two more steps in the same direction; that's the location of the second. Return the dividers to the centerline and repeat the process, this time walking the other direction along the layout line.

CHAPTER 16

Walk this way. With dividers set to 2", you can easily lay out the four spindles with 4" between each mortise.

Boring the mortises is simple work. The sightline for each of the four mortises is 0°, or straight ahead to the front of the seat. The resultant angle for each spindle is 10°. Set your bevel gauge to 10° and tape it to a sightline. Bore a 5/8"-diameter, 1-1/2"-deep hole into the seat.

Make the Spindles & Crest

The grain in the spindles needs to be arrow-straight. If you cannot rive the stock, saw your spindles so the fibers run from end to end as much as possible. The four spindles begin as 3/4"-square blanks (13-3/4"

Tapered octagons. After creating the tenons on the ends of the octagonal spindles, I used a plane to taper the spindles to get smaller at the top.

long) that I shave to octagons. For the prototype backstool I shaved them round and tapered them. For the finished backstool I merely tapered the octagons. (See a fixture for making octagons in the next chapter.)

In the end, the spindles should end up with a 5/8"-diameter x 1-1/4"-long tenon at the bottom and a 1/2"-diameter x 1"-long tenon at the top. These straight, cylindrical (non-conical) tenons can be made with a spokeshave or on the lathe.

The crest can be made several different ways. You can steam-bend it, create a bent lamination from multiple thin plys glued together on a form, or go full-on Welsh: Work with what you got. That means using a crooked stick from the woods or sawing the crest out of a solid piece of wood.

For the prototype, I sawed the crest from a piece of 1-3/4" x 2-1/2" x 17-1/2" red oak. To draw the curved shape of the crest I used a flexible wooden batten that I bent across the crest and traced with a pencil. Then I moved the batten and traced a second line 7/8" away from the first. After sawing out the crest and cleaning it up, it ended up at 3/4" thick.

Before cutting the curves, I drilled the 1/2" mortises for the spindles. I laid these mortises out just like on the seat at 4" apart. The mortises

CHAPTER 16

Driving spindles. Check the diameter of the spindles with care before driving them in. The tenoned section should be a cylinder, not a cone. Fat spindles can split the seat.

Drill, then saw. The crest is more stable on the bench and easier to drill while it is thick and square.

should be 1-1/4" deep.

I sawed the two curves on the band saw and cleaned up the tool marks with a spokeshave and card scraper.

For the finished backstool, I steam-bent the crest rail to a curve that matched the curve along the rear of the seat.

Sidebar: Steam-bending a Crest Rail

Steam-bending wood is no more difficult than cooking pasta. Imagine sticks of linguine; it comes to you straight and rigid. Applying heat and moisture loosens it up so you can bend it to almost any form you please. Then, when the pasta cools and dries, it retains that new shape.

It's really that simple.

Steam-bending is best done on wood that is somewhat green or air-

BACKSTOOL

Hey look, it's furniture. If you live in the city and have trouble getting green wood, try firewood bundles. These are just long enough for many chair parts.

The high-class setup. A steam box with a steam generator makes it easy to get your parts limber enough for bending.

> "Furniture is the servant of fantasy just as much as it is the response to practical everyday needs."
>
> Edward Lucie-Smith (1933-)
> "Furniture: A Concise History"

dried – not kiln-dried. I've tried many tricks to get kiln-dried wood to bend but have had little luck. It's like trying to boil a mess of scorched pasta. It won't bend when heated. It just cracks and breaks.

If you are having trouble finding air-dried wood, buy a bundle of firewood at the local grocery. This material is split, air-dried and usually about 14" to 20" long – enough for a crest rail. Here in the Midwest, our firewood bundles are oak, ash, walnut (!) and tulip poplar – and they are usually about 30 percent moisture content (MC) if they haven't been rotting behind the store's propane tanks for too long.

To bend it you need a steam box and a source of steam. The steam box can be anything, from PVC pipe to some plywood scraps screwed together. You don't want air-tight joinery, otherwise you are building a bomb. My latest steam box took about an hour to build and should last about a decade. It's a leaky box with drainage holes at one end and a hinged door at the other that is held shut with rubber bands.

Don't obsess about it. Don't worry about it. Just put down this book and make one from crap sitting around your shop.

CHAPTER 16

Or in the oven. The oven is a good source of high, continuous heat. You are only limited by the size of the oven itself.

The source of steam can be a teakettle or wallpaper steamer. Or you can spend the same money and buy a steam generator designed for steam bending that includes all the fittings and hoses to make it a snap.

You can bend the wood around the rear curve of the seat blank (squeeze it with a strap clamp) or make a dedicated form from MDF. My form for this crest rail is made from four layers of 3/4"-thick MDF that are glued and nailed together. (No, the moisture won't hurt the form.) The radius is the same as the curve on the back of the seat. (See the next chapter on the staked chair for a plan for the form.)

Crank up the steam while you prepare the stock for the crest rail.

Horizontal press. A vise gives you tremendous mechanical advantage when bending wood. A child can provide enough force to bend a 3/4"-thick crest rail.

Four-square the firewood (this is fun) and plane it to 3/4" thick x 2-1/2" wide x 18" long or longer. Handplane all the faces and edges because this will make your life easier after the piece comes out of the form. Smooth surfaces create smooth surfaces. (Curved surfaces are difficult to smooth.)

Put your rail in the steam box and let it steam for 60 to 80 minutes. Remove the stick and bend it in the form with clamps. (Or pull it against the rear of your seat with a strap clamp.)

Let it sit for two days before releasing the clamps.

So before you leave this sidebar and return to your normal life, know this: Don't read anything more about steam-bending before attempting it. Do not worry about it or over-analyze it. It has been done successfully for centuries with less instruction than above.

Wait, what are you still doing here? Not convinced you should make a steam box? OK, let's try this. Another way to bend wood without fussing over the temperature is to use my mother's recipe for beef brisket.

She would seal the brisket in a roasting pan covered in foil and cook it in the oven until the meat fell apart on your fork. Go to the grocery and buy a bundle of firewood ($3.99) and a roasting pan ($2).

I typically get three crest rails from a split of oak and plane them all

CHAPTER 16

Impressed? Firewood is easily transformed into a crest rail with almost no cost for raw materials or tools.

four-square. Preheat the oven to 450° F. Fill the aluminum roasting pan with hot water, put the oak in and seal the pan with two layers of aluminum foil. Cut a 1/2" slit in the top and roast (actually, poach) the wood in the oven for 75-80 minutes. Then take it to the bending form.

The easiest way to bend a 3/4" crest rail is to use the help of a bench vise. Clamp half the form to the jaw of your vise and the other half to the bench.

Drop the poached oak between the two parts of the form and crank the vise closed. Simple. Put two bar clamps across the form and remove it from the vise. In two days take the clamps off, drill the mortises and you'll have a crest rail for your backstool.

Not fancy. I forget who showed me this trick – perhaps bodger Don Weber. Instead of rigging an odd dog system on your workbench, you can hold the seat in place by screwing a board to its underside. Then clamp that board in your face vise.

Saddling the Seat

Scooping out the seat, even a little, adds to the comfort of the backstool. As I studied old pieces before building this one, I wondered how the makers would do this task if they didn't have an adze, scorp or travisher.

I don't know how they did it. But here's what I did.

As I mentioned earlier, I oriented the grain of the seat so the fibers run from side to side instead of front to back. That allowed me to scoop out the seat using a jack plane with an iron that has a curved cutting edge.

The iron's curve is a segment of an arc with a 10" radius. With the iron set for a rank cut (.02"-thick shavings), I began hogging out the area where the saddle should be deepest. When the plane stopped cutting, I shifted it to the left until it was able to take a cut again. I shifted it to the right and did the same thing.

Then I returned to the middle and planed this area again. I repeated this process, fanning out left and right to create a gradual valley. After 25

CHAPTER 16

Meet jack. With a properly curved iron, a jack plane can easily create a deep valley in the seat. Set the iron rank. Plane until the tool stops cutting, then shift to the side. Repeat. Check your work.

An adequate saddle. While the shape of this seat wouldn't pass muster in a high-style home, it works.

Scrape it smooth. A card scraper finishes the job. No inshave, travisher or spoon-bottom plane is necessary. It's not ideal, but it's not bad, either.

minutes of work, I had created a saddle that was about 7/16" deep and rose gradually to the front and back of the chair.

While this isn't the shape of a saddle you'll see on a high-style Windsor chair, you do see this sort of saddle on vernacular chairs.

After refining the shape as much as possible with a jack, I switched to a card scraper and smoothed out the furrows created by the jack's curved iron.

Clean-up & Assembly

The legs are attached to the seat in the same manner used with the sawbench. Paint the tenons and mortises with hide glue, drive the legs in with a mallet or hammer and wedge the tenons where they poke through the seat.

No matter what the glue instructions say, I let the leg-to-seat joints cure overnight before pushing them around or leveling them to the seat. This joint is the core of the backstool's strength, so I don't want to do anything that will disrupt the adhesion process.

After I sawed, planed and scraped the seat joints level, I cleaned up

CHAPTER 16

Knocked flat. Tap the crest up and down until it is parallel with the seat board. It might look cockeyed, but that's because you haven't leveled the feet of the backstool. Obey the tape measure.

the saddle as much as possible because I won't be able to clean up the rear of the seat once the spindles are glued in.

Here's how I put the back together.

Paint the bottoms of the spindles and the mortises in the seat with glue. Drive the spindles in with a hammer until the tenon stops moving.

To attach the crest, paint glue into the mortises and a little onto the tops of the spindles. Drive the crest on with a mallet. You want the crest to be parallel to the seat. So measure between the seat and crest on both ends of the crest. Adjust the crest up and down with a mallet until it is parallel. Drill a hole through the crest and each tenon, and pin each joint with a bit of a bamboo skewer and dab of glue.

After the glue cures, trim up the wedges and level the legs, much like on the sawbench. The only difference is you want the front of the seat to be 17-1/2" from the floor and the back of the seat to be 16" from the floor.

How do you do this? Easy. Level the front two legs left to right. Then turn the level 90° so it runs from the front of the seat to the rear leg. Keep putting wedges under the front legs until the front of the seat is 1-1/2" higher than the back. You can test this by raising the end of the level that's over the back leg until it is 1-1/2" off the seat. When the bubble in the level hits the middle, your seat is at the right pitch.

Mark the legs for cutting and saw them to final length. (There are detailed instructions for this in the chapter on sawbenches.)

Clean up the backstool for paint. If you built this using poplar and oak, the paint will definitely improve its appearance, hiding the incongruous grain patterns and revealing the form of the backstool. I used black milk paint, sanding between coats.

"In many shops half the things are everybody's business and never done; the others are nobody's business and half done."

— James W. See, "Extracts from Chordal's Letters" (American Machinist, 1880)

STAKED BACKSTOOL

NO.	PART	SIZES (INCHES)		
		T	W	L
1	Seat	2-1/2	17-1/2 *	16*
3	Legs	1-5/8	1-5/8	18
4	Spindles	3/4	3/4	13-3/4
1	Crest	3/4	2-1/2	17-1/2**

* Swap these two dimensions if you want the seat's grain to run left to right.

** Finished size. Start with a longer board.

CHAPTER 16

Stool or chair? What's the difference between a backstool and a chair? A backstool never has arms. And its seat looks more like a rural milking stool than a shield or some other shape you would find on a Windsor chair.

Photo by Narayan Nayar.

STAKED CHAIR

CHAPTER 17

A baby step toward full-bore chairmaking.

It's difficult to convince most woodworkers that it's easy to build a staked or Windsor chair. It seems akin to telling a kindergartner to build a bombé chest.

I was in the same position in 2003 when I built my first Welsh stick chair. Everything about making chairs was a mystery because until that moment I'd built only casework with kiln-dried wood and sheet goods. After reading everything I could about chairmaking, the following was the short list of the things that baffled me.

1. *Working with green wood.* Where would I get this stuff? And processing it with an axe, hatchet, wedges, froe and a brake seemed 100-percent foreign – even though I was used to dressing stock by hand with saws and planes.
2. *Steam-bending.* I was excited to learn to do it, but I was oddly daunted by making a steam box and dealing with the propane-fired boiler (i.e. a bomb) to power it.
3. *Saddling the seat.* This seemed like carving, and again, I was excited to learn it. But I was apprehensive about all the tools – adze, scorp and inshave. Did I really need all three to scoop out the seat?
4. *Shaving the spindles.* I didn't have a shavehorse and I didn't have the room in my shop for one.
5. *The drawknife.* I knew I needed to become good with this tool to

STAKED CHAIR

Photo by Narayan Nayar.

CHAPTER 17

build a chair, but it was such an open-ended thing (like a chisel) that I was overly timid and slow with it.

6. *The compound angles.* Furniture with 90° corners was easy. Furniture with simple angles was do-able. Furniture with compound angles seemed a geometrical nightmare.

Of course, I took on all of the above hurdles. I didn't have a choice because I had enrolled in a chairmaking course and didn't want to look like a crybaby. But would I have attempted a chair like this on my own without taking a woodworking course? Unlikely.

As a result, I am well aware that the above barriers hold back many woodworkers from attempting to make a chair solo.

So when designing a chair for this book I decided to winnow the list of stuff you had to learn, buy or build to make a totally decent chair. I looked at the historical record. And I felt my way through the problem with my butt and my lumbar spine.

Making a chair this way lowers the price of admission in both tools and skills. It will give you a taste for the construction process. It will convince you that you can handle the angles and the joinery. Then, when you are ready, you can start making your chairs more complex by adding new tools and processes.

This chair is a baby step toward full-bore chairmaking.

About the Chair

The chair is built using (mostly) kiln-dried and sawn wood from the lumberyard – ash, in this case. Riven, green wood is stronger and easier to work. But you can accomplish nearly the same strength by carefully sawing the legs and spindles so the grain is arrow-straight through its length. A band saw makes this easy.

Like many early pieces, this chair doesn't have stretchers between its legs. Stretchers can strengthen the undercarriage, but they also complicate construction. Many chairs have survived hundreds of years just fine without stretchers. But you better make sure the joints between the legs and the seat are stout.

The seat is flat and unsaddled. I struggled with this detail. Deeply saddled seats are uncomfortable because they act as a Jell-O mold for your caboose. They might feel comfortable for a short period of time, but they quickly make you squirmy because you cannot shift around.

Staked Chair

Pl. 9

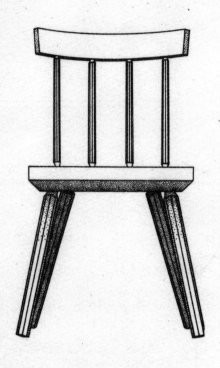
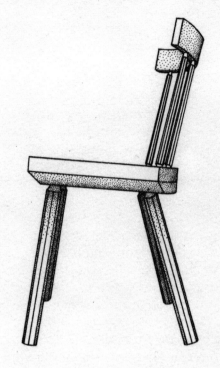

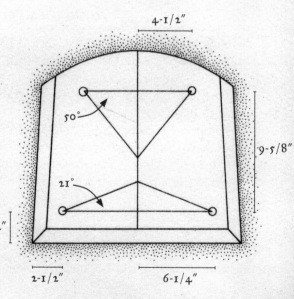

B. Morrow-Cribbs Inv. Del. et Sculp

Slightly saddled seats – say 1/4" to 7/16" deep – seem to work best for me and my customers. They have a little curve for the buns and still allow you to shift around to keep the blood moving.

Flat seats are somewhere between the two extremes. I greatly prefer them to a deeply saddled seat because they allow free movement of the sitter. But they aren't as comfortable as a shallow saddle.

So the flat seat is, to me, a fair compromise for the beginning chairmaker. If you want to saddle the seat, read the chapter on the backstool.

The other seat detail on this chair isn't as obvious. On many Windsor-style chairs, the underside of the plank seat is relieved all around to make the chair lighter, both visually and physically.

For this chair, I chamfered the front and sides of the underside of the seat. But I left the curved back at full thickness – no chamfer. This is a significant timesaver because the curved chamfer is considerably extra work in the round and doesn't lighten the look as much as the chamfers on the sides and front.

To save you some shop space, the spindles and legs are octagonal instead of being shaved round or slightly cigar shaped. Octagons are easy to make with simple home-shop machines or benchwork. So you don't need a shavehorse or spokeshave to make this chair. Oh, and I really like octagonal sticks, especially when they are tapered.

The curved crest rail is bent using firewood, a $2 tin-foil roasting pan and a household oven. I cover this technique in the chapter on the backstool. If you use this technique then you don't need a steam box, a steam generator or tools to rive the firewood crest rail.

All told, this chair isn't much more difficult to make than a staked-leg stool or a sawbench. Yet it looks good and sits surprisingly well.

Construction begins with making the curved crest rail and getting it clamped in a form to dry for a few days.

The Kitchen Steam Box

You can easily make the bent crest with some firewood, either store-bought or homemade. Begin with a stick of it that is about 18" to 20" long. Jack plane one of the triangular faces flat. Then plane off the bark and dress that area so it's 90° to your flat face.

Now you can continue to process the stick by hand or finish the job with machinery. In the end you want a crest that is 3/4" x 2-1/2" x about 20". It needs to be squared and finish-planed neatly all around.

"It seems advisable to make clear at the outset the fact that this is not a book telling how to transform some object that is no longer wanted into some other object that has even less excuse for existence. In its pages will be found no formula or design for making a goldfish tank out of an orange crate, or a Turkish tabouret out of a sardine tin and two broomsticks. What it does attempt is to bring back something of the self-reliant craftsman of early America, when a man's chief pride and satisfaction lay in his ability to practice any or all of the common crafts."

— Henry H. Saylor, "Tinkering with Tools" (1924, Little, Brown & Co.)

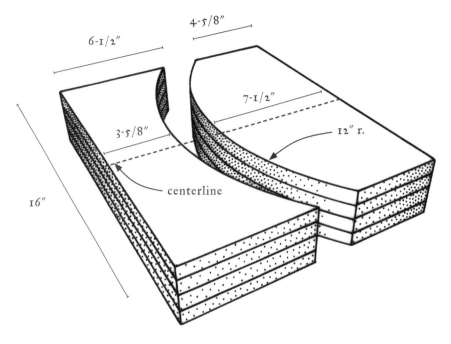

The crest-rail bending form.

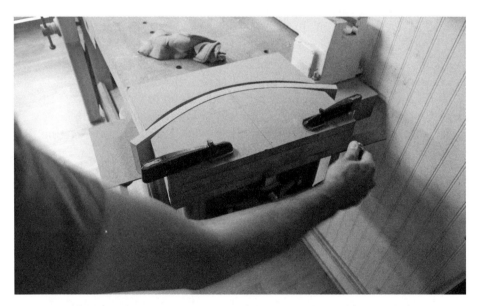

Screwed & bent. You can easily bend the crest in a form (the same form for the backstool) by pressing the two halves of the form together on a workbench's vise.

CHAPTER 17

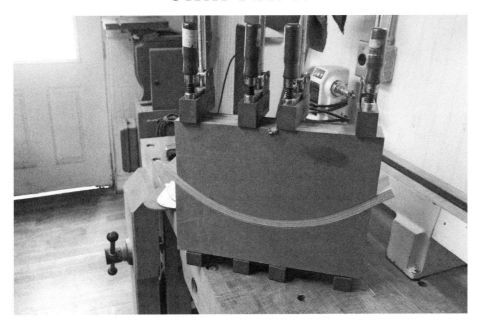

Clamp & set aside. With the form closed on the stick, clamp the form tight. Remove it from the bench and set it aside for a few days.

Place your crest in a disposable foil roasting pan filled with water. Seal the pan with two layers of aluminum foil and cut a small slit in the foil to allow steam to escape.

Put the pan in the oven at 450° for 75 to 80 minutes. Then take the pan out of the oven and scurry to the bending form – it's the same MDF form used for the crest rail on the backstool.

Drop the hot stick between the jaws of the form and press the two halves of the form together with pressure from clamps or a bench vise. Steady and swift pressure works best. When the form has closed on the stick, clamp it up and set it aside for a few days to let the wood set.

The Seat & its Mortises

The seat is solid 1-7/8"-thick ash that is glued up from three equal-width sticks. Arrange the joints in the seat so that none of the leg joints or spindles will land on a glue line. This helps ensure the chair's longevity if any of your edge joints deteriorates.

Awkward angles. It's easy to see if the brace is in line with your body along the sightline. But it's a trick to see if you are doing right by the resultant. The best solution is a spotter to act as an extra set of eyes. Barring that, you can tilt your head around the brace to peek at your progress.

Like all the staked projects in this book, this chair began as a half-scale model with wire hangers for the legs. Making the model let me dial in the exact stance of this chair – I was shooting for an attentive and obedient dog. The front legs use a 21° sightline and a 13° resultant. The rear legs use a 50° sightline and a 25° resultant. These angles aren't anything unusual in the chair world. The front legs are fairly vertical – they slope out and rake forward only enough to fall in the shadow of the seat.

The rear legs slope and rake out more significantly so they peek out from the shadow of the seat and provide some extra stability when the sitter leans back against the crest rail.

Lay out all the sightlines and mortise locations on the underside of the seat. Then chuck a 5/8" auger in your brace. Bore the mortises in the seat, using a bevel square set to the resultant angle as your guide.

Once the mortises are bored, ream them so they are all tapered cones.

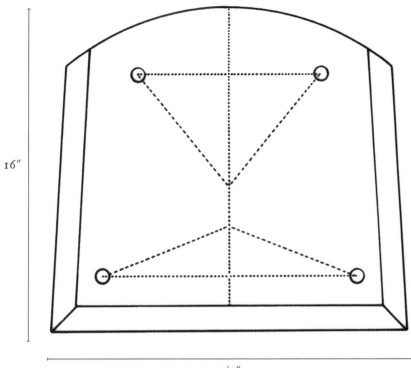

Seat layout.

> "No snowflake in an avalanche ever feels responsible."
> — Stanisław Jerzy Lec, Polish aphorist and poet

Now bore the 5/8"-diameter x 1-1/2"-deep holes for the four spindles. They are located on 4" centers, radiating from the centerline of the seat and 1-1/8" in from the back edge of the seat. Set your bevel gauge to 10°. The sightline for each mortise is 0° – straight ahead.

Now that the seat has gotten beat up by your bits and reamer, it's a good time to plane off the damage. Because this seat isn't saddled, this is quick work. Screw a temporary block to the underside of the seat so you can clamp the blank in your face vise. Then plane it flat and clean.

Make the Legs

These legs taper from 1-1/2" square at the top down to 1-1/8" square at the floor. I usually saw the legs to a square tapered shape first, then plane them into octagons.

Your dummy. A "dummy leg" that is shaved with the correct tenon shape is a valuable aid when dialing in the correct angle of the mortise as you ream it.

CHAPTER 17

Easy seat. A temporary block on the underside – cheated toward the front edge of the seat – allows you to clamp the seat to plane it flat.

To make them octagons, I have a simple bench fixture that holds them against my planing stop. Then I plane down the sharp corners so they create a tapered octagon that looks perfect to my eye – never mind what the ruler thinks.

So taper the legs by eye then work the tops of the legs for the tenons. Before you shave the tenons to their final shape, it's a good idea to rough in the taper with any means possible. You can shave it with a drawknife, spokeshave or (in my case) a lathe.

The roughed-in tenon should be slightly more than 5/8" at the tip and taper at 6° or 12° depending on your tenon cutter.

Once the tenon is roughed in as close as you dare, then it should be just a few twists or so away from perfection. Shaving the tenons for the legs is a two-handed job. Hold the tenon-cutter with your off-hand; twist the leg with your dominant hand.

The first rotation is the most critical. Watch the gap between the leg and the mouth of the tenon cutter. Try to keep that gap consistent as you turn the leg. After a few careful turns the leg will be centered and you

The hard eight. This simple bench fixture holds my leg blanks in position so I can turn them into octagons. Then taper them.

Overly fancy. Once the leg is on the lathe, it's easy to taper the tenon and elaborate. Here I've added a cove at the point where things transition from octagon to round.

Maker's-eye view. This is what I see when I turn the tenons on my legs. My eyeball is glued to the gap between the leg and the tenon cutter.

can focus on removing material instead of focusing on the position of the leg.

It's easy once you get a few legs under your belt. So make a few throwaway tenons. Turn them and burn them.

Assemble the Undercarriage

Like all the staked projects in this book, the assembly process is the same for this chair. Saw a kerf in the tenon of each leg that's about 1-1/4" deep. Prepare wedges that are as wide as the diameter of each hole in the top of the seat.

Paint the interior of each mortise and each tenon with hide glue. Knock the leg home – hard. When the leg stops descending into its mortise, stop hitting it. It's done.

With all four legs seated, flip the chair over. Paint glue on the wedges and knock them home. Just like with seating the legs, stop hitting them when they stop moving.

Clean up any excess glue with hot water and a toothbrush. Set the

Tenons sized. The spindle tenons should be carefully shaped to final size so they have to be driven with a hammer into their mortises. I turned these on a lathe and added a cove as a transition between the octagon and round shapes.

chair aside overnight. The next day, trim the tenons flush and cut the legs to length. This process is covered in the chapter on the sawbench.

This particular chair should have the front of the seat 1" higher than the back edge of the seat. The splay of the rear legs should get you close to this, but some wedges here and there will perfect the slope of the seat.

Make the Spindles

The length of the spindles determines where the crest rail will touch the sitter's back. If you are building this chair for a particular person, it's time to break out the tape measure and find their favorite backbone.

The length of the spindles shown in this chair (14-1/4" long, or 11-1/2" exposed between the seat and crest rail) has worked well with most sitters and customers. So that's a good place to start.

No matter the length of your spindles, first make the four sticks into equilateral octagons using a machine or the same V-shaped appliance

CHAPTER 17

Taper the spindles. The spindles should be skinnier at the top. I tapered mine using a handplane. The guiding light was the shape and size of the shoulders at each end of the spindle.

Ready to assemble. The holes are drilled. The spindles are shaped. Nothing is left to do but glue the thing together.

Protect your back. Where the bit exits the crest rail is vulnerable to splintering. So I clamp a bit of curved wood to the exit point. (You can't see it because it's under the crest rail.)

shown for the legs.

Then create the tenons on the ends. Each tenon is 1-3/8" long. The tenon at the top is 1/2" in diameter. The one at the bottom is 5/8". You can turn these to size on a lathe or rough them in with a drawknife and spokeshave.

Now bore the 1/2"-diameter x 1-1/2"-deep holes in the crest rail for the spindles. The layout should exactly match the layout on the seat.

Also important: the angle on the ends of the crest rail. I tapered the ends of the crest rail by a few degrees and cut it with a saw. This is all by eye.

Assemble the Crest & Spindles

If you have done your homework, this is easy. Paint the mortises in the seat with hide glue. Paint the tenons and drive the spindles in fully.

Don't wait for the glue in the seat to dry. Paint the mortises in the crest rail and paint the tenons on the tops of the spindles. Knock the crest rail in place.

CHAPTER 17

Tight fit. I protect the crest rail with masking tape on both faces before drilling holes for the pins. The tape prevents glue from sticking to the crest rail.

The goal here is to get the crest rail the same distance from the seat on the left side and right side. And you want the spindles to look consistent as they enter the crest rail.

Measure the distance between the crest rail and seat on the left and right sides. Knock the crest rail to adjust things. Twist and shift the spindles so they look consistent – both up and down and left and right. When things look good, let go of the chair and walk away for a few minutes. Then return with a toothbrush and hot water to remove any excess glue.

Pin the Spindles

The weak spot of the chair is the joint where the spindles meet the crest rail. If you lean back enough times, this joint will come loose. So the best thing to do is pin the spindles and crest rail together using 1/4"-diameter dowels.

Lay out the location of the pins so they pierce the tenons in the middle of their length and width. Then drill the holes for the pins.

The diameter of the hole should be slightly – just slightly – smaller than the dowel if you want a tight fit. I skinned my dowels so they were a perfect 1/4" in diameter. The hole was 1/64" less than 1/4". Wood compresses. And it can be beat to shape. So this procedure works.

Drive the pins through the holes. Trim them flush with a saw, chisel and some sandpaper.

Finish the Chair

Dress any rough spots with #220-grit sandpaper and break any too-sharp edges.

The finish I used for this was a Danish soap finish (see the appendix "On Soap Finish" on page 590 for more on this simple finish). I dissolved 1 cup of pure soap flakes into 4 cups of boiling water. After the concoction cooled overnight, I wiped it on the chair using a rag. The finish should have the consistency of shaving cream.

After the finish dries, sand the surface with #320-grit paper and apply another coat of finish. About three or four coats should do the trick. A true soap finish is like an oil finish. It requires maintenance, but the results are tactile and satisfying.

STAKED CHAIR

NO.	PART	SIZES (INCHES)		
		T	W	L
1	Seat	1-7/8	17-1/2	17
4	Legs	1-5/8*	1-5/8*	18-1/2
4	Spindles	3/4	3/4	14-1/2*
1	Crest	3/4	2-1/2	20*

* Rough dimension to allow for shaping.

CHAPTER 17

Sidebar: Charles H. Hayward on Utility Furniture

Perhaps one of the most testing times of furniture-making was that of war time and the immediately following years, when utility furniture came into being. Certain restrictions had to be placed on the methods of construction and the weight of timber used. It was realised that the items had to be reasonably durable, but the stringent requirements of the times made it necessary to keep timber sizes to the minimum. At the same time, although all unnecessary weight was avoided, there was a limit below which furniture would be unsound.

Compared with furniture of the Victorian and earlier periods, utility furniture was lightly built, but most people today have come to realise that much early furniture was unnecessarily heavy, and that in some ways lightness is a virtue providing that strength is adequate.

A problem that confronts the man in the home workshop is that of the thickness and width he should make the various parts. To the furniture designer or craftsman the decision is largely one of appearance only, because over the years a tradition has grown up in which the sections are more or less settled within certain limits.

If this sounds like blindly doing a thing for no better reason than repeating what was done before, it should be remembered that trade practice is generally founded on what experience has shown to be sound. Sometimes you can get away with slighter material, but it is often because you have to, either because the cost is too great otherwise, or because larger stuff is not available.

In any case we have to realise that, except for first-quality things, furniture today is not built for posterity as it used to be. The day when furniture was intended to be handed down to later generations has largely gone. Ask any young couple of today whether they want to start their home with things from the home of their parents, and you will invariably be told that such old-fashioned stuff does not interest them. Perhaps they are right. If the true craftsman dislikes the idea of making a thing that is not intended to last, at least the younger generation is entitled to its view of what it wants.

— *Charles Hayward, from* The Woodworker, *February 1961*

"When I read interior design magazines today or visit rich client's homes, all I see are simple, unassuming, plain lines, devoid of decoration or expensive materials. Each room is designed exactly like a hotel room. Neutral colors, basic functionality, predictable forms and function. Nothing to challenge the senses or intellect. Nothing to draw your attention. In my opinion, completely boring."

— W. Patrick Edwards, "Where Have All The Antiques Gone?," Dec. 31, 2015

STAKED ARMCHAIR

CHAPTER 18

Armbows are difficult creatures.

There's something about building an armchair that tips the mental scales for many woodworkers. Making a stool is easy – it's a board with legs. OK, now take your stool and add a backrest to it. Congrats – you've made a backstool or perhaps a side chair.

But once you add arms to that backstool you have committed a serious act of geometry. You've made an armchair, and that is hard-core angle business.

Yes, armchairs are a little more complicated to build than stools or side chairs. But the geometry for the arms works the same way as it does for the legs or the spindles for the backrest. There are sightlines and resultant angles (if you need them). In fact, I would argue that adding arms to a chair simplifies the geometry because you have two points – the arm and the seat – to use to gauge the angle of your drill bit. When you drill legs, for example, you are alone in space.

OK, I'm getting ahead of myself here. The key point is that arms are no big deal. So let's talk about arms and how they should touch your back and your (surprise) arms.

Floating in Space

The arms of the chair shown here have the same basic shape as the seat below – a curve for the back and some straight parts for the arms of the sitter. But where should this arm go as it sits above the seat?

The answer, as always, is: it depends.

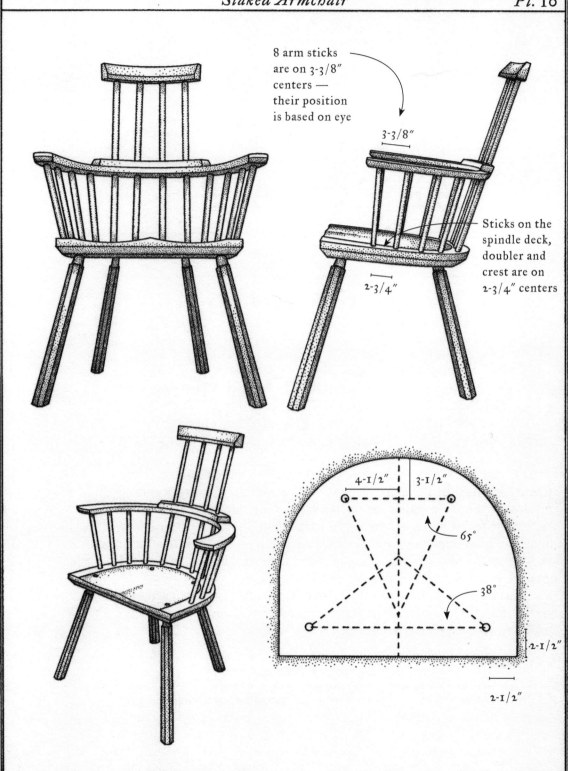

CHAPTER 18

Here. This is where I like the back of the armbow to go. Its inside edge lines up with the outside edge of the seat. The square shows this relationship clearly.

Let's say the arm floats right above the seat. The back edge of the arm is directly above the back edge of the seat. This would make the backrest 90° to the seat. This is a great orientation for torturing people or for Barbie dolls without lower-back problems, but it is an otherwise useless place to put the arms.

The obvious urge is to shift the arm backward so the sitter reclines a bit yet is not in a chaise-lounge on the Lido Deck. But how far should you lean back?

I like my backrests to tilt about 13° to 14° back from the seat. When I first started building chairs I was taught to use 7°. But my back likes to lean back. If you tend to sit like you are in trouble at church, however, go for a more upright backrest.

Here's how to get a tilt of 13° or 14°. Position the arm assembly so it will float above the seat about 8" or 9", depending on how tall you are (most prefer 8" in my experience). Then shift the arm backward so the inside edge of the arm is in the same vertical plane as the back edge of the seat.

Words fail. An image is a better way to explain this.

That's the goal, to get that arm in the correct place above the seat so that the chair is comfortable and the armrests fall in a comfortable plane. It sounds difficult to do, but it's not (once you know a couple tricks). The geometry of the spindles that hold up the arm also seems complex – each spindle can have a different sightline and resultant angle. Argh. But I'm going to show you a way to do this without sightlines and resultants. All you need is a dowel and a friend.

And what about the crest – that bit of wood at the top? You'll position it to suit your sitter. I'll give you some suggestions as to where to start (22" from the seat is a good spot) and where you can go if you want to cradle your skull. The angles on the crest are pretty easy. Many chairmakers just eyeball them. But I'll give you a bit more guidance.

End of the Preamble

OK, feel better about it? Even if you are still tentative, let's build the rest of the chair first then ease into the arms. You might not even notice – I strive to be the Versed of DIY writers.

Before we can build this chair, we have to collect the materials. Luckily, the wood for this chair is easy to get, no matter where you live. As far as species goes, you can use almost anything. If you are going to paint the chair, you can mix species to save money. For example: a poplar or pine seat – plus oak sticks, ash arms and a maple crest are all possibilities. This chair also allows you to use a decorative species if you wish (cherry or walnut, for example) with a clear finish. Though you will have to go to some extra trouble to source the sticks in particular.

You need three kinds of wood for this chair:
- Dead-on straight-grain wood for the legs and sticks
- Curvy-grain wood for the arms and "doubler"
- Thick stock for the seat and crest.

Quick recommendation: If you are looking for a stout chair that you can either paint or apply a clear finish to, use red oak for all the parts. It is cheap, strong and available everywhere in North America. (If you are in Europe, I recommend beech, which is common, strong and fairly inexpensive.)

CHAPTER 18

Around the knot. Your curved components will be stronger if the grain is curved. Look for curved grain around knots and from boards that came from the base of the tree in particular.

How to Find Dead-straight Wood

If you don't get dead-straight grain for your legs and sticks, your chair will be fragile and likely to fracture along any short-grain areas. Early chairmakers would rive their timber to get straight grain. We are going to use our eyes and brains.

For the sticks, you need seven 5/8" dowels (36" lengths) with dead-straight grain. You can get these from the home center in oak. I pull out all the 5/8" dowels from the store's bin and purchase the ones that have straight grain through their entire length. You might get the stink eye from the employees for this behavior, but it's worth it. I can usually find seven or eight straight dowels out of a batch of 30. You might have to visit more than one home center.

If you want a species other than oak, you should splurge and get a dowel-cutting machine. I use the Veritas Dowel Maker. Then you can saw out all the stock for the dowels so they are as straight as possible. Then run them through the Dowel Maker to create the sticks. The device has a bit of a learning curve, but I figured it out in an afternoon. It produces sticks that need only a quick scraping to be usable. And you can fine-tune their diameter.

For the legs, you also need dead-straight grain. Go to any lumberyard and look at the 8/4 (1-3/4"-thick) stock. You want to look at the grain lines on both the faces and edges of the boards. The grain should be straight (or nearly so) on the face of the board and on its edges. If you have a band saw you can saw out your legs so the grain is quite straight.

Curved Wood

The arms are made from three pieces of wood: two arms and a "doubler," which increases the arm thickness for the backrest. For the best results, you want the curved arm pieces to have curved grain. You are unlikely to find boards where the curve matches the curve of the arm exactly. But any curve in the grain helps. Look for curved grain around knots and on the ends of boards that were clearly near the tree's roots.

This curved wood should be at least 3/4" thick – 7/8" is better because it will be stronger.

Thick Wood

The seat and crest are cut from 8/4 stock. The grain for these parts can be whatever looks best to you – curved or straight. If you are going to glue up the seat from two or three boards, take pains to ensure the grain direction of the boards runs in all the same direction. This extra care will make saddling the seat easier.

STAKED ARMCHAIR

NO.	PART	SIZES (INCHES)		
		T	W	L
1	Seat	1-3/4	16-1/2	20
4	Legs	1-5/8	1-5/8	20
1	Crest	1-3/4	5	15
2	Arms	7/8	7	22
1	Doubler	7/8	5	16
7	Dowels	5/8		36*

*Eight pieces cut to 10" long; four pieces cut to 24" long

CHAPTER 18

After I've found all my wood, I rough out all my parts plus a few extras in case I botch a leg or arm piece. Consult the cutting list for the part sizes for the chair shown in this chapter.

Begin with the Seat

If you need to glue up parts for the seat, do that. Then use the drawings (see the appendix titled "Seat Templates" for details) to cut its "D" shape. The grain runs left to right on this seat, though you can make it run from front to back if you prefer. Either way, draw a centerline on the top of the seat and the underside of the seat. The centerline should run from front to back.

Use the drawings to lay out the locations of the mortises for the legs on the underside of the seat. Mark these with an awl. Now draw the "baselines." One baseline connects the two mortises for the front legs. The second baseline connects the two mortises for the rear legs.

Last layout chore: Draw in the sightlines shown on the construction drawing. The sightlines for the front legs are 38° off the baseline. The sightlines for the rear legs are 65° off the baseline.

Now is a good time to cut the bevel on the underside of the seat. The bevel is 45° and is 7/8" x 7/8". You can rough it out with a drawknife or use a band saw. On the band saw, set the table to 45°. Lay out the location of the bevel on the edges of the seat. Cut away the bevel and clean it up with a spokeshave or a rasp (this clean-up can happen at any point before assembly).

Drill & Ream the Leg Mortises

The mortises for the legs begin with a 5/8" hole that are then reamed to a conical shape. To drill the holes, set a small sliding bevel to the resultant angle for the front legs, 16°. (Confession: I now use a 22° resultant for the front legs. The photos in this chapter show the chair with 16°.) Tape the bevel to your sightline and drill the 5/8" hole. Keep your bit in line with the blade of your bevel and you'll be OK.

Before you ream the mortise, make a sample tenon from a 1-1/4"-diameter dowel. I made one of these sample tenons years ago and have used it ever since. Here's how you make one: Take a dowel that is about 18" long. Use your tapered tenon cutter to shave the end to a point – it's like using a pencil sharpener.

Now you can ream the mortise. Use the same setting on your sliding

Obey the bevel. The sliding bevel is taped to the sightline on the underside of the seat. Keep your bit in line with the blade and you are halfway home.

Make a sample tenon. Use your 5/8" tapered tenon cutter to shave the end of a dowel to shape. You will use this to test the angle of your mortise.

bevel and keep it taped to your sightline. Ream the mortise. After every four or five rotations of the reamer, pause and clear it of shavings. If you don't do this, the reamer will stop cutting and merely burnish the hole. And a burnished hole accepts no glue.

Test your angle. If it's off slightly (less than 1/16" variance from the blade of the bevel) don't bother fixing it. You might make it worse. If you are wonkier, here's how to fix the problem: About 99 percent of the time your mortise is off so the leg is tilting a little too close toward the bevel or tilting away from the bevel. This means you'll have to "English" the drill a little toward the bevel or away from the bevel. Rarely will you have to English left or right.

To correct, pull the reamer out of the hole about 1/8". Press the reamer in the direction you want to move your leg. This will make the reamer contact the hole at two points. Run the drill up to full speed. Pause for a second and then plunge. Stop. Now press the reamer straight down

CHAPTER 18

Ream it. Chuck a reamer into your brace or electric drill and ream the mortise.

Test it. Place your sample tenon into the mortise and check your work. Correct the angle of reaming if you are off.

into the mortise and rotate the reamer until you get it to bite. These two movements adjust the mortise and correct its shape to the proper cone. Test the leg again. At most, you will get two chances to correct a cock-eyed mortise. So take your time.

Now set your bevel to 22° (I use 26° for the rear legs at times). Drill and ream the rear legs.

Make the Legs

The legs start out at 1-5/8" square. You have several options as to how to shape them. You can keep your legs as straight octagons. (A second option is to make them 1-3/4" square for a heavier look.) You also can taper the legs. For a traditional Welsh look, make them skinnier at the top. For a modern look, make them skinnier at the floor.

No matter which way you go, first plane your legs to size. Taper them

Tapered on the lathe. The conical tenon is 3-1/4" long with a cove at the shoulder. The base of the tenon is about 1-1/16" diameter.

Tapered on the plane. A trick from fellow chairmaker Chris Williams. You can shave the leg with a plane then use the tapered tenon cutter to finish it.

CHAPTER 18

Dirty cheater. I stick the pattern to the seat with double-stick tape. Then I rout the trough by swinging the router counterclockwise around the pattern. Then remove the pattern and the tape.

(if that's your plan) then plane the corners of each leg with a jack plane to create your octagons.

Making the tenons on the ends of the legs is easy – it's like sharpening a pencil. Before you use the tapered tenon cutter, you should remove a lot of the waste wood with a block plane or a lathe. Mark the top 3-1/4" of the leg. Taper that area so it's about 1-1/16" in diameter at the 3-1/4" mark and 5/8" diameter at the tip. (Note: If you taper with a drawknife, your taper will have to be longer than 3-1/4".)

If you rough out the tenon on the lathe, use the same dimensions, but you'll cut a shoulder at the 3-1/4" mark.

With the tenons roughed out, use your tapered tenon cutter to finish shaping them. It should take about 12 turns or so.

Drive the legs into the seat with a mallet and mark what goes where. They should stick fast in their mortises. If you've done a good job you'll have to whack the tenon hard to get it to release. With the legs stuck into the seat, turn the chair over to reveal your project in its stool stage.

Remove the legs and saw a kerf in the top of each one. This kerf will accept the wedges at assembly. The kerf should be about 3" deep.

STAKED ARMCHAIR

> "It takes half a fool to make chairs and a whole fool to make baskets."
>
> — Verge, an Appalachian chairmaker as quoted in "Craftsman of the Cumberlands" (University of Kentucky) by Michael Owen Jones

Bad idea. We all have dirty design laundry. Here's mine. The arms are separate from the backrest. Bad idea.

CHAPTER 18

A Brief Diversion to the Seat

It's not yet time to saddle the seat, but this is the point during construction when I remove some material on the seat to define the "spindle deck" of the chair. The spindle deck is a 2"-wide swath of wood around the rim of the seat where the spindles get stuck.

So, it's confession time. I use an electric router to waste away some of the material and reveal the raised section of the spindle deck for this chair. My methods are odd, non-traditional and entirely indefensible as a lover of hand tools. Here's the why.

The spindle deck is usually separated from the saddle by a crisp line made by the travisher. Or the saddle and spindle deck flow into each other smoothly. Neither look makes me happy. The hard line is difficult to execute for beginners. And the smooth look just doesn't do it for me.

My solution was to make an MDF pattern to guide a pattern bit in a router. Using the router, I waste away a 1/8"-deep trough between the spindle deck and the seat. Then I saddle the seat right before assembly.

Use a pattern-cutting bit to plow the depression in the seat. Believe me, I've tried to do this operation with scrapers, incannel gouges and the like. A router is the best way.

Assemble the Armbow

The most difficult part of designing this chair was the armbow. I built five different chairs to get to the point you see here (which is a return to where I started in 2003, when I first began making approximations of Welsh stick chairs).

Armbows are difficult creatures. My first designs with this chair were armbows that were separate from the backrest.

Then I tried armbows that were connected to the backrest via one spindle on either end. This looked somewhat better, but it required a crazy amount of jigging to get consistent results. I also decided that the problem with these designs was the shape of the seat. The seat was angular. Very angular. So, I switched to a classic D-shaped seat. This allowed me to use an armbow with a wide and sweeping arc.

With the shape of the seat set, I played around with armbows that were one piece of steam-bent lumber (too much equipment). Then one piece of cold-bend hardwood (too expensive for the first-time chairmaker). So, I went back to a "pieced armbow." This is where you build the armbow out of three pieces of wood that you stack together. If done

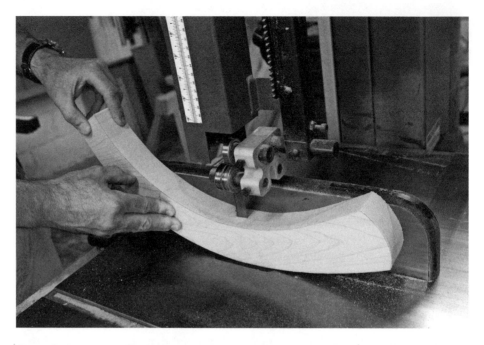

Better looking arms. Resawing the arms from a single thick piece of stock improves the overall appearance of the chair.

right, this armbow sidesteps most problems with short grain and lets you make an armbow out of lumber you can get at a home center.

This is where you need wood with grain that is curved. Before diving into your wood, make two templates for the armbow (the directions for this are in the appendix). One for the hands and one for the "doubler." The hands are joined together at their ends to make the shape of the armbow. The doubler is glued to the top of the hands to double the thickness and reduce any problems with short grain.

I make my patterns from 1/8"-thick plywood or hardboard. After I glue my pattern to the plywood, I cut it out and rasp, file or sand the edges to shape (use whatever you've got).

A Trick Arm

Chris Williams, who made Welsh stick chairs with John Brown, makes his armbows with 8/4 material and resaws them on the band

CHAPTER 18

Pinch it good. Put glue on the ends of the hands and drive in the pinch dogs with a hammer to draw the bits together. Note the wax paper below the hands.

saw to make the grain bookmatched. This makes for a spectacular armbow with symmetrical grain and is worth the effort. After seeing their results, I do the same.

After experimenting a bit with the technique, here's how I like to do it. Lay out the pattern on some 8/4 stock that has curvy grain. Make the grain of the wood match the pattern as best you can. Cut out the shape of the hands and sand or rasp the edges to shape. Then use your band saw to rip the hands through the thickness, producing two identical pieces. Plane these flat.

Put Your Hands Together

After cutting and shaping the hands, cut the doubler to rough shape, about 1/16" oversize all around. But don't rasp or sand it to its final shape or size. You'll do that after you join the two hands.

Joining the hands isn't difficult with a simple tool called a "pinch dog."

Soft hands. The bevel on the underside of the hands is a quick addition to the armbow but makes a huge different to how it looks.

This primitive tool looks like a staple with a hormone problem. You drive it into two adjoining pieces of wood and the wedge-shaped legs of the pinch dog draw the parts together. And it doesn't matter on which side.

If you don't have pinch dogs you can use a pocket-screw jig. Drill the pocket in one of the arms. Use a screw to pull the armbow pieces together – like a clamp. Then remove the screw when the glue is dry.

Before assembling the hands, make sure their ends are straight, square and (when assembled) make for a fair curve. Paint liquid hide glue on the ends of the hands and place them on a piece of wax paper – this will prevent you from gluing your hands to your bench. Clamp one of the hands to the bench to prevent things from shifting around. Press the hands together for a minute until the glue starts to grab.

Drive the pinch dogs into the hands. I start with one dog in the dead middle of the joint. Hammer it in a bit and make sure the hands don't slide around. Adjust them if they move and hammer some more. When the pinch dog is seated, drive in a second.

Let the assembly sit overnight.

CHAPTER 18

Bevel the doubler. The 30° bevel on the front of the doubler avoids some lower back pain for the sitter. Set the table of your band saw to 30° and make the cut. (Note: The pencil line on the stock shows what a 45° cut would look like.)

The next day, use a hammer or screwdriver to pry the pinch dogs out of the wood. Peel away the wax paper and gently (gently!) plane the joint flush all around.

Add the Doubler

The doubler cancels out any (or most) of the short-grain problems in your hands. Yes, you should ponder the wood-movement problems inherent in this assembly. And yes, you should go ahead with it anyway.

The doubler should be slightly wider than the armbow you just assembled. The basic idea is that you should fair the armbow then trace its shape onto the doubler. You then shave the doubler so it's the same shape as the armbow and cut a bevel on the front edge of the doubler. Finally, glue the doubler to the armbow.

Whew. Start by fairing the assembled armbow. Use rasps or sandpaper to make the armbow look nice. Then place the doubler on the armbow

Double down. Glue the doubler to the armbow. Make sure the doubler doesn't move when you apply the clamps. Use liquid hide glue so you have a lot of open time – this gives you the opportunity to shift everything in place.

and trace its shape on the doubler. Use rasps and sandpaper to shape the doubler as close as you dare.

Now cut a bevel on the front edge and the ends of the doubler. The chair as shown uses a 30° bevel. I now use a 45°. Leave a 1/4"-wide flat on the front edge and ends. I usually make this cut on the band saw.

Once you've cut the bevels, clean them up with files and some sandpaper. Leave the flats alone until everything is assembled. Finally, glue the doubler to the armbow.

After the glue has dried, remove the clamps. Now refine the armbow as much as you like. I cut a 30° bevel on the front edges of the hands and rasp them smooth. I leave the rasp marks on the ends of the hands; they are a nice tactile detail for a sitter to find.

CHAPTER 18

A handy notch. This V-shaped notch tells you when to stop drilling the mortises in the seat of the chair.

Sticks & How to Drill Them

The sticks in this chair are dowels (will the blasphemy never end?). But they're not just any old home center dowels, they're... OK, they actually are home center dowels.

Now before you curse my name, let me explain. These dowels have dead-straight grain through their entire length, just like a stick in a traditional Windsor chair that's made with rived stock. How is this possible? The magic of manufacturing.

If you go to the home center and sort through a big bin of dowels, there is a better-than-average chance that you'll find some dowels with arrow-straight grain – usually enough for a chair. I haunt the home centers in my area and find a handful of prime dowels with each visit.

All dowels are slightly oblong in cross section. You'll compress these a bit to fit them in an undersized mortise (more on that in a bit). So, don't worry that the dowels aren't perfectly round or that they aren't perfectly 0.625" in diameter. Just pick ones with straight grain.

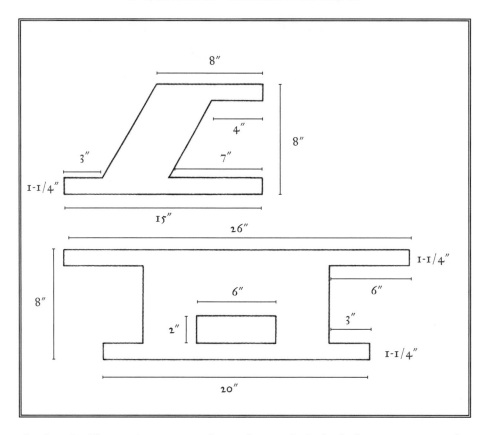

Armbow jig. The top piece supports the armbow at the back; the bottom piece provides support to the hands of the armbow.

Before you drill the holes, you need to tweak your spade bit. For these chairs, I use 5/8" spade bits. They come in two lengths – about 18" long and about 6" long. Get both lengths – spade bits are cheap. Do not buy the bits that have a threaded screw-like tip. These suck for chairmaking.

The beauty of spade bits is that you can grind (or file) their long edges to make the bit drill a slightly undersized hole. I do this on the grinder and it takes 23 seconds, tops. Kiss both long edges of the bit to the grinder's wheel. Try to remove the same amount of metal from each edge. Then use a dial caliper to check your progress – I shoot for a bit that is about 0.010" less than 5/8" – 0.615" or so. If you don't have a grinder, a coarse file will also work.

Before you step away from the grinder, grind two notches in the long

CHAPTER 18

The jig is down. Here's the armbow jig in action. The front piece supports the hands. The back piece supports the remainder of the armbow. This jig – rough as a cob in an outhouse – provides unparalleled drilling stability.

The magic wand. I can see if the drill needs to be adjusted left or right. Brendan, holding the stick, can see if I need to tilt the drill forward or back.

edges that are 1" up from the bit's cutting spurs. This notch will tell you when to stop drilling. Blue tape slips off the bit and allows you to drill all the way through your seat.

Before attaching the jig to the seat, mark the location of the holes through the armbow and the mortises in the seat using the drawings to guide you.

Now it's time to suspend the armbow over the chair seat and drill the mortises in both pieces. To do this, I make a jig from some scrap construction 2x12s. I cut these two jigs out on the band saw. This jig is not fine furniture – it takes about five minutes to make it.

The jig has two parts that are not attached to one another. One part clamps to the seat and holds the hands in position. The second part

The meat bushing. Use your fingers to keep the drill bit centered in the hole in the armbow and it will be difficult for you to botch this job.

clamps to the seat and holds the rear part of the armbow in place.

The only fancy part of the jig is that I mark out some lines every inch away from the centerline of the jig that goes under the hands. These marks allow me to center the armbow over the seat.

Clamp the jig pieces to the seat and put the armbow on top. To get it in position, place a combination square on the seat. Position it so the blade touches the outer edge of the seat. Shift the armbow so its inner edge touches the blade. Move the square to several points on the seat to ensure the armbow is positioned correctly.

If the above description flummoxes you, think of it this way: The inside edge of the armbow should hover directly over the outside edge of the seat.

When you achieve this, clamp the hands in place. Then clamp the rear of the armbow to the jig.

The hard part is over.

Now you just have to drill the holes through the armbow and into the seat. This is easy if you have a friend and a straight stick, which I call the "magic wand."

The magic wand is a straight stick that your assistant holds up to check the pitch of your drilling. The assistant sits 90° to you and holds up the wand so it looks like the wand intersects the location of the mortise in the seat and your drill bit. Then they tell you to lean forward or back.

Before you drill, clamp a backing board under the armbow to prevent massive spelching when your spade bit explodes through the bottom of your armbow.

You might be wondering: What are the sightlines for this drilling operation? Good question. The sightlines are "baked in" to the design. You are trying to join two points (the two mortises) with a line (your drill bit). Only one line in the universe can join those two points. So, align the two points in front of you by eye. You can see if you are lined up left-to-right. Have your assistant sit at 90° to you. He or she can see if you are lined up front-to-back. You will get very close by eyeballing it.

Now listen to your assistant for the fine tuning….

After drilling through the armbow, place the lead point of your spade bit in the mark on the seat. Use your fingers to keep the bit centered in the hole you just drilled in the armbow – I call this the "meat bushing." It works. Drill until the notch in your spade bit reaches the seat.

Now move the backing board under a new hole and repeat the drilling process.

A little compression. The pliers press and burnish the wood a bit. When the tenon encounters the warm hide glue (which is nearly 50 percent water) it will swell up to its full size and lock the joint.

Scrape up. Here I'm using a Veritas chair devil to scrape the stick so it is round and will pass through the armbow.

Fashion Your Sticks

The good news is that your sticks shouldn't need a lot of work. You likely need to compress the ends of the sticks that go into the seat. And you need to scrape the four back sticks a little to pass through the armbow.

Cut your sticks to length. Leave the back sticks about 24" long so you can adjust the position of the crest for the sitter.

Sand or scrape all the sticks. I prefer (greatly) the scraper. If you prefer to sand them, start with #180-grit and finish with #220-grit. You might have to start at a coarser grit depending on your dowels. After everything has been sanded or scraped, use "non-scratch pliers" to compress the tenons on the short sticks. Non-scratch pliers have plastic jaws that won't chew up the wood. If you don't own this tool, wrap the jaws of your

CHAPTER 18

Fit sticks. Here you can see the back sticks that slide smoothly into the armbow.

pliers with masking tape to mimic the action of the non-scratch pliers.

Here's how you compress the tenons. Squeeze the tenons gently and rotate the stick. You'll feel the tool's handles flex as they encounter the oval shape of the dowel. The pliers can squeeze most of this out and create a round tenon that will fit into the undersized mortises in the seat and armbow.

After your first few tenons, check the fit of the tenons in the seat or armbow. The tenons should need light mallet taps to seat them. If you are whaling on the stick it's too tight. If it drops into the mortise you are too loose.

With chairmaking, it's easy to make the joints too loose or too tight. If they are too loose, the glue will fail and the chair will fall apart. If things are too tight the chair won't go together without self-destructing. The margin for error is pretty low, I'm afraid. The good news is that most chairmakers learn the margin of error by rote after only one or two

A is for Adze. Adzes are an important part of the pre-industrial method for processing lumber. You can also use it to scoop out a seat, as shown here.

missteps. I did.

For the four long sticks, you'll need to shave the section of the sticks that passes through the armbow. This is done with a card scraper or a scraper shave – a tool you can buy or make. Sometimes called a "gunstock scraper" or a "chair devil," this is a tool much like a spokeshave that scrapes instead of slices.

To scrape the long sticks, wrap some tape around the point where the scraping should stop and get to work on everything above the tape. I clamp my sticks in my face vise and work them with a scraper – no spokeshave required.

Scrape the four sticks and test their fit in the armbow. When everything fits, saw a kerf in the top of each short stick – just like you did for the legs. The kerf should be about 3/4" deep. Now set the sticks and armbow aside. It's time to saddle the seat.

CHAPTER 18

Across & angled. The grain in this seat runs from left to right. So, when I scorp the material, I work across the grain but have the cutting edge skewed slightly toward the right. This helps control tearing. As the saddle gets deeper you'll have to adjust the tool to always work downhill.

Safe scorping. If you have trouble nicking the spindle deck, apply a thin layer of plywood over it to protect it. I stuck mine on with carpet tape.

From the hill to the valley. If the grain in your seat is dead straight, use the travisher to cut from the high points to the low points. Cutting uphill is difficult and mostly naughty.

Seat Saddling

I've saddled a lot of seats, but I am not an expert. If you want a master's thesis on the topic, read Peter Galbert's "Chairmaker's Notebook." If you want the "Dick & Jane" version, read on.

I prefer seats that are lightly saddled – about 3/8" to 1/2" deep at maximum butt projection. I have a lot to say about why I prefer shallow saddles, but the short answer is that I don't want to create a Jell-O mold for my customers' butts.

There are lots of ways to carve away the seat and make room for your butt cheeks. While I've tried many ways – both hand- and electric-powered, I prefer the simple hand-powered ways. They don't take too long – I can saddle a seat to completion in three to four hours – and you are unlikely to mess one up with hand tools.

Using an angle grinder or router jig, on the other hand, can botch a seat in seconds.

CHAPTER 18

Shave your thighs. Use a spokeshave with a curved bottom to dress the front edge of the seat where your thighs grow. With this tool you'll work (mostly) parallel to the grain.

Sandpaper is not evil. As you get better with your edge tools, you will sand less. Until you get really good, don't be ashamed of a little sandpaper. Abrasives pre-date handplanes, after all.

To begin the process I usually start with a "scorp," also called an "inshave." It's like a drawknife that was wrapped around a cylinder. Recently, I have begun using an adze at the start instead. The adze is a like a carving gouge and an axe had a baby. It also works well. Work across the grain. In oak, this is a bit of a slog. In pine, it's a breeze.

Cut as deeply as you dare without marring the spindle deck of your seat. Then get ready to switch to the scorp.

Scorping

The seat needs to be flat on the bench to quickly scoop out the wood with a scorp. To keep the seat in position, I screw a 2x4 to the underside of the seat and affix it in my face vise. Arrange the seat so you can work across the grain – called traversing. Scorping parallel to the grain is asking for abuse.

Learning to use the scorp (especially in oak) is a challenge. Do not clench the handles with your hands. Use your arms to set the angle of the tool. Use your body to pull the tool across the grain. Repeat to yourself: Keep the wrists loose.

Travishing

The travisher is a curved-edge tool much like the adze and is used in the same direction as its coarser brethren. The only difference is the travisher takes a lighter cut.

Like all the tools before it, cut across the grain but skew the tool in the direction of the grain in the seat. But, as the cut deepens, you will need to adjust your approach to cut the seat based on the feedback it provides. Learning to read and follow the grain is the single-most important lesson when saddling.

When you have done everything you can with a travisher the seat will be a little lumpy. Dress the front edge of the seat with a curved-bottom spokeshave. This tool will avoid spelching if you use it mostly parallel with the grain. Again, work from the top of the hill to the valley.

Now scrape and sand the sucker. I use a card scraper with a broadly curved edge. Then I follow that with coarse sandpaper (#120-grit) if necessary, and finish with finer sandpaper.

CHAPTER 18

Cut & flip. The advantage to using the miter gauge is it's faster. The downside is that your fingers get closer to the blade at the end of the process.

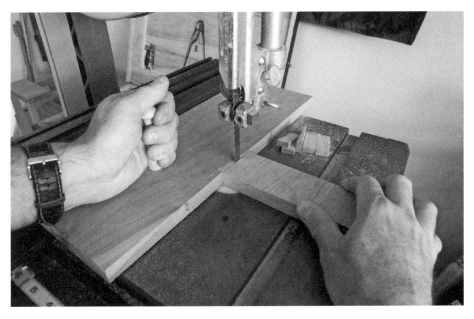

With a fence. For this jig, you need a fence on your band saw (or clamp a piece of stock to your table). The jig is a block of wood with a wedge-shaped notch cut into its side. The jig passes between the fence and the blade. Press your wedge wood into the notch, push the jig forward and cut a wedge free.

A close shave. Here you can see how closely I cut my tenons before finishing them off with a flush-cut saw. You might prefer a chisel here – that's fine, too.

Make Pretty

Before assembly, derail your head for a moment. Take a walk, drink a beer or do some yoga. Then come back and look at all the parts with a critical eye. Look at them in raking light for defects or damage. Repair that stuff. Feel the edges for bumps and try to fix them.

Spend some time dressing the spindle deck. This is the last time it will be easy to do. Ditto for the armbow.

Take all the sticks and blunt the corners of the tenons that will enter the seat. Sharp corners can scar the spindle deck during assembly.

Clean off the underside of the seat if you like (I like).

When nothing else can be improved, it's time to assemble. I prefer hide glue in all instances. It is reversible and easily cleaned off, even when dry. Make sure your glue is fresh and the correct viscosity (like runny snot) before beginning. Lay out rags, glue brushes and a toothbrush for cleaning glue out of corners.

CHAPTER 18

Wiggle up. Here I'm rotating the short stick as I push it upward. This spreads the glue around the joint and allows me to position the kerf in the stick correctly.

Assemble the Undercarriage

The undercarriage is easy on this chair because there aren't stretchers. Basically, you glue the legs into the holes and wedge them.

But wait, where do wedges come from?

I make wedges on the band saw using a variety of methods. Both methods use a blank of oak that is 5/8" thick, 8" wide and 1-1/2" long. If you think about it for a minute, this makes sense – you want the grain to run the length of the wedge.

One method uses a miter gauge set to 2° to rip wedges from the blank. Make a cut, flip the blank over and make a second cut.

Or you can make a dedicated jig that passes between the band saw's blade and a fence. There's a wedge-shaped notch cut into the jig. You press the blank into the notch and saw. Flip the blank and saw again.

Make a ton of wedges with thin tips and thick tips. You'll be glad you have a variety of wedges to choose from when the glue is getting hard.

Glue is cheap. Don't skimp on glue. The surfaces need to be wetted with glue to get the best bond.

CHAPTER 18

Hand fit. It takes a few minute to get all the sticks in place. This is why liquid hide glue – and its long open time – are an asset.

Bring on the mallets. Drive in the back spindles until they bottom out in their mortises. Then start knocking the arm-bow and the short spindles down.

To assemble the undercarriage, paint each mortise and the tenon with glue. Rotate the leg so the kerf in its tenon is perpendicular to the grain of the seat. Drive it in hard with a small sledge. After driving in all the legs, turn the chair over.

Likely the kerfs in the tenons have closed up. Don't panic. This is normal. Fetch a 5/8" chisel and drive it into each kerf to open it up. The bevel of the chisel will deform the kerf enough that you can slip a wedge in there.

Paint a wedge and drive it into the kerf. Keep striking the wedge until it stops moving. When the wedge stops moving, stop hitting it.

Let the glue dry overnight – even if you are in a rush. Leveling the tenons with soft glue around is ruinous to your tools and results.

The next day, trim the tenons with saws and/or chisels. My preferred method is to cut the tenon as close as possible with a saw, then use a fine

Wedged for good. The wedges ensure the armbow won't go anywhere.

flush-cut saw to finish the job.

After you trim the tenons, dress the seat again with a scraper and sandpaper. Then you can assemble the armbow and sticks.

Assemble the Top Stuff

This part is easy if you do it correctly. First thread the four long sticks into the armbow. This is important. Here are the next steps:
1. You'll glue the sticks into the armbow.
2. You'll add glue into the seat mortises.

3. You'll wrangle the armbow and sticks into position on the seat.
4. You'll knock the armbow in position.
5. You'll wedge the short sticks.

It's easy to get in the weeds quickly. Follow the steps above and it's difficult to make a fatal error.

So, let's begin by gluing the short sticks into the armbow. Put a short stick into a mortise in the armbow only about 1/32". Paint the inside of the mortise with glue and wiggle the stick up and rotate it so its kerf is perpendicular to the grain of the armbow (just like you did with the chair legs).

Repeat this process for all the short sticks. Then add glue in the mortises in the seat.

Now dock the armbow into the seat. This takes some wiggling and bending and cussing. Try to use hand pressure only to get the sticks started in the seat. You'll switch to the mallet in a bit.

Seating the short spindles is a game of eyeballs and tape measures. The chair has to look right. The tape measure can guide you, but the eyeball is the ultimate judge. The goal here is to knock the armbow around until it hovers 8" above the seat. It will want to tilt on you. Dive. Rise up. Sticks will move up and down.

Knock things around. Check your work. Don't say you are done until it looks good to your tape measure and your eye. Then walk away to get the wedges.

Wedge the sticks into the armbow just like you did the legs. Let the glue sit overnight. Level the tenons the next day.

Make the Crest Rail

The crest rail is sawn out of solid 8/4 material – no steambending here. But it pays to use wood that has some curvy grain, both for looks and for strength.

Cut the crest on the band saw. Lay out the locations of the mortises in the crest. Their spacing matches the spacing of the holes in the armbow and the seat. That consistency is what gives the back its straight appearance.

Drill the 5/8" mortises in the crest. These mortises need to be angled and the angle should match the lean of the back sticks. Use a sliding bevel gauge to determine the angle that the back sticks lean. Then use that same setting on your bevel gauge to drill the mortises in the underside of the crest.

Also angled. If you drill these holes vertically, the crest will look very odd. Drill them at the same angle as the back sticks intersect the seat.

CHAPTER 18

Three fingers. On my hand, three fingers is about 2". Prop up the bubble level with your fingers. When the bubble level reads level, the slope is correct.

Note that the sightline is at 0° – straight ahead. These mortises should be 1" deep.

Now shape the crest to your liking. I sawed a 30° bevel on the front edge of the crest and cleaned off all the machine marks with spokeshaves and scrapers. Test the crest on your spindles. Sit in the chair and see if the crest hits you in a nice place. Lower the crest by shortening the back sticks as needed.

Then glue the crest to the back spindles. Again, this is a case where the tape measure and your eyeball need to come to a compromise. Once you are happy, clamp the crest in place overnight.

Sawing the Legs

Leveling the legs is straightforward. In the end, you want the top of the pommel about 17" from the floor. And you want the back of the

An artificial floor. Think of the scrap as an artificial floor. Here I've planed a carpenter's pencil in half and have it held tightly to the scrap. Mark all around all four legs.

seat 15" from the floor. Here's how to do it.

Create a level surface on your bench. Shimming a piece of plywood is a good solution if your shop floor is a wreck. Place the chair on top and level it left to right using a bubble level and shims below the feet. To get the seat to slope backward, prop up the front legs until a bubble level reads as level when it is floating 2" off the back of the seat.

Now let a tape measure hang down from the pommel 17". The space between the end of the pommel and the floor should be about 2-1/2" or so. Measure that distance and crosscut a scrap of wood to that length.

Use that scrap of wood to scribe the final length on all of the legs.

Then it's just a matter of sawing on your lines.

After all the legs are cut to length, use a rasp to chamfer the feet a bit so they resist splintering when the chair is dragged across the floor.

CHAPTER 18

Follow the lines. Make shallow kerfs on three facets on the legs. These kerfs will guide your sawblade as you finish cutting the leg to length.

Finishing

There are lots of good and easy finishes for chairs. Milk paint followed with a coat of oil or wax wears nicely. Many woodworkers like shellac. I love shellac, but it can get too shiny for my tastes. When I use shellac, I knock down the sheen with wax and an abrasive pad.

My two favorite finishes for chairs are soap (for maple, ash or beech chairs) or a blend of linseed oil and wax (for oak, walnut and cherry). Neither finish provides much protection, but they are easy to apply, maintain and repair.

ALL ABOVEBOARD

CHAPTER 19

The path to boarded furniture began and ended with boards.

You might find this pitiful, but I have lost more nights of sleep to furniture than to love, anguish, guilt or bawling infants. When I fall hard for a furniture form, I get a rock in the pit of my stomach. Nothing will make that sharp-edged feeling go away until I have read everything about that form. And I have figured out how to build it. And I have drawn it in my sketchpad. And, if I'm lucky, I have built it.

Only then does sleep come, usually as I hear my wife blow-drying her hair at about 6:15 a.m.

Yet, I'm not what anyone would call an emotional guy. I struggle to maintain human friendships or even look most people in the eye. Take me to a ballgame and I'll meditate. At parties I'm the weirdo staring at the sky or the tree line in your backyard, usually thinking about furniture.

I wasn't always this way. I think it might have started in Owen Riley's apartment.

So it's late 1990. I'm 22 and living in Greenville, S.C., where I've landed my first job as a newspaper reporter at *The Greenville News*. The editors do not know what to do with me. My writing is clean and competent, but I don't have the killer instincts of a good reporter. Still, they try. First up: the cops beat.

One night I return to the newsroom from the police station, and my editor asks for a run-down on the crimes on the blotter. Instead I pitch him a story about how the police were filling cigar boxes with rocks,

The new News. They tore down the charmless brutalist structure that housed The Greenville News *when I worked there and replaced it with this charmless glass box.*

wrapping them with duct tape and giving these "magic boxes" to homeless people who were hearing voices.

"Shake the magic box when you hear the voices," they said, "and the voices will go away."

Soooo, next up: the suburban government beat. Then the disas-

CHAPTER 19

My first church. We lived in the bottom-right apartment. Owen lived in the top left. His apartment would put most decorative arts museums to shame.

ter-of-the week beat. The trailer-fire beat. Then a lot of eye rolling and Wrigley's spearmint gum-smacking on the part of my superiors. My days at the newspaper seemed numbered.

The bright spot in all this was meeting Owen Riley, one of the senior photographers at the newspaper. He helped Lucy (my girlfriend and eventually my wife) and I rent an apartment in his building on Atwood Street. It was a gorgeous brick structure on a tree-lined street with a reporter-friendly rent of $350 a month.

After we moved in, Owen invited us up to his apartment. When Owen opened the door to his place that afternoon I wasn't expecting my entire life to take a hard turn. But it did.

The entire place was decorated like it was right out of a 1907 American Arts & Crafts catalog. It wasn't just a few pieces of Stickley. Every single object in the apartment was an antique piece of Arts & Crafts. Yes, the furniture. But also the textiles, paintings, books, rugs – even the pots and pans in the kitchen. Everything was connected to the American

Arts & Crafts movement.

I fell in love.

Owen spent weeks educating me on the Arts & Crafts ethos. He loaded me up on vintage books by William Morris and John Ruskin. He explained everything he knew about every object in his possession. How it was made. Where it was made. I learned about craft communes, the Stickley family lineage and Elbert Hubbard and the Roycrofters.

I embraced it all. Within a month I was haunting flea markets, auctions and derelict houses with Owen on the hunt for objects from the Arts & Crafts period. I bought my first Arts & Crafts rocker for $15 and began restoring it. I attended the Arts & Crafts Conference at the Grove Park Inn in Asheville, N.C. When I gave Lucy an engagement ring we celebrated at the Grove Park Inn, where I spent most of the time studying the furniture there – picking out my favorite Gustav Stickley Morris chair.

At the time I was making about $300 a week, and that wasn't enough to buy the pieces that I really wanted. Though Arts & Crafts pieces were cheap then – a Gustav Stickley Morris chair might go for $500 to $700 – there was no way I could swing a purchase like that. Instead, I scraped together about $200 and bought a Shop of the Crafters Morris chair (which I am staring at right now) and a few other pieces by Charles Limbert. These were second-string makers, but it was still pretty good stuff.

I decided that if I wanted to own a Gustav Stickley Morris chair, I was going to have to build one.

My bedside table was stacked with copies of Stickley's *The Craftsman* magazine, which offered plans and encouragement for anyone who wanted to make their own chairs, beds or even houses. But at the time, I didn't own a single woodworking tool. For the most part I had memories. I had helped my father build our houses on our farm in Arkansas. And I had spent years tinkering at my workbench in our family garage making stuff – a tool tote, model airplanes and even a few bound books. I loved making things, but I wasn't a woodworker by any stretch. The best I could say is that I was a failing newspaper reporter.

It took a couple twists of fate for things to snap into place.

Death & Hand Work

To avoid being fired, I took a year off from newspapers to get a master's degree, teach copyediting and figure out what I wanted to do with my life. I bought a few more Arts & Crafts pieces, but with a week-

CHAPTER 19

My kitchen companion. I built this bench in the early 1990s and it remains a sturdy (if somewhat homely) part of our abode.

"I made my song a coat

Covered with embroideries

Out of old mythologies

From heel to throat;

But the fools caught it,

Wore it in the world's eyes

As though they'd wrought it.

Song, let them take it

For there's more enterprise

In walking naked."

— William Butler Yeats, "A Coat"

ly salary of $200 at the university, I could afford only copper letter-openers and tattered Elbert Hubbard books.

After 12 months, I graduated. Newly married, Lucy and I moved to Lexington, Ky., where she got a job with the city's newspaper. I got a job with a government-affairs magazine (dull doings, indeed).

Then my maternal grandfather died. And I inherited all his woodworking tools.

I drove my inheritance from Connecticut to Kentucky in 1993 in a U-Haul truck, barely making it over the West Virginia mountains in the snow. I unloaded the tools, workbench and machinery into the shed in our back yard. Then I waited for something to happen.

In the years since leaving South Carolina, Lucy and I had continued to haunt antique stores wherever we were. While I was looking for Stickley, I mostly encountered things that were made in the sticks – farmer furniture. This vernacular stuff wasn't of interest to me at the time, but I had to sort through tons of it to find the few Arts & Crafts pieces buried beneath.

In hindsight, I think the vernacular stuff got under my skin.

One day, as I was sitting at our kitchen table, I decided we needed a sitting bench to go by the back door. I had seen hundreds of these benches in antique stores. I thought: Farmers build these all the time. I owned the tools. And I had a napkin. I drew my design on said napkin and went to the lumberyard to buy the wood. The design was all flat boards affixed to one other using dowels and glue.

I talked a friend, Chris Poore, into helping me build the bench. Neither of us had any real skills or knowledge of joinery. But within a few hours it was done. I still use that bench, 26 years later, and can't believe it's still together and is solid enough to dance on.

After that, I built more "boarded" furniture – bookshelves and weirdo cabinets, mostly. Then Chris and his wife, Lee, got the idea that we should all take a woodworking class at the University of Kentucky.

What I was waiting for had – miraculously – happened.

Real Joinery

About a year after taking that class on hand joinery, I became the managing editor at *Popular Woodworking* magazine in Cincinnati, Ohio, and embraced the "real joinery" that would help me build the Gustav Stickley Morris chair I still coveted.

Like many good woodworkers, I became obsessed with mortises,

CHAPTER 19

All nails. Troy Sexton's dry sink. I served as the photographer and ghost writer on this 2001 article. The experience made me re-think nails.

tenons, dovetails and all the other intricate solid-wood joints that were used to build high-end antiques. I built my Gustav Stickley Morris chair (I'm now staring at it to my left) and forgot all about building rinky-dink stuff out of softwood boards and nails.

Then I was assigned to be the ghostwriter for Troy Sexton. Troy, who lived north of Columbus, Ohio, had been a subcontractor for the Workshops of David T. Smith for several years and then struck out on his own. Troy is likely the most-clever woodworker I've met (he transformed a table saw into a handy deer grinder). And while he loved making fancy furniture with difficult joinery, he also knew how to bust things out when the situation demanded it.

He once recounted how – because of a miscommunication – he had to build an entire stepback cupboard with glazed doors in just 24 hours for Smith. After working with Troy for a year, I had no doubt that he was telling the truth.

One day in 2001, I was working with Troy in his shop on an article on a simple dry sink with two drawers and two doors below. It was a straightforward and traditional piece for a customer, and I was there to photograph the construction process. I thought the whole thing would take three days of shooting.

It took one.

The entire piece was in curly maple, and Troy knocked it together with dados, glue and 15-gauge nails spit from his pneumatic finish nailer. When he first grabbed the nail gun, I thought he was making a joke. Three minutes later I knew it was anything but. The carcase was assembled and – with the face frame and back nailed in place – was as solid as can be.

I drove home that day thinking about the sitting bench I had built years before and pondered the simple idea of boards plus nails.

Well, why the hell not?

That night I had a rock in the pit of my stomach, and I didn't get much sleep.

"To know and not to do is not to know."
— *Wang Yangming (1472–1529), Neo-Confucian philosopher*

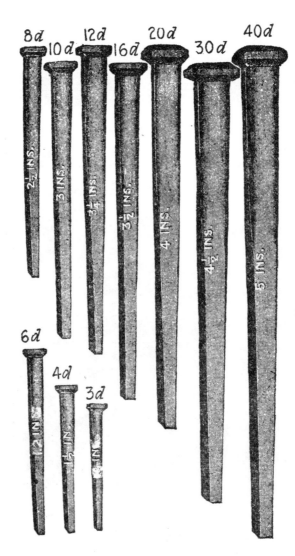

FIGS. 17 to 26.—*Cut nails* showing *actual sizes*, Cut nails have considerably greater holding power than wire nails. Cut nails made from iron are generally preferred for use in exposed positions. There are three regular shapes of cut nails known as 1, common, 2, finish, and 3, casing. The common nails are used for rough work; finish nails for finished work, and casing nails for flooring, matched ceiling and sometimes for pine casings, although the

BARE BONES BASICS OF NAIL TECHNOLOGY

CHAPTER 20

The herpes of the furniture-making world.

I'm often asked why I prefer nails to screws. Here are three reasons: Nails look better. They are quick to install with a hammer. They allow for wood movement during changes in temperature and humidity.

Screws are ugly (I know, this is in the eye of the be-screwer or be-nailer). They should not be installed with a hammer, though the historical record confirms that they were regularly hammered home. And they can crack your work when the seasons change – unless you take extra precautions by elongating your clearance holes.

That said, properly installed screws hold better than nails. It's a fact. And they are more accepted by the modern woodworking elite.

Nails, on the other hand, seem to be the herpes of the furniture-making world. I was taught this hierarchy: Wood-to-wood joinery is the best. Screws are OK. Nails are for rough, temporary or indifferent work.

But that's not true. Nails have been at the core of fine woodwork since Roman (likely Egyptian) times. We are just too blind to acknowledge it. Nails are often invisible to the eye – they are toenailed under a shelf or divider. Snaking into a plinth. At the back of a piece and facing the wall.

I think that nails are as important as the hardware you choose for a piece – the hinges, knobs and locks. Cheap nails look like crap. Good nails enhance the piece. But what's a good nail? Allow me to sidestep that question for a moment and present an historical aside. I would rather show this to you than simply tell it.

Friends, Romans etc. The so-called Roman nail is made by a blacksmith and tapers on all four of its long edges.

Wrought, Forged, Cut & Wire Nails

Nail nerds divide the nail world into four broad categories based on how the nail was made:

1. Wrought or Roman Nails: These are blacksmith-made. The nail's shaft is roughly square in section and tapers to a point on all four of its edges. The head is formed with hammer blows and typically has three or four facets.

Once you master these nails, they are iron joy. They bend and move readily. They cinch down hard. They will rob your body of a kidney if you don't have a trust fund. A blacksmith will charge you more than $1 a nail. That will seem like a lot of money until you start to use them in your work. Then you will realize that you are being undercharged.

Oh, and they look fantastic.

To use the nails, you need to drill a pilot hole in many cases to prevent splitting the work. In softwoods or green wood, these nails are forgiving and almost any pilot hole will do. In hardwoods, you will need to drill a tapered hole or a stepped hole to prevent splits.

CHAPTER 20

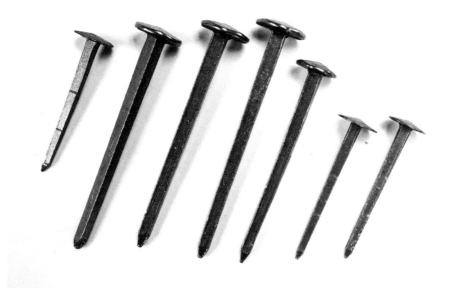

Done with a die. These modern nails resemble Roman nails but are made by a machine. They cost considerably less than blacksmith-made nails, but they don't quite have the same authentic look.

The tapered shape of the nail's shaft is what makes it hold your work together. It's a beautiful wedge that tapers shallowly on all its surfaces. When used correctly, it holds like crazy. When driven indifferently, it splits everything in its path.

2. Machine-Forged Nails: One of the benefits of modern technology has been the development of a nail that is shaped like a Roman nail (tapered on four sides) but is made with modern hammer-forging. These nails are inexpensive and hold quite well.

Because they are machine-made they don't have the handmade quality of a blacksmith-made nail, but for the price they can't be beat. These require a tapered pilot hole like a wrought nail.

If I could ask for one improvement to these nails it would be to rough up the shaft of the nail during manufacturing. Wrought nails and cut nails (see below) have a rough surface finish that adds to the fastener's holding power. As of now, the only nails like this that I know of are made in France.

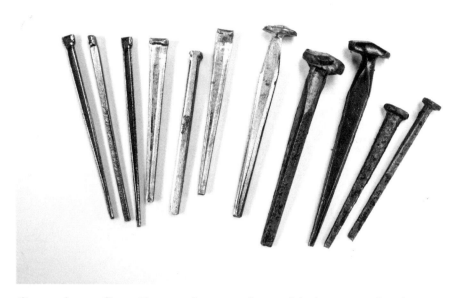

Cut one for me. Cut nails taper along two edges and don't taper on the other two. This taper is a result of the way they are sheared from a plate of steel or iron. Then the fasteners are headed by the machine.

3. Cut Nails: In the late 18th century (as near as I can tell), ingenious mechanics developed machinery that could shear out a ton of nails in a short period of time. All that was required was a flat bar of steel and a machine that could "cut" the steel.

Cut nails are rectangular in section. In one view of the nail it has parallel sides. In the other view, it tapers. And it usually has a head.

Because of the shape of its shaft, a cut nail needs a pilot hole (except in some soft woods) and it usually has to be oriented a certain way to avoid splitting the work. Think of the nail as a wedge. It is. Apply the wedge so it is parallel to the grain of the top board you are nailing down. Otherwise you are splitting mini firewood with your nail.

If this confuses you, don't worry. You will do it wrong only once.

As of now, the only maker of cut nails for furniture is Tremont Nail in Mansfield, Mass.

4. Wire Nails: These are the venereal disease of the nail world. They have a round shaft. They don't hold for squat. They're cheap. They don't

CHAPTER 20

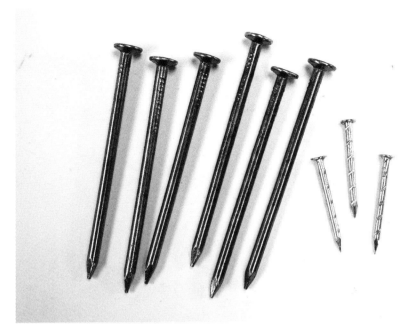

Wary of wire. Though wire nails have their place, I don't think they are useful for furniture that you want to last more than a few years.

require a pilot hole. They are the reason people think nails are for rough and temporary work.

I avoid using wire nails in my work unless I want them to work loose about a week after I drive them in. Which is never.

Bottom line: I use wrought nails when I (or the customer) can afford it. I use cut nails when I cannot afford wrought nails or machine-forged nails. I use wire nails to sprinkle the driveway of my enemy.

On the Naming of Nails

Nails have a ridiculous number of confusing names. For the most part, I suggest you ignore the names at first and focus on how they look. That will usually tell you what they are good for. For furniture work, we usually use four shapes of nails.

1. Brads. This generic name refers to a nail with a smallish head. The brad is used to lock shelves into dados with what is called a "toenail

Brad, the small head. A good general-fastening nail, a brad has some holding power because of its head. But most of its strength is in its shaft and in resisting shear forces.

Give it a clout. Rosehead nails have a somewhat-decorative head, perhaps looking like a flower if you are delusional. The pronounced head makes it ideal for fastening on cabinet backs and bottoms.

Chapter 20

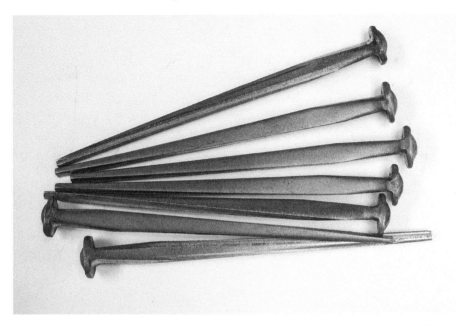

Can't pull this. A clenched nail passes though two pieces and its tip is bent back around like a staple into the work. That's why these nails are ridiculously long and soft.

joint." Or to fasten one piece of wood to another when the head should be small. Because the head is small, the brad's holding power is in its shank. So it's not ideal for attaching a cabinet back or bottom boards.

2. Clouts or Roseheads: Nails that have a prominent head have the most fastening power. They can keep a cabinet back or chest bottom from being pulled off a carcase. Think of the head like the washer on a bolted joint. The price of this holding power is that the nail's head is quite visible in the finished piece – for better or worse.

Many times this form of nail is used for "clenching," which is when an extra-long nail is driven through two pieces and the too-long tip is driven back into the work.

3. Headless Nails: These thin nails have little or no head. They are used mostly for attaching mouldings to hold the work in place while the glue dries.

4. Pins: These are usually wire nails with a head that are used for attaching lightweight pieces of hardware, such as an escutcheon for a lock, or for temporarily holding pieces of veneer in place.

"A writer has nothing to say after the age of 40; if he is clever he knows how to hide it."

— George Simenon (1903-1989)

Square wire. Headless brads hold small bits and mouldings in place while the glue dries, and not much else.

On the 'Penny Size' of Nails

The origin of the so-called "penny system" of sizing nails is murky – on par with the stories surrounding the "nib" on the tips of old handsaws. Suffice it to say that the reason we still use the old penny system is because it is fecking brilliant.

How long is a 5*d* nail? (The "*d*" stands for "penny.") I think I know the answer, but I'd have to look it up first to be sure. The point is that it doesn't matter how long a 5*d* nail is, as long as you know the trick.

Here's how it works: When you nail things together you have a top board and a bottom board. The nail enters the top board first then passes into the bottom board.

So how thick is your top board? Let's say it is 1/2" thick. Now convert that fraction, 1/2", to eighths – 4/8". The top number, 4, is the penny size you need: or 4*d*.

There are exceptions. When working in soft pine, you should increase the nail size by one penny, to 5*d* in our example. And the second exception is this: Use your intelligence. Is the bottom board thin? Are the particular boards easy to split? Are you clenching the nail? Do you need

CHAPTER 20

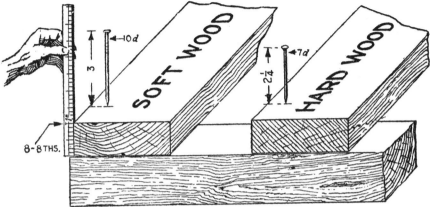

FIG. 156.—Application of rules 2 and 3 in determining the proper size of nail to use.

A good guide. Nailing advice from "Audels Carpenters and Builders Guide No. 1" (Theo. Audel & Co., 1947).

massive amounts of holding power? Then you need to adapt and adjust.

But what about woodworkers who use the metric system? You are in luck. One of my students in England had a flash of inspiration and figured out how to calculate the penny size required when using metric.

Here's the rule: Take the size of the top board in millimeters and divide it by three, rounding up or down as is usual in math.

So if you are nailing down 19mm work, you should use a 6*d* nail (19 divided by 3 is 6.33). If you nail down 13mm material, use a 4*d* nail (14 divided by 3 is 4.33).

On the Pilot Hole

Wrought nails, machine-forged and cut nails usually need a pilot hole, otherwise you will split the top board. The size of the pilot depends on many factors, mostly how close your nail is to the end of your board and the species being nailed.

NAIL TECHNOLOGY

CHAPTER 20

"Here is Edward Bear, coming downstairs now, bump, bump, bump, on the back of his head, behind Christopher Robin. It is, as far as he knows, the only way of coming downstairs, but sometimes he feels that there really is another way, if only he could stop bumping for a moment and think of it. And then he feels that perhaps there isn't."

— A.A. Milne (1882-1956), "Winnie-the-Pooh"

Right & wrong. The cut nail on the left is oriented properly. The one on the right is oriented wrong – its wedge shape is likely to split the wood.

My best advice is this: If you are unsure if you will split the work, make a test joint that is identical in every way to the real joint. Start with a pilot hole that is the same size as the tip of your nail. For example, my 4*d* clout nails have a tip that is about 3/32", so that's where I begin.

Drill the pilot to a depth that is one-half to two-thirds the length of the nail's shaft, otherwise the joint will be weak. If the top board splits, move up a size in bit diameter. Repeat until the joint holds and does not split.

This sounds arduous. It isn't. After a few projects you will get a feel for the right pilot hole.

One caveat: With wrought nails, I like to use a drill bit that tapers along its length. This greatly reduces splitting.

What size? That's a tough one when using a tapered drill bit. I use

CHAPTER 20

Clenched. The tip of this nail has been diverted back into the wood to hook two pieces of wood together. The only way the joint will fail is if the wood or nail is destroyed.

What you see is what you get. Different nail heads from left to right, top row: blacksmith-made wrought-head nail; machine-forged nail; decorative "wrought head" cut nail; rosehead cut nail. Second row: fine finish brad; cut headless brad; wire sinker.

tapered drill bits that are intended for drilling pilots for wood screws. So what I do is set the bit so the top of the pilot hole it makes is the same diameter as the section of the nail under its head. And just like with cut nails, the pilot hole's depth should be two-thirds the length of the nail.

Driving & Setting Furniture Nails

If you've done your due diligence, then driving the nail is the easy part. I like a hammer with a 16-ounce head for most nails. For pins and headless nails I use an 8-ounce cross-peen hammer. The cross-peen, sometimes spelled "pein" or "pane," is ideal for starting the nail without whacking your fingers – the peen can sneak between your finger meat.

If your hammer has a slightly domed striking face, you should be able to set the nail flush to the wood without denting it (called "Frenching" by the English).

Setting the nails is done with a nail set, also called a nail punch. You usually don't set clouts or roseheads because the head will splinter the work badly if forced below the surface of your work. For brads and headless nails, set the nail 1/32" below the surface – and no more than 1/16". Setting the nail deeper will make the nail hole difficult to putty or it will simply call more attention to itself if you don't putty the nail.

CHAPTER 20

Bounce then clench. Put the work on a metal plate and drive the nail into the work. When the tip encounters the metal surface below the batten, as shown above, it will bend over back into the work, clenching things together.

Nail sets/punches for furniture making usually come in three sizes. Use the one that most closely matches the size of the head.

The above description is the shortest treatise I could write. There is more to learn, but the education should come from the end of a hammer, not a book. So don't read another word on nails until you've driven a few cut nails or wrought nails using the instructions above. Most of the questions in your head will evaporate as soon as you get busy.

Sidebar: Clenching Nails

Clenching nails is one of the most effective nail-based joints I know. You can build a boat with this technology. Or a door that will last 600 years, easy.

There is not much to clenching nails. Use a headed nail. The head acts like the head of a bolt on one side of the joint. The shaft of the nail

NAIL TECHNOLOGY

Not much to see. When done correctly, the tip of a clench nail hits the metal surface and turns back into the work. What you see on the exit side is a rectangle of metal.

> "In preference to what is modern, one loses one's view and precludes the best aid, namely to build on the experience gained through the centuries. All the problems are not new, and several of them have been solved before."
>
> — Kaare Klint (1888-1954), the father of Danish Modern furniture

passes through both parts of the work and emerges.

The part that is too long is then directed back into the wood and diverted across the grain. It acts like a staple or a hook, holding the two pieces together until the wood or the nail is destroyed by Vikings.

Nails for clenching are soft, which makes them easy to bend back into the work. If you don't have clench nails handy, you can soften and point any headed nail by holding it with pliers and shaping it on a belt sander. The heat from the belt sander will soften the nail in no time.

How do you bend the tip of the nail back into the wood? Some people first drive the entire nail through with the tip poking out 1/2" to 2". Then they back up the head of the nail with a steel plate, and hammer the tip of the nail until it bends back into the work.

You also can divert the tip by backing up the work with a plate of iron or steel. The nail tip hits the plate and bends back into the work automatically. (Angle the pilot hole to steer the bending action across the grain of your work.)

Practice clenching in test pieces before you dive into clenching nails in a finished workpiece. Clenching can go bad quickly if you aren't familiar with the particular nails, the pilot hole and the work at hand.

Despite the above warning, clenching nails is one of the best tricks to create a permanent joint.

CHAPTER 20

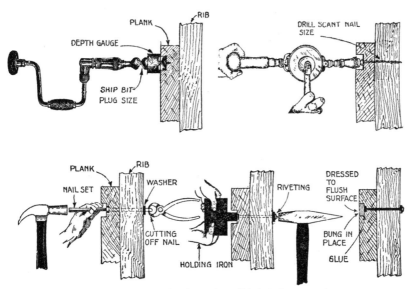

FIGS. 172 to 176.—Various operations in making a riveted copper fastened joint in fine boat construction.

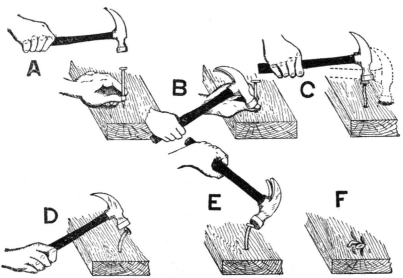

FIGS. 177 to 182.—How not to drive a nail, or method employed by greenhorns and some amateurs. **A**, *stroke 1*, hits nail (accident); **B**, *stroke 2*, hits thumb; **C**, *stroke 3*, oblique blow causes hammer to slide off nail and hit board (first dent); **D**, *stroke 4*, second oblique blow bends nail; **E**, *stroke 5*, side blow to straighten nail; **F**, appearance of nail and board after "driving."

How-to. Nailing advice from "Audels Carpenters and Builders Guide No. 1" (Theo. Audel & Co., 1947).

BOARDED LOW BENCH

CHAPTER 21

Bite off exactly what you can chew.

This low bench is one of the first projects I made as a beginning woodworker. And I've returned to the project many times because this furniture form has a lot of things it can teach you.

For the dead-nuts beginner, this bench is a way to build a useful project for your home using just a few tools, a few hours of shop time and two 8'-long 1x12s. And if the result is a little crooked or ragged, then it fits in with all the boarded benches you'll see at antique stores.

For the intermediate woodworker, this bench is a chance to focus on processing stock by hand, planing surfaces to perfection and using a shooting board. If you are trying to become proficient with hand tools (especially saws and planes) this project is an ideal exercise. Saw the pieces close and plane them to a perfect fit and finish.

I've also built this bench to achieve other goals. When I was learning to make and fit drawers, I built one of these benches and incorporated a dovetailed drawer. I painted a checkerboard on the seat and stored its checkers in the drawer. (Then I sold it to a customer.)

And when I was warming up to build a Nicholson workbench with angled legs, I built one of these sitting benches with angled legs to wrap my head around some of the complementary angles. (If you squint your

Boarded Low Bench   Pl. II

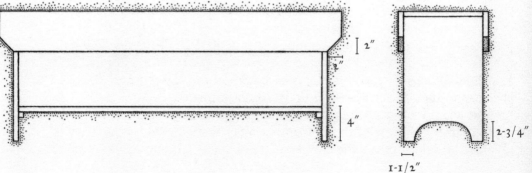

B. Morrow-Cribbs Inv. Del. et Sculp

CHAPTER 21

eyes you'll see how this sitting bench is built similarly to a Nicholson workbench.)

The bench is also an ideal project for learning to use cut nails or blacksmith-made rosehead nails. None of the nails in this bench is located close to the ends of the boards, so you can experiment with different pilot holes without much risk of splitting your work.

But mostly, I just like this bench. I still have the one I built in my first workshop in Lexington, Ky. in 1993 or 1994. Despite my lack of skill at the time, the bench has survived and now sits under a window in our place in Covington, Ky., where our cats use it to hunt squirrels and the neighbors. I've sat on this bench a thousand times as I worked out recipes in my kitchen. And lots of woodworking luminaries have (I think) farted upon it while visiting me.

I hope you'll consider building one because they are loads of fun to make. Here's how I go about it.

Pine is Fine

I've always used white pine 1x12s to make these benches. Full stop. Pine is cheap, easy to work and doesn't move much with changes in humidity. Those qualities make it ideal for this project. If you insist on using a fancier wood, pick one that doesn't move much in service. There is some cross-grain joinery in this project, so wood movement is something to watch out for.

All you need to make this bench are two 8'-long 1x12s. The cutting list and construction drawing show the seat and legs as 11" wide. If your 1x12s are 11-1/4" wide, then go with that. Don't rip off 1/4" of wood on my account.

Saw the seat, aprons and legs to close size – as close as you can get with a handsaw. (Leave the shelf 1" overlong until the rest of the bench is assembled.) Then shoot the parts to finished length. The legs need to be the exact same length. The seat and the aprons should also be bang-on the same length as well (though you can true up small inaccuracies after things are assembled).

I do this with a shooting board. You don't have to own a shooting board, though the appliance makes the task a snap. If you don't have a shooting board, clamp together the boards that need to be the same length (48", for example) and plane the ends simultaneously.

Shoot & confirm. Here I'm shooting the ends of the legs, then checking them against one another. They need to be the same length. What that length is exactly isn't as important as long as it is in the neighborhood of 17".

Saw the Legs & Aprons

Many of these benches feature some sort of cut-out at the bottom of the feet. These cut-outs aren't necessary, but they add a little style to the piece. Pick a curve, an angle or an amoeba if you like. Draw it on the feet. The feet as shown are two 2-3/4"-radius arcs joined by a straight line. But that shape is no better than any other.

Saw out the shape, then clean up your cuts with a rasp and sandpaper.

I also sawed off the corners of the aprons, which is another traditional detail that is not structurally necessary. Mark the 2" x 2" triangle on the bottom corner of each apron. Saw it off and plane off the saw marks.

CHAPTER 21

Better for me. I like to hold a coping saw vertically when making scrolling cuts such as these. My saw cuts end up more square through the thickness of the work.

Clip the corners. This old miter box is handy for angled cuts that have to be repeated several times. These tools are common in the used tool market as they were popular among garage woodworkers and carpenters before the age of electric miter saws.

Get it flat. Here I'm working on the interior surface of a leg panel. It needs to be flat so it meets the shelf without a gap. But it doesn't have to be beautiful because it's not very visible. So a little tear-out or a few plane tracks aren't going to matter.

Cleaning Up

Most of the work in building this bench is done with a plane. The joints between the seat and the aprons need to be tight, strong and exactly 90°. This is all done with handplanes. If you are using pine 1x12s (like me) then you might need to remove some cup and twist from the boards to get the parts to fit together accurately.

This is also an opportunity to work with a pre-industrial mindset about stock preparation. Some surfaces, such as the exterior of the seat and aprons, need to be beautiful but not flat. Other surfaces, such as the interior surfaces of the aprons and seat, need to be flat but not beautiful. Still other surfaces, such as the underside of the shelf, can be almost rough-sawn and still work.

So focus your attention on what needs to be flat and clean.

Dress the edges of the seat to exactly 90°. These need to be straight, 90° to the faces and clean to make a good glue joint. This is a great place to practice with your long planes. Or, if you own a Stanley No. 95

CHAPTER 21

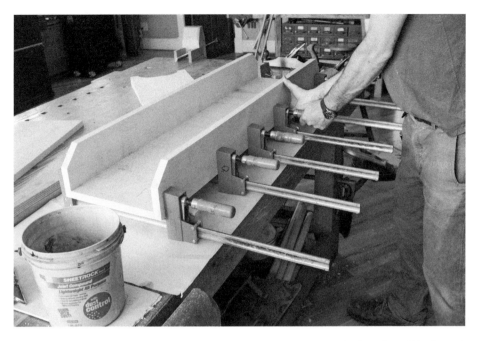

Glue the 'U.' Tight joints between the seat and aprons ensure the bench will look good and last a long time. Clamp the parts together, adjust them as needed to ensure they are flush and clean off the glue. Then wait for an hour before removing the clamps.

edge-trimming plane, you can get the job done without much thought.

After cleaning up the parts, get out the glue. It's time to assemble the seat to its aprons.

The Slow Way

If you are in a hurry, you can glue and nail all these joints together and whip out this bench in an hour or two. I prefer to take a slower approach. I glue the parts together, clamp them until the glue cures, then add the nails. I find this is the better approach when working alone.

If, however, I have an extra set of hands that can hold things in place while I nail them, then I might take this quicker route.

First I glue the seat to the aprons. I prop the parts up on some 2x4s to get them up off the benchtop. Then I apply the glue and clamp things together. With the parts held off the benchtop, I can easily feel if the mating surfaces are flush and make small adjustments. It also makes it

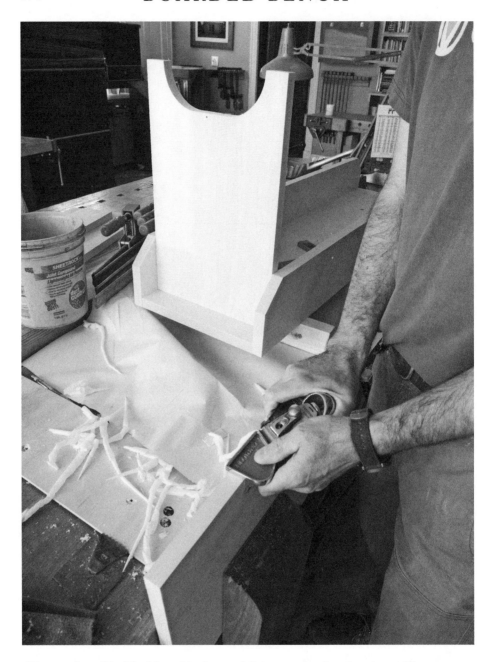

Cheater plane. The No. 95 and its integral fence ensures that the edges will stay square as you fit the legs. It's the ideal plane for the beginner who is still struggling with a jointer plane.

CHAPTER 21

Square all around. Clamp the leg in place and use a mallet to tap it around until it is perfectly 90° to the seat and the aprons.

easier to clean off the glue squeeze-out while it's wet.

After an hour in the clamps, remove them then fit the legs between the aprons. This is done with a handplane (I used a No. 95 plane to keep the edges square). Take a few shavings then test the fit of the leg. The leg should slide in smoothly without bending the aprons out. Take your time with this process.

Once the legs fit between the aprons, glue them in place. First "size" the end grain of the legs. Sizing is where you apply a thin coat of glue, let it soak in for a minute or two, then apply a fresh coat over that. When used on end grain, this technique increases the strength of a joint that contains a lot of end grain.

After sizing the end grain, apply a bead of glue to the inside of the aprons. Press the legs in place then clamp the aprons to hold them. Use a square to ensure the legs are 90° to the underside of the seat and the interior faces of the aprons. Take your time with this joint and try to get it perfect. It will make fitting the shelf much easier.

Fit the Shelf

If you did your job with the square, then fitting the shelf should be a snap. The first task is to attach the cleats that fasten the shelf to the legs. Drill both the clearance holes and countersinks into the cleats for fastening both the shelf and the legs. After you bore these holes, clamp the cleat to the leg and bore the pilot holes. Then screw the cleats to the inside surfaces of the legs with #8 x 1-1/4" screws.

Now you can fit the shelf. Saw it to close size then shoot it until it slides right in. When it fits, take it out then clean off all the machine marks with a handplane. Don't forget to plane the long edges of the shelf so it is the same width as the legs.

Clamp the shelf to the cleats and drill pilot holes into the shelf. Screw the shelf in place.

At Last, Nailing

I put off nailing up all the joints until the end. Why? The nail heads can interfere with cleaning up the surfaces of the bench. So I plane up the entire bench – true the ends, remove any glue and make sure the seat and aprons are trued up. Then you can drive the nails.

I use 2" (50 mm) Rivierre nails, which have a square and tapered shank like a Roman nail. These work best with a tapered pilot hole, though you can easily get away with a straight hole. The depth of the pilot should be about one-half to two-thirds the length of the shank. I start with a drill bit that is the same approximate diameter as the tip of the nail. That usually works in soft pine. For this bench I had to jump up a size because the nails were splitting the work a bit.

As always, it's best to experiment with a test joint or two if you are unfamiliar with the nails or the wood species.

To lay out the spacing of the nails, I use masking tape and mark out my pilot holes on that. Then I can drill my holes and transfer the layout to other places on the bench.

Finishing Details

Break all the edges with fine sandpaper. Then apply a finish. I used a homemade wiping varnish (equal parts boiled linseed oil, mineral spirits and spar varnish). I wipe on thin coats, let them dry then lightly sand them with #600-grit paper. Then repeat until the bench looks nice.

CHAPTER 21

First, secure the cleat. Screw the cleat in place – the clamp helps hold it while you drill the pilot holes.

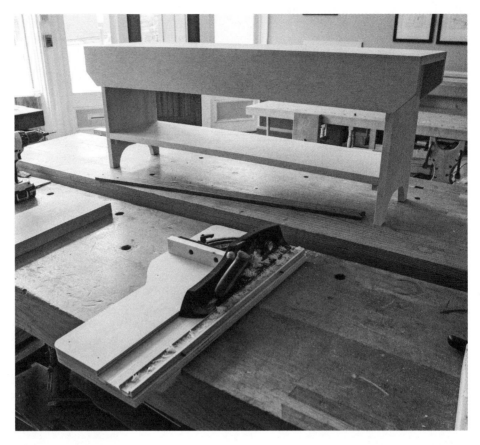

An easy shot. If the legs are square, then the shelf should slide right in. If the legs aren't square, you'll have to taper the ends of the shelf to fit the odd-sized hole.

This usually requires three or four coats.

Historically, these benches endured almost every finish imaginable, from wax to polyurethane. Milk paint always looks good on these benches, and I've used it many times to good effect.

No matter what finish you use, don't be disgruntled if it doesn't come out perfect. You'll build another of these low benches soon enough and get a chance to try a different finish.

CHAPTER 21

Driven. Headed nails hold the aprons in place much like a nut and washer hold machine-screw parts in place. So I recommend headed nails (such as roseheads) for a long-term joint.

BOARDED BENCH

NO.	PART	SIZES (INCHES)		
		T	W	L
1	Seat	3/4	11	48
2	Aprons	3/4	5-1/2	48
2	Legs	3/4	11	17
1	Shelf	3/4	11	43-1/2*
2	Cleats	3/4	3/4	10

* Part is oversized for fitting

BOARDED TOOL CHEST

CHAPTER 22

Resistant to water, wear and whacking.

Every household – even those devoid of a proper woodworker – needs a tool chest. On the day we closed on our first house (correction: our first slightly frightening shell) in Lexington, Ky., I bought a shiny red metallic toolbox, a hammer, screwdrivers and a wooden miter box.

That metal box filled up within a month of work on the house and soon my tools took up two kitchen cabinets. A tool chest like the one shown here would have been a far superior choice, and it was in the range of my fresh-out-of-college skills (e.g. getting hammered and trying to nail something).

This chest is based on a lot of agricultural examples I've studied at antique stores, in private collections and at museums. It is designed to hold a kit of tools you need to maintain a household or farm, or to begin woodworking.

It is long enough to hold full-size handsaws – which are more common than the panel saws used by joiners – plus any planes, levels or bigger tools you might need. And the two sliding trays and any interior racks you might add can swallow all the little hand tools.

It's a great choice for a person who starts work on his or her house and makes the jump to furniture maker – the path that most North American woodworkers seem to take. It's also the chest I recommend new woodworkers build before tackling the full-size English tool chest presented in "The Anarchist's Tool Chest."

Tool Chest

Pl. 12

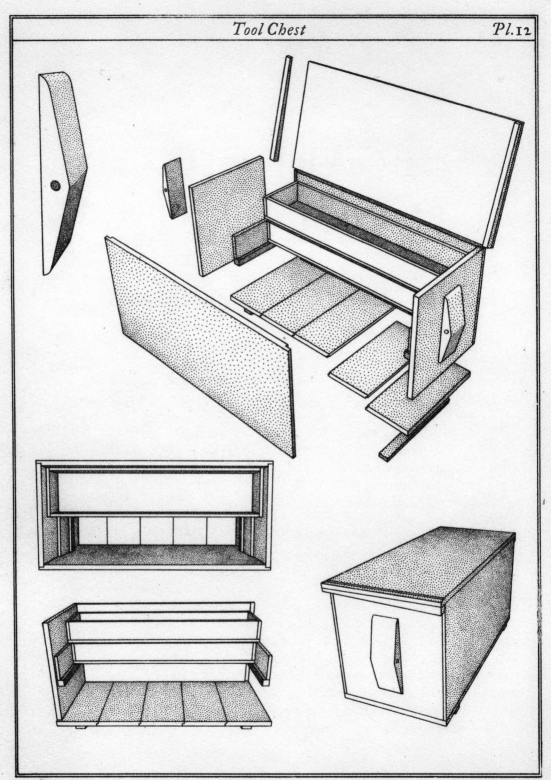

B. Morrow-Cribbs Inv. Del. et Sculp

CHAPTER 22

How it's Built

This chest is simple but, if made with care, stout enough to last a couple hundred years. The ends, front and back are rabbeted, glued and nailed – and the type of nail you choose is the key to the chest's long life.

The bottom is simply nailed to the underside of the carcase to make it easy to replace the bottom boards should they rot. As further protection against rot, there are two water-resistant "rot strips" screwed to the bottom to lift the chest off a wet floor.

The lid is a simple panel of wood with a batten screwed on at either end. The battens help keep the lid flat and also repel dust from penetrating your chest.

Inside the chest are two sliding trays – also nailed together – that slide on oak runners secured to the interior walls of the chest.

Woods for Building Chests

To make the chest easy to move, use the lightest-weight species you can find. My first choice: one of the white pines. Clear cedar or cypress are almost as good. If you come up empty-handed, poplar will do. Tool chests get moved around. Even if you are a stay-at-home woodworker, you want a lightweight chest.

That said, there are a few bits and pieces of the chest that need to be resistant to water, wear and whacking. The rot strips take the most abuse. Consider using white oak or even something exotic (purpleheart or teak) if you have some scraps lying about.

The runners and the bottoms of the trays need to resist wear, so white oak is a good choice for these thin bits. And the battens that restrain the lid need to be straight and stout – oak again.

Prepare the Panels

Dress the stock for the front, back and end panels. Cut the panels to width and length (see the cutting list at the end of the chapter) and remove any machine marks with a handplane.

Before cutting any joinery, mark the four panels using a cabinetmaker's triangle, a simple but effective marking system that will reduce the chance of an error during joinery or at assembly.

"We've been slaves to our tools since the first caveman made the first knife to help him get his supper. After that there was no going back, and we built till our machines were ten million times more powerful than ourselves. We gave ourselves cars when we might have learned to run; we made airplanes when we might have grown wings; and then the inevitable. We made a machine our God."

— John Brunner (1934-1995)

Two triangles. Mark the triangles on the top edges of your panels. Each triangle should point toward the front of the chest and be marked when the panel and its opposite part are placed together.

Extra step. Scribe in the width and depth of your rabbet with a cutting gauge. Use these lines to guide you as you fine-tune the setting of your moving fillister plane.

Now lay out the rabbets on the ends of the front and back panels. The 3/4"-wide x 3/8"-deep rabbets will strengthen the corner joint and assist you when you align your corners at assembly time.

This rabbet is cut across the grain of the panels, so you need to prevent the joint's shoulder from splintering as you cut it. A moving fillister plane has a nicker that knifes in a clean shoulder before the iron levers out the waste. So it's the best choice for this joint.

Even if you use a moving fillister, I recommend you first use a cutting gauge to define the waste. The cutting gauge's lines act as further insurance against splintering. Plus they will point out if your plane's fence or depth stop have moved during the operation.

Even the best moving fillister planes are fussy. The tool's iron and

CHAPTER 22

Head games. Get your head over the tool and use your hands to crowd the body of the tool against the work.

Verify. It's not a rabbet if it slopes down and the shoulder isn't 90°. That's a beveled moulding, and it is no good for joinery.

nicker need to be in perfect alignment and extend out from the body of the tool the tiniest amount so the plane will cut a square shoulder. The fence and depth stop can slip. And even if they don't slip, they won't save you from making a sloping, out-of-90° rabbet.

Making square rabbets requires practice and (until you are good) continuous inspection as you make the joint.

How you hold the tool is important. The fingers at the front of the tool should press the fence against the work. That hand's thumb should be in front of the mouth of the tool. The hand at the rear of the tool should push the plane forward only. If you grip the tool too tightly you will tilt it and cut a sloping rabbet.

Also important: where you put your head. It sounds odd, but you are much less likely to tilt the tool if your head is over the tool and you are looking at the place where the tool's sidewall and the joint's shoulder meet.

Get in position. Start the tool at the far end of the work and pull it backward toward you. The nicker and your scribe line should be one and the same. If they aren't, you need to adjust the plane's fence.

If they are the same, then push the tool forward. When working across the grain you can take a thick shaving with ease. I usually start with a slightly thinner shaving on the first rabbet to make sure everything is in working order. After about four strokes, stop planing and check your work with a square. The floor of the rabbet needs to be 90° to the end of the board, and its shoulder should be perfectly vertical.

If things are out of whack, adjust your hands, and lean in or out slightly to correct the problem. Take two strokes to see how you did.

The next step is to nail the carcase together, so this will be your last opportunity to clean up any dings on the interior faces of the case.

Nail the Case

"The things we make show to the world what we are. The furniture of a period is a sure index to the ideals and aspirations of that period – or to the lack of them."

— Elbert Hubbard (1856-1915) American writer, publisher, artist and philosopher

The case is assembled with glue and nails. Considering all the end grain that is in these corner joints, you might not expect the box to be very strong. But if you apply the glue and nails in the correct way, it will outlive you.

As to the glue, I prefer hide glue for furniture in almost all cases, but if you have only yellow or white glue, it will be fine here. What's most important about the glue is that you use it to "size" the end grain in the joint before adding glue to the face-grain surfaces.

"Sizing" is simple. Paint a thin layer of glue on the end grain and let it sit for a minute, maybe two. This first application of glue will get sucked into the end grain and clog the wood's vessels. Then, when you apply the second coat of glue, the end grain will not be able to suck the glue away from the joint (that's what normally weakens a joint that uses end grain).

This procedure was developed by a glue scientist, but I've tested it in the shop. When these sized joints are intentionally broken, you see a lot of wood failure and little glue failure. That's a good thing.

The second factor is the nail you choose for the joint. You should use a tapered nail that has a significant head – either a cut nail or a blacksmith-made wrought nail. These nails have a shank that tapers, and early 20th-century studies showed that these nails hold as much as 400 percent better than a same-size wire nail. That's because the nail's tapered shank acts like a wedge.

As to the size of nail, you can use a *4d*, *5d* or (in a pinch) *6d* cut nail. The larger nails are more likely to split your work, but I'm going to show

Chapter 22

Exposed joinery. You are going to see these nails every time you look at the chest, so I recommend spacing the five pilot holes at each corner with care.

Tape marks the stop. The pilot hole should stop short so the nail has to burrow its way into the material. Here I'm using a tapered drill bit for the pilot holes. It isn't strictly necessary, but it helps.

A minute for strength. The thin coat of glue size on the end grain is an important component of a strong rabbeted butt joint.

you how to get around that by clamping across the joint.

Lastly, you will strengthen the joint if you drill your pilot holes at alternating angles, kind of like dovetails. You don't want a lot of angle, just 5° or so. Mark out the locations of the five nails at each corner and get out the glue.

The most difficult part of using cut (or wrought) nails is drilling the correct pilot – both its diameter and length. The best way to approach the problem is to do some test joints in the same kind of material and get a feel for the correct diameter bit. With typical 4*d* and 6*d* nails I start with a 3/32" pilot hole and adjust up or down in size from there.

The pilot depth should be about two-thirds the length of the nail. If you make the pilot the full length (like with a screw), the nail's hold will be weak. The nail has to do some of the work.

CHAPTER 22

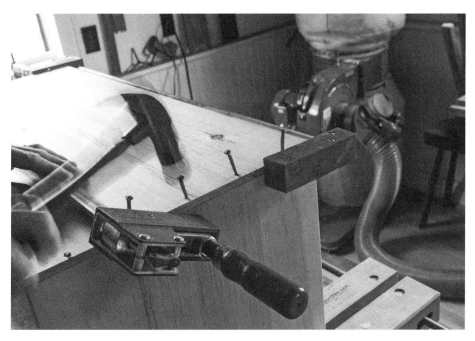

A clamp for safety. Clamping across the joint significantly reduces the chance you will split the top part of the joint or the board below. Note the alternating slopes of the nails – sometimes called "dovetailing" a nail.

The last thing to remember before driving the nails is that the tapering action of the nail should be parallel to the grain of the top board. If you apply the wedge across the grain, it's like splitting firewood. This confuses some people at first until they do it wrong. Then they never forget the rule.

Now it's time to put the box together. Begin by attaching the back to the ends.

Size the end grain of the end boards with a thin coat of glue and let it dry for a minute. In the meantime, apply a thicker coat of glue in the rabbets on the back panel.

Place the back panel on the end panels and drill your pilot holes – don't forget to angle each hole slightly to increase the wedging action of the nails. If you are even the slightest bit worried about splitting (and I am always worried), put a bar clamp across the joint to reduce (greatly) the chance of the work busting apart.

Drive the nails and set the heads flush with the surface. Headed nails,

"Apart from panel and veneer pins the furnituremaker has little use for nails except for softwood work etc."

— *Ernest Joyce, "Encyclopedia of Furniture Making"*

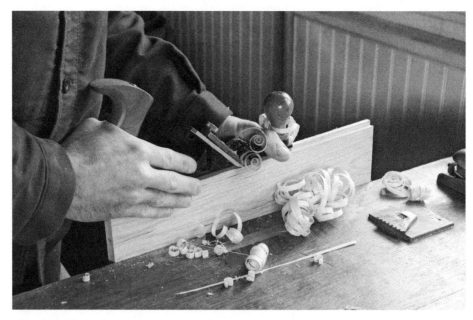

Special planes. While you can make a tongue-and-groove joint with plow and rabbet planes, it's much faster if you have a dedicated set of match planes or a metallic tongue-and-groove plane dedicated to the task.

A strong bead. Bead the shoulder of the tongue section of the joint. If you bead the groove section you will weaken the joint.

CHAPTER 22

Nails all around. Don't glue the bottom boards, just use nails. I drive three nails into the ends of the carcase. Then I space the nails every 4" or 5" when nailing into the front and back of the carcase.

such as clouts, roseheads and wrought-head nails, are not typically set below the surface of the work like a brad. Setting the head only increases the chance for splitting.

Affix the back panel. Flip the carcase over and repeat the process for the front panel. When the glue is dry, level your joints with a plane, including the top and bottom rim of the carcase.

Bottom Boards

The bottom boards are merely nailed to the bottom rim of the case. The individual boards should have some sort of edge joint to allow for seasonal movement. I used a tongue-and-groove joint; shiplaps would be another good choice.

Note that the grain of the bottom boards runs from front to back, not side to side. This is for strength.

Cut the edge joints on your bottom boards, then remove the machine

Automatic chamfers. Consistent chamfers are easy with a block plane. Clamp the work in your face vise so it is about 3/8" above the benchtop. Rest one corner of the plane on the benchtop and plane for 20 strokes. Flip the board over and repeat.

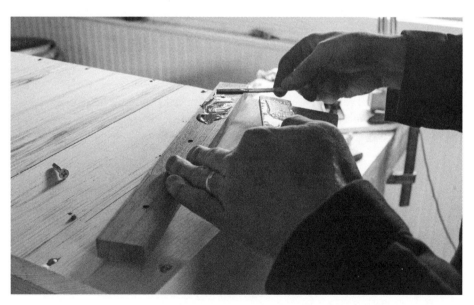

Waterproof. Teak and epoxy will prevent water from migrating from the floor into your bottom boards.

marks. If you'd like to dress up the bottom boards, you can cut a small bead on the boards. If you are using a tongue-and-groove joint, cut the bead on the shoulder of the tongue section of the joint.

Now you can nail the bottom boards to the rim of the carcase using 6d clouts or rosehead nails. Use the same pilot hole you used earlier for the carcase and apply a clamp across the carcase if you want to reduce the chance for splits.

After the bottom is on, true up the carcase all around to flush the bottom boards to the carcase.

The Rot Strips

The last bit of work on the bottom is to affix the two rot strips to the underside of the bottom boards. There are three (at least) philosophies when it comes to rot strips. One philosophy is to make them from pine and affix them with iron nails. If these start to rot, they will fall off and you will know it's time to replace them.

The second philosophy is to make the rot strips from a water-resistant species and attach them with epoxy and brass screws. Then oil and wax them. These rot strips will refuse to rot or soak up water.

The third method? Skip the rot strips and screw casters to the chest.

All three methods protect the chest from moisture.

I had some teak scraps so I used those for the rot strips. After cutting them to size, I planed a small chamfer on the edges to make the chest easier to slide around on an uneven floor.

On this chest, I glued the rot strips on with epoxy and screwed them down with brass screws. A few coats of linseed oil on the teak and bottom boards will also help moisture from wicking into the carcase.

Add the Chest Lifts

The last bit of work is to make and attach the chest lifts on the ends. You can use metallic lifts or make your own using wood and rope.

There is no real advantage to either. Wooden lifts take time and effort to make, and they can break at times – I've seen it happen. Metallic chest lifts cost more to purchase, but they can be installed in a few minutes and are quite durable.

Your call. Chest lifts made from wood and rope, called "beckets," are one traditional choice. Iron lifts are another. There is no real functional advantage to either.

The Lid

The chest's lid is a simple flat panel with battens screwed to its ends. You can decorate the edges of the panel anyway you please – a thumbnail profile was a typical edge treatment.

To make the thumbnail profile, fetch your moving fillister plane. Use the same fence setting (a 3/4"-wide cut) as you did for the rabbet joinery. Adjust the depth stop so the plane takes a cut of about 1/8" deep.

Cut the profile on the ends first. Then rabbet the front edge of the lid. To complete the profile, use a block plane to round over the top lip of the panel.

Now affix the battens. On early chests, the battens were secured with clenched nails. This works really well, but it takes a little practice to get good at the operation. If you don't want to attempt clenched nails, the other option is to use wood screws in holes that are slightly elongated to allow for seasonal wood movement.

The first step is to shape the battens. At the least, ease the lower corners to make them nicer to handle. I sawed a bevel on the corners and cleaned up the cuts with a block plane.

CHAPTER 22

For decoration. It's OK if this rabbet slopes a bit. After cutting the rabbet on three sides, round over the sharp corner all around until it looks nice.

Quick cut. Many early chest lids had rounded corners on the battens. Or the battens would taper toward the front, ending in a rounded corner.

Screws that move. By elongating the clearance holes in the battens, the threads of the screw will stay tight in the lid (usually) without splitting.

CHAPTER 22

Permanent Jenga. The pine board shown at the bottom puts the lower runner in its correct position. After the first runner is in place, install the second runner on top of it. Then remove the spacer and repeat the process on the other end of the chest.

Remove any machining marks and drill pilot holes and clearance holes for your wood screws. The clearance holes in the batten need to be slightly elongated parallel to the grain. This slight elongation allows the top to move without cracking.

Elongating the holes is simple, quick work. After drilling each clearance hole, put the bit back into the hole. While the bit is spinning, tip the drill forward then back about 10°. That's enough.

Shoot the bottom. After cutting the till bottom to a close size, shoot its ends until the bottom slides smoothly on its runners.

CHAPTER 22

Familiar operation. The trays are assembled with the same joints and procedures as the carcase.

Screw the battens to the lid. Then attach the lid to the carcase with hinges. Strap hinges look best here.

Interior Trays

The two sliding tool trays hold all your small tools and grant you access to the large well below. The bottom tray sits on oak runners that are 5-1/2" above the floor of the chest. This space is critical because it allows you to put a typical bench plane on the floor of the chest with the sole of the tool flat on the bottom boards.

So the first task is to make a 5-1/2"-wide spacer so you can nail the lower runner in perfect position on either end of the carcase. Cut a scrap to this dimension and stand it on the floor of the chest. Place the lower runner on it. Glue and nail the runner to the wall of the carcase. Then glue and nail the remaining runner above it. Repeat at the other end.

With all the runners glued and nailed in, cut the bottom pieces for the trays to size and fit them to the inside of the carcase. It's easier to do this before you add the walls of the trays.

Slightly proud. Leaving the bottom end slightly proud of the tray solves a variety of potential problems.

"By this process men gradually become mere machines, and lose all the moral and intellectual characteristics which distinguish the skilled artisan…"

— Henry Mayhew (1812-1887), The Morning Chronicle, July 11, 1850, on the system of sub-contracting and piecework in London

The trays are built a lot like the carcase with rabbets bonded with glue and headed nails. The rabbets on the end boards are 1/2" wide and 1/8" deep. The only significant difference between the trays and the carcase is that you want the bottom of the trays to poke out of the end of the assembled trays by 1/16". This slight proudness makes the trays simple to fit and ensures the nail heads won't rub against the interior walls of the chest and jam the trays.

You can attach the bottom to its tray with screws or nails. Just be sure to slightly elongate your clearance holes if you choose screws (nails will bend on their own without any further help).

A little beeswax on the trays and runners will help them slide, but that's really all the finish you need on the inside of the case.

On the outside, a few coats of a long-wearing paint is the typical choice for a tool chest. I used varnish alone on the lid, though that doesn't offer near the same protection as paint.

The rest is up to you. You can make racks for the inside walls to hold small tools. And there should be room to affix your handsaws to the inside of the lid.

CHAPTER 22

BOARDED TOOL CHEST

NO.	PART	T	W	L
			SIZES (INCHES)	
2	Front & back	3/4	15	33-1/2
2	Ends	3/4	15	14-1/4
	Bottom boards*	3/4	33-1/2	15
1	Lid	3/4	15-1/2	35
2	Lid battens	3/4	1	15-1/2
2	Rot strips	3/4	1-1/2	15
2	Lifts	1-1/2	3-1/4	10
2	Top tray, front & back	1/2	3	32
2	Top tray, ends	1/2	3	7
1	Top tray, bottom	1/2	7	32
2	Bottom tray, front & back	1/2	3	31
2	Bottom tray, ends	1/2	3	7
1	Bottom tray, bottom	1/2	7	31
2	Runners, lower tray	1	1	13-1/2
2	Runners, top tray	1/2	3-5/8	13-1/2

* Made up from multiple boards

TO MAKE ANYTHING

CHAPTER 23

Embrace or reject the history lesson.

If you want to make historical furniture reproductions or pieces that are inspired by vintage work, you must devote yourself to studying old work – in person, up close and without prejudice.

But if you want to make things that are new or modern, you instead must devote yourself to studying old work – in person, up close and without prejudice. Otherwise, how will you know what it is you are rebelling against or rejecting?

In other words, no matter what sort of furniture maker you are, understanding the furniture record will make you a better one. Otherwise you might end up like some members of the Bauhaus, for example, who rejected historical work and set out to reinvent architecture, furniture and other crafts from first principles. As a result, they made a lot of unnecessary and time-consuming mistakes to create a new world. (See armchair F 51 designed for the director's room of the Bauhaus.)

As I see it, every generation of makers has goals that fall upon these three lines:

1. Exalt old work to revive principles that have been forgotten by our degenerate society.
2. Create new work that rejects the principles of our degenerate society.
3. Make birdhouses.

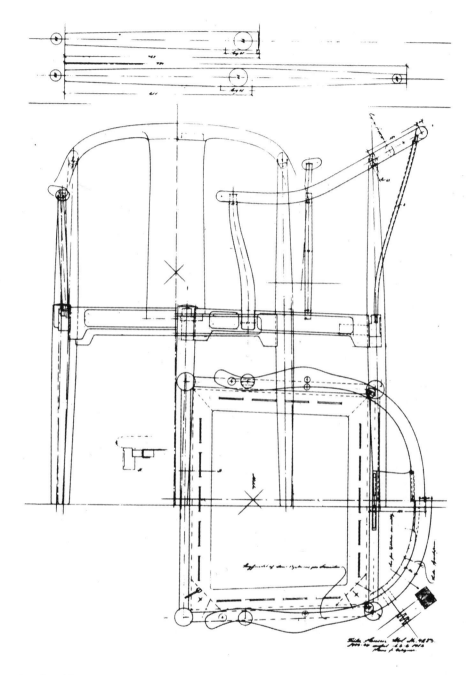

Another Chinese chair. Hans Wegner's Chinese Chair No. 1 (1944).

CHAPTER 23

All three are completely valid ways of approaching the craft. Only No. 3 allows you to skip the furniture record and create something useful with minimal effort.

As I write this, I am surrounded by hundreds of books filled with thousands of pieces of furniture that I'll never build. Many of those pieces are somewhat ugly or, at the least, too ornate for my taste. Yet I am thrilled to study every line and curve of every William & Mary, Georgian or Seymour piece that I can lay my hands on.

Some of these pieces are brilliant because of their technicality. Their talented makers found clever ways of making extremely complex pieces in a shockingly simple way. (If you have studied furniture bandings, then you know what I mean.)

Other pieces are notable because of the sheer patience and focus of the maker (see French marquetry).

Still other pieces are forms that are perfectly proportioned in silhouette.

In my personal work, I seek to combine all three of those properties (though I rarely succeed). And the only way I can try to reach that goal is to study old work. So every day I open an old book, go to a museum in a strange city (thank you, crazy teaching schedule) or plumb the Internet.

Example: In a manor house in Cornwall there's a beautiful Chinese chair. Why is it there, surrounded by 300-year-old English stuff? The house's docents don't know. So I buy a book on the history of the manor house and its contents. I explore Chinese chair construction on the Internet. I turn up some Hans Wegner chairs in my search and find a bright string from traditional Chinese furniture through Danish Modern.

Suddenly, the curve of the chair's crest rail makes sense, across time and cultures. What I do with that information is up to me as a designer – but if I decide to incorporate a wishbone shape into a future design, I have a path to explore all the possibilities. And I can embrace or reject the history lesson.

> (W)e want an architecture adapted to our world of machines, radios and fast cars.
>
> — Walter Gropius (1883-1969), founder of Bauhaus

"A book makes a good staff, but a poor crutch."

— Julia Ellen Rogers, "Trees" (Doubleday)

SIX-BOARD CHEST

CHAPTER 24

The puzzle isn't how they go together.

Like many American families with a traditional bent, I grew up with a six-board chest in our home, where it led a romantic existence in my sister Robin's room. I was one of those kids who always liked digging through old stuff in the attic, the bottoms of closets and our family's chests. So sometimes I'd clear off all of Robin's swimming trophies from the top and lift the pine lid. Inside were bits and pieces of my family's history that made us seem more interesting than we really were. My dad's medals from Vietnam, old letters with exotic postmarks, a boxed acupuncture set.

While I never used the acupuncture needles on my sisters, I can't make the same claim about their Barbies.

The term "six-board" chest is a bit of a misnomer used by antique dealers and grandmothers in describing this particular form of furniture. The name is half-right in that there are typically six boards nailed together to make the chest – top, bottom, front, back and two ends.

A better name might be "boarded chest" because you are nailing together wide boards instead of making a frame-and-panel chest with mortises and tenons.

But I like the term "two-board chest" because that's what you need to build one. When you examine these chests as a builder – instead of as an antiques dealer – they are a bit of a puzzle. The puzzle isn't how they go together; it's how they stay that way.

Six-board Chest

Pl. 13

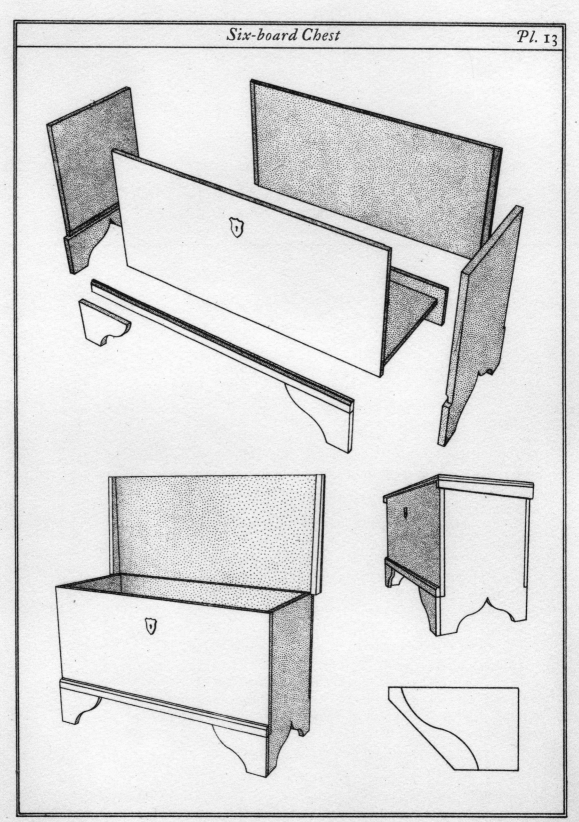

B. Morrow-Cribbs Inv. Del. et Sculp

CHAPTER 24

These chests disobey almost all of the rules of wood movement. The grain on the front and back of the chest runs horizontal. The grain on the ends runs vertical. The front and back should have split and fallen off. And take a gander at the lid. The grain of the battens that help keep the lid flat and the dust out is 90° to the grain on the lid.

By all rights, the battens should have fallen off and the lid should have split. The whole chest should be just a collection of interesting splinters.

Yet these chests survive in droves.

Now the snarky woodworker would claim that only the oddball chests survived, or the ones that were extremely well-made or cared for. In other words, the typical chests actually did succumb to cracking and splintering and what's left are the "superlignum" examples.

Of course you cannot directly refute this claim – there are no birth certificates and death certificates issued for chests. But even a casual antiques collector can tell you that you'll find 20 (maybe 200) boarded chests for every highboy you stumble on.

So perhaps highboys are rare because only the best highboys survived?

You can see how this can get ridiculous in short order. Here are the facts. There are lots of these boarded chests out there because they were easy to build. Highboys are rare because they were expensive to build and only the rich could afford them (both then and now).

But why do the six-board chests survive? I have some clues and theories that relate to the raw materials used for the chests and the makers' understanding of that material. Let's start with the wood.

Pine, Oak & Wood Movement

A lot of these chests are made of softwood – usually single, wide boards of the stuff – not panels that have been pieced together from narrower boards. Some of these chests are made of a combination of softwood and oak – oak for the ends and softwoods for the other components.

Most woodworkers I've met have a misconception about softwoods that needs to be dispelled. Here is the misconception: Softwoods move a lot during the yearly change in seasons.

In fact, the opposite is true. Take a look at the Forest Products Laboratory's numbers on shrinkage and expansion for North American hardwoods and softwoods. In almost every case, softwoods at equilibrium move less than hardwoods.

"The taste or style (or lack of it) of the hollowed tree-trunks of far back in the Middle Ages was probably founded upon (1) necessity, (2) usefulness, (3) the primitive tools of that day, and (4) the fact that there was no previous furniture from which their primitive imaginations might wander to other things."

— The Woodworker, April 1933

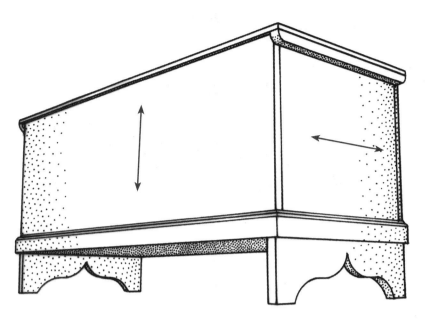

Wood movement in a six-board chest.

This is important. Remember it.

Why does this misconception exist and thrive? Easy. Most softwoods are purchased wet compared to hardwoods. Though both softwoods and hardwoods are commonly kiln-dried, consumers are willing to buy softwoods that are not at equilibrium moisture content with the environment.

For example, when I buy kiln-dried cherry or walnut in the Midwest, it will usually be about 9- to 10-percent moisture content. After a few weeks it will drop a couple points in my shop (which has forced-air heat and air conditioning).

When I buy softwoods, on the other hand, they will typically be 15 to 18 percent moisture content. Again, after a few weeks they also will reach equilibrium with my shop. However, that usually means the softwood has to lose half of its moisture content. Softwood moves a lot as it pumps out all this extra water.

But once it reaches equilibrium, softwood doesn't move much in service, no matter where it is stored in the house, attic, shop or basement.

So the bottom line is that softwoods are more stable, less expensive, easier to work and tough enough for most furniture (especially chests).

CHAPTER 24

Rough & tough. The surface finish and wedging action of these wrought nails makes them ideal for a six-board chest.

All this sounds nice and neat until you see an American chest that is made from both pine and oak. Typically the ends of the chest will be oak. The rest of the parts will be pine, though sometimes the front and back will also be oak.

It might seem like a bad idea to combine a wood that moves a lot (oak) with one that moves little (pine). But as it turns out, the way these chests are constructed is smart.

With the ends made from oak, this will cause the chest to contract from front to back. So the chest's lid and bottom will move in the same direction as the ends – front-to-back. So far, so good.

Then you nail the pine front and back onto the oak and you have created a cross-grain construction. The front and back will move up and down. The ends move the opposite way. But still it works. Take a look at each corner of the chest. That's where the face grain of the front and back intersects the edge grain of the ends.

In this joint, the front and back are moving up and down. The long edges of the oak end pieces aren't moving at all because wood doesn't move much along its length. And because the front and back are made

Clenched batten. The nail passes through the lid batten and the lid, then is bent back into the wood like a staple.

from softwood, there isn't much movement at all in this joint.

Don't be fooled – there is some movement. But the movement is minimized by using softwood for the front and back. The rest of the story about why this joint works is in the nails.

The Most Forgiving Nail

Nails – the right nails – allow you to get away with serious crimes of wood movement. Nails are almost always more flexible than screws or even dowels. So a nail will allow the wood to expand and contract, bending back and forth through the yearly humidity cycles.

With the exception of hardened masonry nails, I've found that all nails will bend, including wrought nails, cut nails, wire nails and pneumatic ones. The reason I've always preferred cut nails for making furniture is that they hold better than wire or pneumatic nails. Cut nails are a wedge that – when properly driven – bend and crush the wood fibers in a way that holds the nail fast.

CHAPTER 24

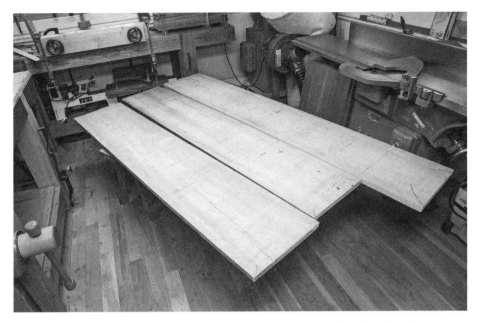

Close to the chest. These pine boards are a few sawcuts and a handful of nails away from becoming a six-board chest.

Wire and pneumatic nails aren't wedges, and while they do compress some of the surrounding wood fibers, they are just not in the same league as cut nails (or wrought nails).

Another bonus: A good cut nail or blacksmith-made nail will have a rough finish, especially compared to a wire nail. That rough finish also gives the nail some extra bite. This is why many pneumatic nails are coated with glue that helps them stick in the wood – every little bit helps.

Nails are also the reason that the cross-grain battens stay attached to the underside of the lid. In this joint, the nails are typically clenched (some would say "clinched"; some might say "bent") to improve the grip of the nails.

The nails are driven through the battens so the tips poke out through the moulding in the lid. The first time you see this, you'll think it looks like crap. But after you've had a batten fall off, you'll come around.

Once these nails are driven in, the tips are bent around like a fishhook and driven back into the moulding. The hook shape of the tip, the thick head of the nail and its bendability all conspire to keep the battens attached to the lid for many years.

But Why Not...

Whenever a project has a cross-grain construction such as this, many modern woodworkers will try to fix it or avoid it. Even though it has already been fixed by the stock selection and the particular fastener.

Here are some suggestions that have been lobbed at this enduring form.

Why not attach the battens with sliding dovetails? You can do this, but it will take considerably longer to cut the sliding dovetails and fit the battens into the socket.

Why not make the grain on the ends match the grain on the front and back? That way the chest would expand and contract in only one direction (vertically). Problem solved. Yes, you can do this, but there are multiple problems. You are unlikely to find a single board that is wide enough to make the ends without gluing up a panel. Even if you did this, the legs would be weak and prone to breaking. And you would weaken the grip of the nails. Nails don't hold as well in end grain.

OK, so why not dovetail the front, back and ends? Then add a separate base with stronger feet that are backed up by glue blocks. Yes, you can do this, but it will take a lot more time, and you're not making a six-board chest anymore – it's more like a 10-board chest, minimum.

As I hope you can see, the design of this chest form is closely tied to the raw materials that make it possible. Fixing one part that isn't broken causes another problem – usually it slows you down or requires you to own an additional tool or acquire another skill.

And as you move into actually building this piece, you are going to see that the techniques I use flow both from the design of the chest and the materials. None of these elements can be easily separated from the other without making a mess – or a different form of furniture.

As with all the pieces in this book, six-board chests are designed to be made with the fewest number of boards, the fewest number of hand motions and the most efficient material yield possible. After all, if you are going to build these projects by hand and build them for the non-rich, you have got to be efficient. And the end product must be durable.

So About Those Two Boards

As I mentioned before, these chests are somewhat of a puzzle. Some people might be puzzled about why they survive. I'm more puzzled

---

"All told then, it is quite a good idea to remember the advice of Dr. Primrose in 'The Vicar of Wakefield,' who chose his wife on account of her good wearing qualities. Possibly it will not give you the immediate thrill that something rather more flamboyant would have done, but in the long run you will be the better pleased."

— The Woodworker, January 1955

CHAPTER 24

Rip, then crosscut. Rip the moulding from your boards before crosscutting the front and back pieces. It will make the moulding process easier and faster.

by how they were made – how many sawcuts were required, what is the order of operations that produces the chest with the least amount of effort, least amount of time and the fewest tools?

The only way to answer these questions is to examine the furniture record for clues, make some guesses, then build some chests using those

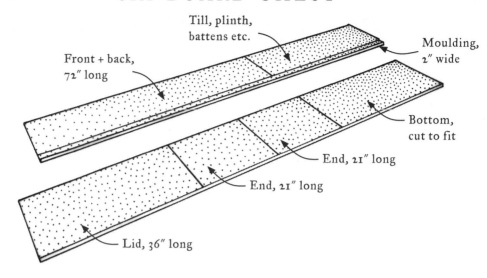

Sample cuts for a typical chest.

guesses. Every chest built with these principles in mind should bring us closer to unraveling the lessons that have been baked into this form by their makers.

Design Begins with the Boards

When you look at a lot of these chests, you see a lot of variety in their sizes, yet the chests look like they were built using the same design principles. It's tempting to explore these chests using dividers and look for different proportioning systems. I've done some of that, but it was mostly a dead end for me. Sometimes you simply find whatever you are looking for.

So instead, I started the design process by thinking how I would build these chests with simple tools, a short timetable and the minimum amount of material. When you look at these chests, you'll notice that typically the lid is the widest piece of lumber in the project and is usually a single board of pine. These chests typically range in size from 15" to 18" deep overall, which is the width of the lid. So I started my design process by basing the depth of the chest on the widest board I could get my hands on. In this example, I found some 18"-wide sugar pine.

CHAPTER 24

Note: Finding wood this size is not as difficult as you might fear. Just because your home center doesn't carry this stuff doesn't mean it's not readily available at auctions, through the Internet or at specialty dealers. I paid about $200 for the pine to build this chest. Yeah, that's more than if I had bought 1x12s, but it also looks a lot better.

So I crosscut the 36"-long lid piece from a 10'-long-board and set it aside. Why 36"? These chests are typically 32" to 48" long, and 36" was the clearest length of wood I could get – no knots or checks.

A logical question might be why these chests were about this length, and it's probably a question that is unanswerable in the absolute. If they were longer than 48", I suspect they would be unwieldy. Typical casework rarely contains components that are more than 48" long. If the lid were shorter than 32", then you'd lose out on storage space and your chest would take on the characteristics of a box or a miniature chest.

With the lid cut, I needed to find two boards for the ends. The ends need to be almost as wide as the lid, so I sawed them from the same board where I got my lid.

These chests typically range from 18" to 27" tall – that's a good height for a chest when it comes to lifting the lid and bending over to get something out of storage. It's not too high and not too low for our bodies.

In this example, I could manage two boards almost 22" long and a piece for the bottom from what remained of this 10'-long board. This allowed me to cut around some knots and eliminate some checks on the end of the board. I then set the two end boards aside and grabbed a second 10'-long board.

From this board you need to get your front, back, moulding and other bits. This is where things get a wee bit tricky. The order of operations is critical. Why? The moulding.

When you cut moulding by hand, the best way to do it is to "stick" one long piece of moulding then cut your pieces (three, in this case) out of that one finished piece of moulding. Sticking three separate pieces of moulding is tricky. Even if you are using a complex moulding plane, it's unlikely that you will be able to create exactly the same moulding profile on all three pieces.

So you need to find a piece of moulding that is long enough to wrap around the front and two ends. Moulding on the rear is uncommon.

The best place to find this moulding is in this board – before any crosscutting.

Decide how wide your moulding piece will be. Something about 2" wide is typical, but it depends on the moulding profile you want to use

"If the crafts survive, their work will be done for love more than for money ... People are beginning to believe that you cannot make even toothpicks without ten thousand pounds of capital. We forget the prodigies one man and a kit of tools can do if he likes the work enough."

— *David Pye (1914-1993), "The Nature and Art of Workmanship" (1968)*

and your eye. Rip that moulding from this long board.

Now find the clearest section of the board. This is the front. Make it a little shorter than the lid. The board next to your front is the back of the chest. It can have knots and look like poo – it's the back. It is, of course, the same length as the front – in my case about 36".

You can now crosscut the front, separating it from the back. The hard part is done. The remaining stock will be your lid battens and miscellaneous pieces. Those will be cut later, after everything else is assembled.

Congratulations. You just designed your chest with a saw. And the tree helped.

Techniques, Assistance & How to Avoid Them

When choosing how to build this chest, it's a bit of a balancing act that depends on the tools you own and whether or not you have a helper monkey in the shop.

For example: cutting shallow rabbets on the ends of the front and back boards makes the chest easier to assemble by yourself (it also lets you use less-expensive nails – more on that later). So even though cutting those rabbets requires an extra tool (a rabbet plane) and extra effort, it's worth it if you are alone in the shop without racks of clamps and other workholding gizmos.

In fact, you don't need a single clamp to build this chest – aside from your workbench. A couple handscrews would be helpful, but they aren't strictly necessary.

The first step in creating the joinery for this chest is to deal with the end pieces. They have long notches cut into their long edges to receive the front and back. Not all chests had these notches, which create feet at the floor of the chest, but they look nice and they make assembling the chest by yourself a bit easier.

Some woodworkers create this notch by scabbing on a small piece at the floor. It seems like a good idea, and it's especially easy to do if you have woodworking machinery. However, I have yet to find evidence that this was done on historical chests. I have looked and looked. Perhaps the joint is so seamless that I cannot see it, perhaps I haven't seen enough chests, or perhaps they didn't do it that way. I cannot say for sure.

But what I can say is that cutting these long notches is easier than it looks. Sandwich the boards together and lay out the long notches – each is about 3/4" wide and is as long as the front and backboards are wide.

CHAPTER 24

An easy rip. Cut the notches simultaneously and you will get better results. The thickness of the two pieces will make it easier to stay 90° to the face.

Pinch the sandwiched boards in your vise and saw the long notches. With the boards still pinched in your vise, use a chisel or plane to true up the notch if it is not 90° to the faces.

The last task while the ends are sandwiched together is to cut the decorative profile on the bottom that creates the feet of the chest.

The simplest profile is what antique collectors call the "bootjack" – it's a simple inverted "V" that resembles the tool used for pulling your boots

Always together. Plane the notches flat and true with them pinched together. I always seek to do one operation on multiple boards whenever possible.

off your feet. This profile is just two lines, two cuts and done.

A fancier profile is a half-circle or an ogee. Both of these are laid out with a compass, cut with a frame saw and smoothed with a rasp if necessary. While laying out the half-circle is obvious, the ogee is not.

CHAPTER 24

One setting. Here you can see the arc struck by the compass both above and below the baseline. That's all it takes to make a symmetrical S-curve.

Lay Out an Ogee

There are multiple ways to lay out an ogee, but this is my favorite. Now the fastest way to lay it out is to eyeball it and wing it, but I like to take the extra minute or two to make the ogee, which is sometimes called a "cyma recta" or "cyma reversa."

Step 1. Draw the inverted "V" shape as if you were making bootjack ends for this chest. The point of the "V" should be slightly lower than where you want the bottom of the chest to lie.

Step 2. Set your compass so it bisects one of these lines at the halfway

Together again. OK, it's a theme. Here I have the two ends pinched together to cut the ogee shape of the feet.

point of the line segment. This is the only compass setting you need, by the way. Mark the center point of each line segment.

Step 3. Use a compass to strike four intersecting arcs as shown on the previous page. Two arcs are from the ends of the line segment. Two are from the center point. Note that where you strike these arcs determines if the ogee will be a cyma recta – where the curves bend to a horizontal – or a cyma reversa – where the curves bend to the vertical. This ogee is a cyma reversa.

Step 4. Place the point of your compass at the intersection of an arc. Draw an arc that bisects your line segment. Move the point to the other intersecting arc. Strike a second arc that bisects your line segment.

Step 5. One side of the ogee is complete. Move to the other leg of your inverted "V" and repeat the same process to make the mirror image of the first ogee.

Cut out the foot profile on the sandwiched ends. Smooth the cuts with a rasp. Now mark the ends with a cabinetmaker's triangle so you know what is the inside, outside, front and back of the chest.

CHAPTER 24

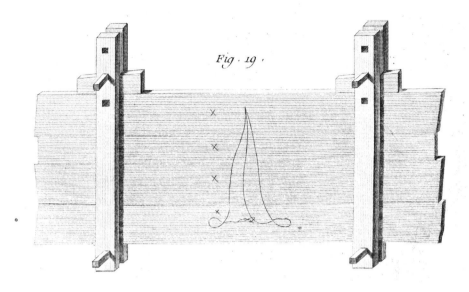

Forever together. The marriage mark – or cabinetmaker's triangle – keeps parts oriented before and after assembly. A better or simpler system has yet to be devised.

Sidebar: The Marriage Mark for Parts

Woodworkers are prone to come up with all manner of whack-a-doodle methods for keeping track of parts. What's the front, the back, the inside, the outside etc. These hair-brained systems usually involve lettering the parts – AA, BB, CC and so on – with big arrows.

These systems work, but they are so needlessly complex that it's easy to get parts turned around and put in the wrong place, especially when there is open glue involved.

Ditch your system and use the "cabinetmaker's triangle" instead. It uses the fewest marks, it tells you all the information you need to know at a glance and you don't even have to know your ABCs and 123s.

Here's how it works:

Bunch together the parts of your assembly as if they were all in the correct position. A classic example is with four legs of a table. You bunch the four legs together in the same orientation that they will be in when the table is finished. Then you draw an equilateral triangle on the top edge of the parts.

Work across. Chiseling out the waste in a dado is easy work. Begin with the chisel bevel-up as shown. Then switch to bevel-down when the handle gets in the way.

The point of the triangle faces the front of the assembly or the top of the assembly. The base of the triangle represents the rear or bottom of the assembly. That's it, you are done. The rest is learning to interpret and respect your triangles.

These triangles are powerful stuff. If you mark them properly, then you will always know what is outside, inside, left, right, front and back with every assembly. As anyone who has taken a class with me already knows, the only thing you need to remember when you have wet glue are these two words that I shout when we assemble: Triangle check!

Whoever is nearby will look over and confirm that all the triangle points and bases are lined up. Doing this will save your skin.

In the House

It's best to finish up the joinery on the end pieces while these pieces are in your hands. The next decision for you – the builder – is whether or not you want to plow dados in the ends that will grasp the bottom board.

Here are some pros and cons.

Pros: A dado allows you to slide the bottom board in without any battens or glue blocks to support it. You don't even need to add any glue when sliding the bottom in place. Also, thanks to the dados, it's easy to put the bottom in the correct location.

Cons: Cutting these dados requires extra tools and skill. You can cut the dados' walls easily with a panel saw, but removing the waste between the walls can be a fussy and slow-ish job with a chisel alone. You can reduce the fuss factor if you have both a chisel and a router plane. But again, that's an extra tool you'll need in your chest.

I have a router plane and love it, so I always opt for cutting the dados.

The first time you cut a long dado like this one, you'll probably want to nail or clamp some sort of fence to your work to guide your saw. That's OK. Work through that problem – I did. After a dado or two you will realize that the stiffness of your saw's plate is enough to keep you on the straight and narrow.

So define the walls of your dados (the width of the dados should match the thickness of your bottom board), then remove most of the waste with a chisel driven by a mallet. Some woodworkers opt to skip the chisel and go directly to the router plane. Those woodworkers are still cutting their dados an hour after sawing the walls.

Router planes aren't designed to take a big bite. Even if all the cards are in your favor – that is, you are working across the grain and in a soft wood – the tool's design works against you. A router plane isn't supposed to eject huge shavings like a jack plane. So when you take a big bite with a router plane, the shaving usually gets jammed in there and stops the cutting action.

So clean out the waste first with a chisel. Stick the tool in the waste

One of many ways. Cutting cross-grain rabbets can be done with a moving fillister (shown), a simple rabbet plane or even a shoulder plane.

of the dado, leaving about half the waste above the bevel and half below. Drive the tool in and try to find the sweet spot by moving the handle up and down. Work bevel-up at first, then bevel-down. The sweet spot is where you can take a huge chip without the chisel diving down into the work or rising out of the cut. You'll find it after a few cuts.

After clearing as much waste as possible with a chisel, follow up your work with the router plane. Try to remove only about 1/32" or so with a pass. And you should attempt to clean up the bottom of a dado with only one or two passes. After that, it becomes a drag that you should have taken care of with your chisel. By the way, it's OK if your dados are a little too deep in the middle. It won't hurt a darn thing.

Front & Back

The front and back pieces are a blank canvas – both for decoration and for joinery. You can cut shallow rabbets on their ends. Or not. And you can carve the living bejesus out of the faces. Or make some

CHAPTER 24

By yourself. I like to assemble the carcase like this because it lets me do it without any assistance from friends or family.

simple scratched decoration. Or do nothing.

Let's talk about the joinery first. The reasons to cut the rabbets on the front and back are simple:

1. They help prevent the case from racking after assembly – especially when moving the chest around.

2. They make it much easier for you to assemble the chest by yourself. The rabbets lock into the notches in the end pieces. All you have to do is hit a few nails. Without the rabbets, it's best to have a helper there to keep the parts in alignment while you nail.

3. You can get away with using shorter (and cheaper) nails. If you make this chest using 1"-thick stock, then you will want to buy 8*d* nails to assemble the carcase. However, if you cut 1/4"-deep rabbets in the front and back pieces, you will be able to use 6*d* nails instead. This might seem like a nominal savings. But if you buy handmade nails, the savings add up.

So how should you make the rabbets on the ends? That depends on the tools you have. If you have shot the ends of the front and back boards so they are square and smooth, then you can use some sort of fenced rabbet plane – such as a moving fillister plane – to cut the rabbets. A moving fillister plane has a fence and depth stop that will help make your rabbets consistent.

If, however, the ends of your front and back boards are rough or wonky, then you need to take a different approach. Here are the two typical techniques:

1. Knife a line where you want the shoulder of the rabbet to fall. Use any kind of rabbeting plane to make the rabbet. First tilt the plane and put a corner of the tool's sole into the knife line to turn the knife line into a "V"-shaped trench. Then continue to plane the surface until you complete the rabbet. You'll need to tip the plane a little off vertical at first. Then you'll need to tip it vertical.

2. The second method is similar to the first. Knife in the shoulder of the rabbet. Then clamp (or nail) a fence on that knife line. The fence will guide the plane. Simply press the tool against the fence (no need to tip it) and plane away until you reach the desired depth. As mentioned before on dados, the fence is a great teacher. You will quickly outgrow the need for it.

Cut the rabbets. They don't need to be deep – 1/4" to 3/8" is fine – but they need to be consistent in depth so that your carcase is square.

With the rabbets complete, clean up the inside surfaces of your ends and the front and back. This is the best time to do this because you are about to nail some things together.

Nail the Back to the Ends

If you've cut rabbets and dados in your parts, then there really is only one way to assemble the chest. Nail on the back (add glue if you like). Fit the bottom in the dados. Nail on the front. Then nail the bottom in place all around.

You need to use a nail with a sizable head for fastening the front and back pieces – such as a rosehead nail. Headless nails won't do.

Depending on your stock, you might need to drill pilot holes. In some pines and with some nails, you don't. So make a test joint in some scrap to find out what holds and what doesn't split. After some experience you will get a feel (or a bad feeling) about what will work and what will blow to bits.

One last detail: You should angle these nails slightly, as if you were cutting dovetails instead of driving nails. It should be just a small slope –

about 5°. And the slopes should alternate every nail. This slope will help keep the front and back wedged onto the ends.

You don't have to set the nails. The heads should be proud.

With the back nailed to the ends, cut down the bottom board to slide into the dados so the fit is snug and the unfinished carcase is square. Usually when I make the bottom, it ends up too thick for the dados. Instead of reducing the thickness of the entire bottom, I bevel the underside of the bottom – like a raised panel – until it slides in. Beveling the edges is faster.

I glue the bottom in place all around – then nail it in after assembly. The glue only helps here because all the expansion and contraction is in your favor. So take advantage of it.

You don't need to use fancy nails with roseheads to secure the bottom. Just use big 6*d* or 8*d* cut finish nails – four through each end and five or six through the front and back. Set these below the surface because they will be covered in moulding.

Sticking it to the Moulding

You can skip the moulding if you are going for a Bauhaus chest. But the moulding adds the appearance of a classic plinth – the visual separation between the base section and the not-base section. So I recommend the moulding.

What moulding profile you use is up to your tools. On a typical piece of casework, the moulding should bulge – something like an ovolo or a bead. A cove mould looks all wrong – those are the arches that support the top of a carcase.

But it's your chest.

This is the time to dress up that long 80"-plus offcut you ripped earlier. Dress the board, but don't cut it to length. Length is your friend. You want to stick the entire profile at once. Then cut the miters. This ensures your profiles will match at the miters. Try cutting moulding on three separate pieces – then you'll know one of the reasons they invented powered routers and shapers.

I cut the moulding on a sticking board – a long and flat board with a high fence. I use a 3/8" square ovolo. Why? I have a sweet old moulder that cuts this profile. There are worse reasons for picking a profile.

"...(V)isual harassment can be stimulating. What good is taste if it doesn't betray you? Hate can turn to love with just one close glance, or maybe a few."

— *Roberta Smith, art critic,* The New York Times, *April 18, 2009*

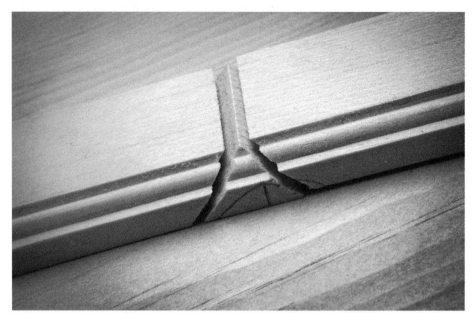

Remember that long rip? Ripping the moulding from a long bit of wood allows you to do this. When these two miters go together they will match perfectly.

On Mitering

The less you fuss about mitering the better your miters will be. Just cut them with confidence and calm. Sweet baby Moses I wish someone had told me that when I was starting out. Or if they did, I wish I could have heard them.

Wrapping moulding around three sides of a carcase is cake compared to making the full 360°. Focus on getting one corner good and tight. Then clamp those two pieces in place on the chest and mark the other corner for its miter.

With both miters cut on the front piece, focus on getting the fit tight on the returns (the pieces that "return" down the ends of your chest).

I leave the returns long until after everything is glued and nailed in place, so don't mess with those until you have to.

Planting moulding is an art. There are lots of ways to do it. I learned this from a trim carpenter: I drill pilots for my finish nails or brads through the moulding and push them into the pilots with my fingers until the tips of the nails protrude slightly from the moulding.

I fit the miters on the carcase then tap the nails into the carcase so

CHAPTER 24

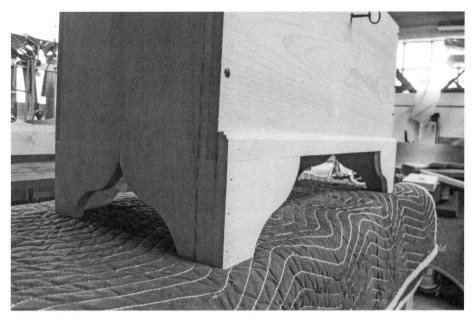

Base bits. Here you can see how the additional foot pieces are added to the carcase to enclose the base on the front of the chest. It's all glue and nails.

they bite into it. Then I remove the moulding and add glue to the back of it. Glue the entire front of the moulding. On the returns, glue the miters and only the front one-third of the moulding to the ends.

Press everything in place for a minute or two. Then drive the nails. The moulding should not shift. Set the nails. Then saw the returns flush at the back of the carcase. The base is complete.

And if You Like Fancy...

Another option for the base of the chest is to add the front moulding, then add a couple ogee-shaped pieces below that to enclose the front of the carcase.

It's much easier than mitering anything, and it looks nice.

The two ogee feet are made from the same scrap from making the moulding, so it will be the same thickness. And the layout is exactly the same as you did for the ends of the chest.

Across the grain. Cut the moulding across the ends of the lid first. Then cut the front edge with the same moulding plane.

About the Lid

The lid has two important components: the moulding profile around the rim and the battens attached to its underside.

The moulding profile makes the lid look like something more sophisticated than leftover siding.

First cut the moulding profile on the lid. It can be almost any profile you have on hand. I have a larger ovolo plane (this one is 1/2" wide) that cuts a moulding similar to one I've seen on other chests. Cut the profile on the ends first, then cut the front edge of the lid. This allows you to erase any splintering from working across the grain.

I know that you aren't "supposed" to make mouldings across the grain. But you can. And you should. It works just fine.

The battens on the ends of the lid keep it flat – if you attach them correctly. Nailing the battens to the lid won't do; the battens will fall off in short order. Gluing the battens won't do. Nailing and gluing the battens? Ditto.

You have two choices: old school or modern. The modern approach is to screw the battens to the underside of the lid and ream out the clearance holes for the screws so the lid can move.

The other approach is old school. The old-school method is entirely awesome. Screw the screws.

With this method you drive nails through the battens and through the lid so that the tips of the nails protrude through the moulding. Ugly? Perhaps to modern eyes. But I think they look permanent.

Choose nails that are long enough that when you drive them through the battens and lid that they protrude about 1/2" or a bit more beyond the moulding. Then turn the tip of the nail over like a fishhook and drive it back into the moulding. Hard.

This secures the batten to the lid and keeps the lid flat(ish). It is called clenching. Or clinching. Whatever you call it, it ensures that your battens won't simply fall off your lid one day when the weather changes.

I used 2" cut fine finish nails for this. I'd have preferred 2-1/2" fine finish nails, but I was out. If you need to use a shorter nail than typical, first drill a 1/4" counterbore for the nail's head into the batten. The depth of the counterbore should ensure you can get 1/2" of the nail's tip sticking out of the moulding on the lid.

After drilling a counterbore, drill a pilot hole through the rest of the way and through the moulding profile on the lid. Use a small bit – 1/16" or 3/32".

Drive the nail into the hole. Then push it so the head is at the bottom of the counterbore and the tip sticks out of the moulding.

Then turn the tip with needlenose pliers and drive it back into the moulding like a staple.

Hinging the Lid

There are a variety of ways to attach the hinges to the carcase and lid. Snipe hinges are an old solution (you can make your own for almost nothing using 2" cotter pins).

Strap hinges are also traditional. But you can use butt hinges or whatever else you have on hand. After you hinge the lid you can add a lock if you like, plus an escutcheon for the keyhole. The goal with the lid is to make it fit as tightly as possible. These chests were supposed to ward away bugs from textiles, so a tight seal was important. And it still helps today.

SIX-BOARD CHEST

Entropy & Finish

With everything assembled, it's time to take the lid off, ease the sharp edges and prepare the exterior for paint. The inside of the chest should remain bare wood. This is traditional. It will impart a nice smell to the textiles inside.

You can make your own paint – there are lots of recipes out there, from lead-based paint to milk-based paint. Or you can buy your own from the paint store. What you choose should be based on:

1. Do you have children? Avoid lead-based paint unless you want to always outwit your young ones.
2. Do you hate strong smells? Use latex paint.
3. Does the paint need to be bombproof? Consider oil-based paint.
4. Do you want a traditional look with modern convenience? Use commercial milk paint.
5. Are you a glutton for punishment? Make your own paint.

At this stage in my life, I'm developing my own paint recipes and haven't found the magic formula for the results I want. So at this point I've been using commercial "milk" paint. I know it's not historically accurate, but it does give me a look I like. Plus it is quite durable and fairly low on the toxicity scale.

I apply two coats of paint and sand between the coats with a #320-grit sanding sponge I've owned for about a decade.

"Humble and touching pine, which can rot in decent fashion, which must not show its dirty hue at any price, which modestly wears the painter's color –

Let us be old fashioned together and out of touch with the times.

Our chance will come again, sooner or later."

— *Poul Henningsen (1894-1967), Danish author, architect and critic, written Oct. 28, 1953*

SIX-BOARD CHEST

NO.	PART	T	W	L
			SIZES (INCHES)	
2	Front & back	3/4	15	34-1/2
2	Ends	3/4	15-1/2	21
1	Bottom	3/4	33-1/2	15
1	Lid	3/4	17	36
2	Lid battens	3/4	1	17
	Moulding	3/4	2	68

CHAPTER 24

Photo by Al Parrish.

MULE CHEST

CHAPTER 25

It's a six-board chest – with drawers.

The mule chest is the slightly more complex cousin of the six-board chest. Like the six-board, its carcase is assembled with rabbets, dados, nails and glue. The only significant difference is that you add a drawer or two at the bottom of the chest.

The drawers improve the chest in two ways. First, the addition of the drawers makes the entire chest taller so you don't have to bend down as far to reach the chest's lid and its contents. Second, the drawers are convenient for storing things you need to get to frequently. Simple chests have to be thoughtfully packed with the most-used items at the top and in the till (if the chest has a till). So, the mule chest is a more flexible, friendlier furniture form. It's not stubborn at all (like its name suggests).

Much ink has been spilled on the origin of the word "mule" in relation to the chest. While the furniture form is old – examples abound from the 17th century – the term "mule chest" is not. It appeared in our language in about 1911, according to the Oxford English Dictionary.

Most accounts claim that "mule" refers to the idea that it looks like a hybrid between a chest of drawers and a simple chest. This seems the most likely explanation, especially when you consider the alternatives:

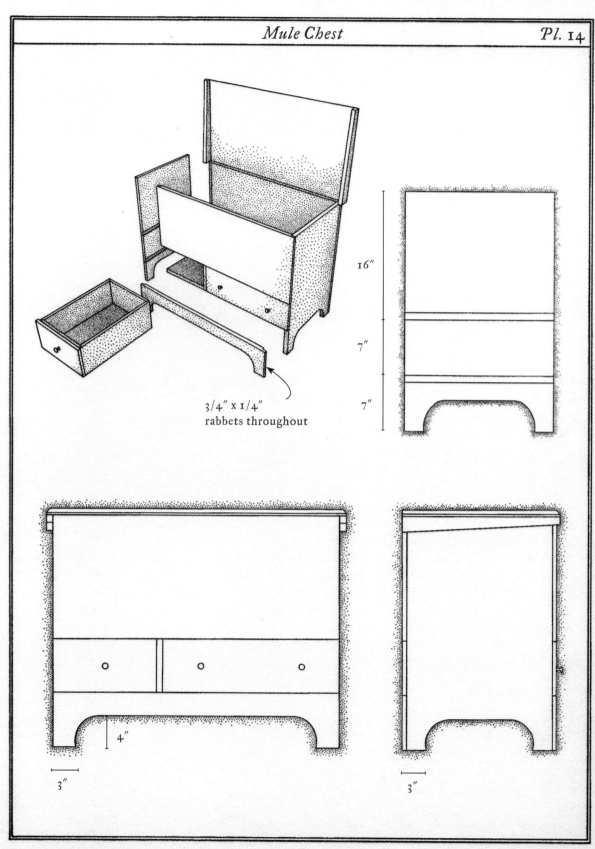

- The drawers were good for storing women's slippers, which were called mules. The word "mules" was indeed used for women's slippers from the 16th century on. But it seems unlikely to name a piece of furniture after one very particular item of footwear. Contrast the general terms "blanket chest" and "linen press" with a Queen Anne jockstrap box.
- Peddlers would strap this sort of chest on both flanks of a mule, allowing the roaming merchant to get at goods in the drawers without removing the chests from the animal. That would be quite a rigging job, and I've yet to see an image or description of the practice that wasn't in the "theory" section of a furniture book.
- The chest had secret compartments, allowing you to hide or "mule" items. (This is the least likely explanation because the term "mule" as it relates to contraband didn't emerge until the 1970s.)

Despite the murky explanations and sketchy origin of the word, I still like to call this form a "mule chest." If anything, it's shorter than saying "a chest with drawers below."

Construction Details

Many of these chests were painted, so feel free to use any inexpensive softwood for all the components. I used white pine because it is inexpensive and easily available in wide widths. While sorting through your stock, look for boards that are 8" to 11" wide. Those will give you the most efficient yield when gluing up panels.

The overall construction of the chest is simple, especially if you've ever built a six-board chest. The chest's bottom and the panel that supports the drawers sit in dados in the chest's side pieces. Then you rabbet the front, backboards and plinth, and nail them to the sides. Then you nail in a divider between the two drawers and build the drawers (I use nails or dovetails). For the lid, battens keep it flat; hinges allow it to open and close.

Panels & Dados

Glue up your panels all a little oversized (1" over-long and 1/2" over-wide). Then cut only the side pieces and two interior panels to finished size. You might have to make adjustments to the sizes of the other components as you go, so don't cut a part to finished size until you must.

Lay out the locations of the 1/4"-deep dados on the inside faces of

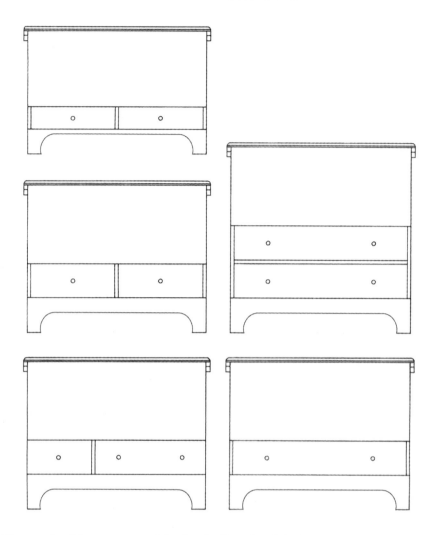

Many mules. Here are some of the sketches I made while designing this mule chest. You can vary the drawer height and arrangement to suit.

the side pieces. Use a knife and darken the lines with pencil lead. Saw out the walls of the dados.

Here's a tip that took me many years to learn. If you are right-handed, saw the right-hand wall of the dado. Use your left hand to guide the saw (which will obscure the left-hand wall). Then turn the piece 180° and – bingo – you have another right-hand wall that is easy to saw without

CHAPTER 25

A little crutch. If you lack sawing confidence, you can clamp a batten to the work to help guide your saw. If you are only minorly insecure, a small block of wood pressed against the sawplate can help keep the tool at 0°.

obscuring your lines with your hand.

Remove the bulk of the waste using a chisel. I start at the ends of the dados with the chisel bevel-up. Then I work the vast middle with the tool bevel-down. Feel uncertain? It's easy. After your first dado you'll be an expert who can direct chunks of work at the walls or your coworkers.

To complete the dados, clean their bottoms with a router plane. Work from the outside edges of the side panel and into the middle. This strategy avoids spelching (aka splintering or "blowing out the backside").

Fit the panel into its dado. If it's too tight, plane off a little material on the underside of the panel. If it's too loose, vow to drive wedges into the joint at glue-up to fill the gap.

Shape the Feet

Lay out the shape of the feet using a compass and straightedge. If you are finicky (I am) then repeat the layout on both the inside and outside faces of the sides. Saw the feet to shape and clean up the cuts with a coarse cabinet rasp. The extra layout step will help with the rasping.

Repeat this process on the front and back plinth panels. You can do it now or wait until the joinery is all cut on the plinth panels.

MULE CHEST

NO.	PART	SIZES (INCHES)		
		T	W	L
2	Internal panels	3/4	18-1/2	37
2	Ends	3/4	19	30
1	Drawer divider	3/4	6	7
1	Drawer divider scrap	3/4	3	11
2	Plinths	3/4	7	38
2	Front & back panels	3/4	16	38
1	Drawer cavity panel	3/4	7	38
2	Lid battens	7/8	2	20-1/2
1	Lid	3/4	20-1/2	39-3/4

Small drawer: overall dimensions of drawer box: 7 x 13 x 18

1	False front	1/2	7	13-3/4

Large drawer: overall dimensions of drawer box: 7 x 22-3/4 x 18

1	False front	1/2	7	23-1/2

CHAPTER 25

Guided by wrist. Raising or lowering your wrist controls how deep the chisel will cut. Find the right bite, then lock your wrist against the work and drive the tool forward with a mallet.

Press & push. After you clean the bottom of the dado, you can also clean up the joint's sidewalls by pressing the cutter of the tool against the wall and pushing. The bevel of the cutter will scrape the sides of the joint.

Sawing alone. My grandfather taught me to use a coping saw (and bowsaw) in the vertical position. The work is horizontal. This might be an echo of some Sloyd education somewhere in my family tree. I find this method makes it easy to keep the cut 90° to the faces.

Assemble the Sides & Panels

Plane up the panels. I use a jack on the interior faces and a smooth plane on the exterior. (Confession: I personally prefer the texture left by a jack plane on the exterior faces as well.)

Check the fit of the panels in their dados. If things are too tight, jack off the underside of the panel – just at the ends. If the joints aren't perfect, say a blessing to the nails and the glue.

To assemble, first paint a thin coat of liquid hide glue on the end grain of the interior panels. This will seal the end-grain pores and increase the strength of a questionable joint. Then apply glue to the dados. Put the pieces together and clamp.

CHAPTER 25

Correcting pressure. Here I am shifting a clamp to pull the rear of the case square. By applying the pressure above one dado and below the other, the case changes its shape. This is handy when clamping across the case diagonally isn't an option.

Check the assembly for square both at the front and the back of the carcase. Shift the clamps around to pull it square.

Add the Nails

After the glue is dry, drive in some headed nails to secure the ends to the interior panels. I used 1-1/2"-long nails. I usually create a template for drilling the pilot holes using some blue masking tape. I lay out the pilot holes on the tape then move the tape to where it needs to be.

Drawer Divider

Now is the best time to add the divider between the two drawers (if you want two drawers). The divider is a scrap piece of pine that is 7" long and as wide as you can find in your scrap pile. Nail it in place between the two interior panels. Examine the photo for a tip on keeping

Template tape. Blue masking tape helps guide you as you drill your pilot holes. Once you finish one row of nails, pull up the tape and move it to the next location.

Two squares. The divider has to be square to the front of the carcase and dead square up and down between the internal panels. Use two squares to position the divider. Drive one nail in, then correct the divider's positions using the squares to guide you. Then add more nails.

CHAPTER 25

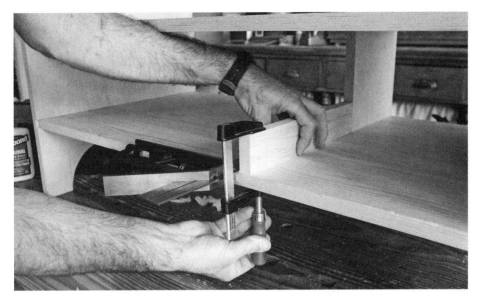

Guides the drawers. Clamp the low divider in place, then affix it with screws from below. Done.

the divider square.

After the divider is nailed in, hunt up a scrap of pine to finish the job at the back of the carcase. The scrap can be narrow – its width doesn't matter. It is just keeping the drawers on track. Affix this scrap with glue and screws. The pine won't move much in service, so wood movement really isn't a problem here. Promise.

Cutting Rabbets

All the boards that are attached to the carcase – front, back, plinths etc. – are rabbeted on their ends. The rabbets add quite a bit of strength to the assembly from racking forces. Don't skip them.

All the rabbets are 1/4" deep x 3/4" wide. There are a dozen ways to cut them. Among the hand-tool options are using a moving fillister plane, a wooden rabbet plane or a shoulder plane. The moving fillister is tempting here because it has a fence and a depth stop.

If you don't have a moving fillister, the next best option is to mark out each rabbet with a gauge then clamp a batten to your work to guide a wooden rabbet or shoulder plane. The batten keeps the plane vertical.

Batten down the rabbet. Here I've clamped a batten to the end of a plinth. The rabbet is marked in with a cutting gauge. And I've relieved the end of the cut with a bevel to prevent the "spelch."

Can't miss. A simple wooden rabbet plane hogs off material. The only tricky part is learning to stop. After a couple rabbets you'll get good at spotting the gauge line.

Chapter 25

Clean rabbet. The batten helps ensure the shoulder of the joint is crisp and square. If it's a tapered mess, clean it up with the rabbet plane run on its side.

Your eyeball tells you when to stop.

No matter what method you use, I have two words of advice: Always relieve the wood at the far end of your cut so you don't splinter (some say spelch) the exit area of the cut. And know that you'll have to adjust the rabbets (or the rest of the board) to get the boards fitting correctly on the carcase.

Attach the Panels

Fit all the rabbeted boards, adjusting the rabbets and the interiors of the panels to make things fit. Then glue the front, back and plinth boards to the carcase. The laws of wood movement decree that gluing the 16"-wide front and back boards is a recipe for disaster. In theory, yes, you shouldn't glue that much wood cross-grain. But when it comes to the white pines (and many other softwoods), these rules are flexible.

White pines simply do not move much in service after they have reached equilibrium with their environment. I've had joints such as this survive for many years with no problems when I used white pine. And

All glued. Despite the data and despite the dramatic cross-grain construction, I've glued all the rabbets. Experience tells me that the chest will survive just fine.

Read the tape. I lay out the nails' locations on a piece of masking tape. Then I can transfer the tape to other parts of the project. This greatly reduces the time setting out the nails' locations.

CHAPTER 25

I've seen them self-destruct when it was a hardwood such as oak, walnut or cherry.

So, I've taken to gluing the entire joint when I have a white pine chest, even with the dramatic cross-grain. All I can say is to follow your own path and keep your mind open that you might be wrong (or right).

Add the Nails

When you nail things up near the ends of boards, things get dicey fast. Driving in the nail can bust out the end grain of the topmost board. Splitting the end grain does not signify the commencement of the burn pile. But it isn't ideal. And if all the nails result in splits….

Years ago, I came up with a trick to reduce this splitting and have written about it quite a bit. I've caught flak from people who say it's not true. So much so that I've been doubting my own shop experience.

Here's the problem: Driving a tapered nail is a delicate balance. You need the nail to bite hard, so you don't want to use a cavernous or too-long pilot hole. But if you use a pilot hole that is too small or short, the nail will split the work and spoil the joint. Oh, you also have to account

One clamp. Clamping the end grain – hard – helps prevent splits.

No clamp & with clamp. Without a clamp, the nail dislodged the end grain and split the work. With the clamp pressed hard against the end grain, there was no problem. There are limits to this trick, I'm sure.

for the wood species and how thick it is.

It's a balance of factors to get a good joint. (And that's why I recommend you make a test joint before nailing together anything – especially if you've never worked with a particular brand of nail or species of wood.)

All this is a lot of set-up for…

Here's the Trick

If you apply a bar clamp across the end grain of the joint, you can reduce the tendency of the wood to split out the end grain. The clamp has to apply significant pressure for this to work.

I tried a variety of strategies as I nailed together this mule chest using 40mm Rivierre nails. All the joints were in Eastern white pine. All the pilot holes were the same diameter (7/64") and depth (7/8"). And all the holes were located the same distance (7/16") from the end of the board.

CHAPTER 25

Without a clamp, about half of the joints busted out the end grain (good thing I started at the rear of the chest). When I added a clamp and applied hard clamping pressure – what you would use to close a joint – the failure rate dropped to zero.

I wondered if I needed to have the clamp at full pressure. What if the clamp's pad simply acted as a wall to prevent the end grain from fracturing? Nope. Clamp pressure – lots of it – was important to keep the joint intact while driving the nail.

I have all sorts of thoughts on why this hard clamp pressure works. But I am weary of theories. Let's just say it works. Prove me wrong.

Nail the plinths, front and back in place. This will leave an open space at the rear of the mule chest at the drawer cavity. I temporarily screw the drawer cavity panel in place back there as I might have to make some adjustments in the drawer cavity before it's all over. When I'm done with the project, I'll replace the screws with nails.

The Lid

The lid of the chest is a simple panel with hardwood battens attached at the ends – these keep the lid flat and help keep out dust. The decorative details of the lid are up to you. I cut a 1/4"-deep x 3/4"-wide rabbet on the top edge to reflect the rabbets throughout the project (all hail Mr. Rabbet). You can skip this.

The hardwood battens are 7/8"-thick ash left over from some chairmaking. Each batten is 2" wide at one end and 1" wide at the other. All that seems normal, but how I attach them is non-standard.

Usually battens are nailed or screwed from the underside of the batten. This gives you a clean look (no fasteners are visible on the lid), but getting everything to hold right is an effort.

For this mule chest, I screwed the battens in place through the top of the lid. Why? It's stronger. The screw threads are in the hardwood instead of the softwood top. But isn't it distracting seeing the screw heads? Maybe. But there are 40 nail heads showing on the outside of this carcase. A few more fasteners aren't going to ruin things.

What about wood movement?

Ah, the most deflating expression I know. Wood movement is real. I believe in it. But you can become a sycophant. In the white pines, wood movement is minimal (look it up). Plus, its soft fibers crush against metal fasteners. So, you can nail and screw pine projects tightly and (usually) they hold up fine.

Hold it. A couple F-style clamps hold the batten and lid in place while you drill the pilot and clearance holes for the screws. Here I used four #8 x 1-1/4" screws in each batten.

So I didn't ream out the clearance holes for the screws or make any accommodations for wood movement. I merely screwed the battens down as best I could.

Attach the Lid

I attached the lid using some inexpensive steel strap hinges. No matter what hinges you use, here's how I recommend you attach them.

First, screw the hinges to the underside of the lid, pressing the barrel of the hinge to the back edge of the lid. (If you are using butt hinges, mortise the hinge into the underside of the lid with the hinge barrel tangent to the back edge of the lid.)

Position the lid on the carcase. Shift it around until it is centered on the carcase and the hinges' barrels are tangent to the back of the carcase. Use a knife to mark the hinge locations on the carcase. Take care not to bump the hinge or lid. Small shifts will ruin your day.

CHAPTER 25

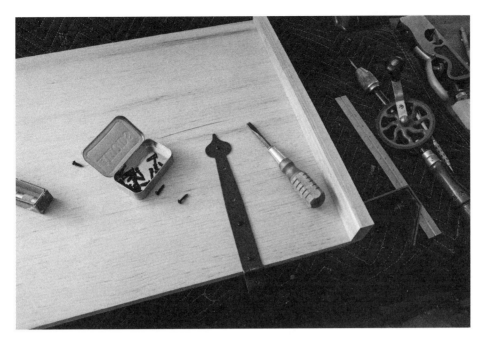

Lid first. I prefer to attach the hinges to the lid first, then transfer the hinge locations to the chest's carcase. It's just my habit.

A little nick. I use a marking knife to nick the carcase on either side of the hinges. Then I remove the lid to mortise the carcase.

Remove the lid and lay out the mortises to receive the hinges in the carcase. Cut this out with a saw, chisel and router plane. Then screw the hinges to the carcase.

On to the Drawers

I tried to avoid dovetailed drawers in this book because they intimidate many beginners. But I've been cutting dovetails for so long (since the early 1990s), that they are many times the easiest and fastest joint for me. Note: I'm not special. Most woodworkers get this way after being at the craft for a while. You will, too (if you want that).

So, I built my drawer boxes with through-dovetails, then glued on a false drawer front to each. Why? To fill in the open spaces at the ends of the drawers. To be honest, I made the drawers more complex than necessary. This was in servitude to my sketch. I wanted the front of the mule chest to be a smooth and unbroken façade. You don't have to do this.

To skip the dovetails, assemble the drawers with rabbets, glue and nails. Use the drawing as a guide. Rabbet the drawer sides and affix them

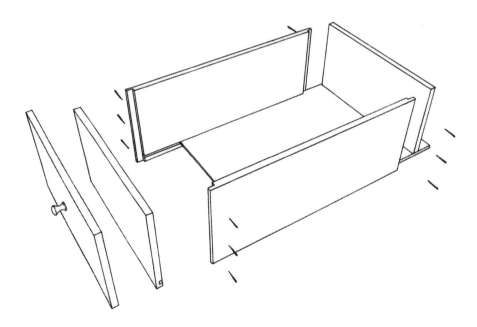

Realistic drawer. Skip the dovetails and assemble the drawer using rabbets and headed nails. The drawer bottom slides into grooves in the side and front pieces.

CHAPTER 25

False front. Here you can see one dovetailed drawer with a false front glued and clamped in place. The false front creates a rabbet that fills in the empty area between the plinth and the chest's front (also seen in the background).

A scab. You can see the thin filler piece I added to the carcase to make the drawer sit flush and tight when closed. This error was caused by making the false drawer front too thin.

Another scab. I added the vertical divider between the drawers with some glue and headless brads. My original plan was to have the drawers' false fronts fill in this area, but I changed my mind and decided I wanted a vertical element to break up the façade.

CHAPTER 25

to the front and back of the drawer with glue and nails.

The 1/2"-thick drawer bottom sits in a 1/4" x 1/4" groove that's plowed in the drawer sides and drawer front. The drawer bottom – also rabbeted – slides into these grooves and under the drawer's back. You can glue on a false drawer front to fill in the gaps in the chest's façade. Or you can glue on some little scraps to the carcase to fill in these gaps.

With the drawers assembled and fit to the carcase, attach some wooden knobs or pulls to the drawers. My knobs are inexpensive commercial ones in oak – this chest is going to be painted.

In the name of style, here are two mistakes I made as I worked my way through this design. I made the drawer divider flush with the interior panels – not flush with the plinth and front panel. I made a little 3/4" x 3/4" x 7" filler block to make the façade look correct. Also, I made the false drawer fronts a little too thin. So, I added 1/8"-thick filler blocks to the carcase to correct this problem.

Finishing

Most mule chests end up painted at one time or another. Like their six-board cousins, the paint job could be a bit wild. Grain painting was common. As was a variety of swoopy patterns in multiple colors.

I opted for a boring darkish blue paint with some yellow pinstripes. Even worse, I took the chicken route on the pinstripes and masked them in using painter's tape.

BOARDED SETTLE CHAIR

CHAPTER 26

A moose at a mouse rave.

Building a chair out of flat planks of wood seems a recipe for a sore backside – like sitting on a crate. And yet, if you take the basic principles of making a comfortable staked chair and apply them to a boarded chair, you can create something quite nice.

Best of all, this chair is easy to make. Once you get the planks prepared, constructing the chair takes about a day.

These settle chairs – also called plank chairs, winged chairs or "lambing" chairs – were common in Northern Wales and North England in the 18th and 19th centuries. They could be simple, as shown here, or have an elaborate frame-and-panel back, scrolled arms and a drawer under the seat.

There is no evidence you did anything with a lamb in these chairs. They were designed to be used by the fireside to capture its heat. Cushions, pillows and blankets all add to the coziness (and comfort) of these chairs. If you are an avid reader, you will enjoy the cocoon-like environment they offer.

Boarded Settle Chair

Pl. 15

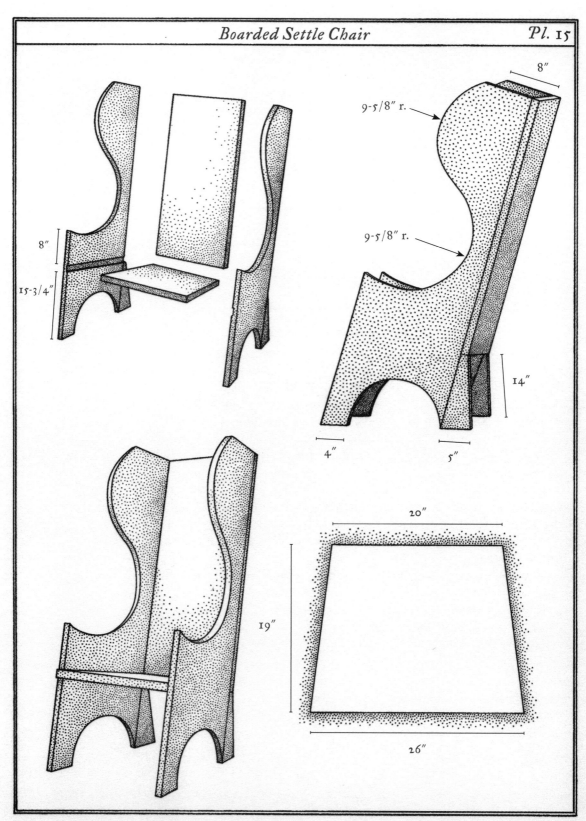

CHAPTER 26

About the Angles

I am of the mind that 90° is not special. It is but one of 360 angles, and you can cut a 93° or 97° angle just as easily as a 90°, especially if you use hand tools. With that said, here's how the chair goes together.

You start with the big side panels. These start out square all around, and you cut the through-dados for the seat in both side panels at a 7° slope. Surprisingly, the seat slopes down from the back to the front. This seems backward, but it's correct. After the chair is together, you cut the feet to make the chair lean backward.

Then you cut (or handplane) a 9° angle on the back edge of the side pieces. This angle opens up the wings of the chair, making it less crate-ish and more inviting. Then you screw the sides to the back piece, which is square and flat in all dimensions.

Then plane a 7° angle on the back edge of the seat board and fit the seat between the dados.

The last important step is to cut the feet so the chair leans back and is comfortable. Everything else on the chair is decoration. If you follow these steps, you'll find the process forgiving, even if you botch an angle or two.

Your Materials – Pine is Fine

Many of these settle chairs were made in pine and painted. I think that's still a good idea. Even in pine, these chairs are massive and heavy. Oak would be expensive and be a (literal) burden if you ever wanted to move house. And painting them can help them blend into a room instead of looking like a moose at a mouse rave.

This chair was built using 2x6s construction timbers from the home center. About six 12' planks do the job. The species? SPF, which means it could be spruce, pine or fir. The price? About $55. Not bad for a big chair. Glue up the panels you need and use the cutting list as a guide.

A second (tempting) option is to buy premade 1-1/8"-thick pine panels from a home center. I gave these a try; they have pros and cons.

Pros: Speed. You don't have to glue up any panels. You just unwrap the panels like a 7-Eleven burrito and go.

Cons: Expense – you'll spend about twice as much for the panels as for 2x6s. Moisture – some of the panels are wet and warp after you open them. Some don't. Mine didn't. Appearance – these panels are typically glued up from many narrow strips and have lots of knots. If you like that look, you are in so much luck.

Sealed for your protection? Premade pine panels can speed you up, but they have some headaches built-in – moisture and knots, for example.

Angled Dados

Two 1/2"-deep dados in the side pieces hold the seat in place and are angled at 97° to add comfort. Lay these out from the front edge of the chair, 15-3/4" up from the bottom edge of the side panels. Use the actual panel for the seat to lay out the width of the dado. And don't forget to lay out the depth of the dado at both ends of the side piece.

CHAPTER 26

Start a dado. Lay out the dado using a knife. A knife will sever the grain, making for a clean arris. Once you lay out one wall of the dado, use the seat to lay out the second wall.

Two-handed saw. Nibble next to the knife line along the entire wall of the dado before trying to make significant progress in the depth of the cut. Once you have laid in a kerf all along your knife line, use your off hand to keep the toe of the saw engaged and square to the work.

I say all this because you should cut these by hand. It's faster and much less prone to error. You might have an AccuGauge 2000 that works to a 10th of an angstrom when cutting on your table saw. Don't use it. It's too easy to get turned around and upside down. And even a tiny bit of slop in your gauge or saw will spoil this joint.

You have been warned.

Cutting dados is one of the easiest hand-tool joinery operations. Saw out the walls, chisel out most of the waste and clean the bottom of the joint with a router plane. It takes longer to read about it than it does to do it. (And I'm not going to write a lot about it.)

Don't worry if the dado's walls aren't perfectly vertical. If you want them dead on, clamp a wooden fence to the work and use that to guide your saw. You'll quickly tire of that crutch.

CHAPTER 26

A ripper. Bash out most of the waste between the walls of the dado with a chisel. Begin working bevel-up. Then work bevel-down. Get as close to the bottom of the dado as possible. Chisels are fast. Router planes are slow.

A clean bottom. Shave the fur from the dado's bottom with a router plane. Light cuts work best with this tool.

Angled edges. The angle doesn't look like much, but it dramatically changes the chair. No matter how you cut this angle, clean it up with a smoothing plane and confirm the angle is correct along its entire length.

Angle the Back Edges

To make the sides of the chair open like wings, you need to cut an angle on the back edges of the side pieces. I used 9°, but there are historical examples that are much more dramatic. Note that if you increase this angle, you will need to make a bigger seat.

Lay out the angle and cut it with a jack plane, a table saw or a circular saw. Again, it's easy to get turned around during this step and cut the angle the wrong way. So lay it out. Then show the side pieces to the chair's back piece and make sure your sides angle out and not inward.

Believe it or not, it's now time to temporarily assemble the sides and the back with screws. You need to assemble things so you can get an accurate measurement of the seat and its angles. There are lots of ways to screw the back and sides together. I placed the back on some sawbenches

CHAPTER 26

One way to do it. You might devise a better way to hold the parts in place while screwing them together. This is the best I could do on a Saturday.

Tricky clamping. This is a second (and ultimately unsuccessful) chair I made, which is why things look odd. Here's how to clamp the back feet to the sides. Apply glue to the edges. Use a handscrew to pinch the two parts to keep them aligned. Then apply bar clamps. Start clamping next to the handscrew and work down. Place bar clamps on both faces of the joint.

CHAPTER 26

and propped up the sides below until they were in the right position.

Then attach everything with #9 x 3" screws, or something in that neighborhood. Don't get too worked up about it. You can replace the screws with glue and fancy nails during the final assembly.

Add the Back Feet

Because this chair will lean back and because it is so top-heavy, you must add some back feet at the bottom of the sides to keep the chair from tipping over.

Because the back edges of the sides are angled at 9°, you'll need to cut a 9° angle on one long edge of each foot as well. That's easy enough. But gluing the feet to the sides can be frustrating. The joints want to slide apart.

You could add loose tenons or dowels to the joint to keep the parts aligned. Or you could just be smart about it and use a handscrew to keep the parts in line while you clamp the feet to the sides.

When the glue is dry, fit the seat.

An Easy Chair

Fitting the seat is simple, even though it's an odd shape and has a weird angle on its back edge. All you have to do is measure the opening in the assembled chair and lay that out on the blank for your seat. You cut to your lines and you are done. Really.

First cut the angle on the back edge of the seat that will allow the seat to mate tight with the back plank. This angle should be 7°, but I recommend you simply record it from the chair itself using a sliding bevel and transfer it to the seat.

Now determine the width of the seat at the back. Pinch together two pointed sticks and use them to probe the distance between the dados at the back.

Now measure the width of the seat at the front – that's easy to do with a tape measure. Finally, measure the depth of the seat from the front of the chair to the back. That's also easy. Lay a stick over the dados so it imitates the front edge of the seat. Now measure from the stick to the back of the chair. Record this measurement.

You have everything you need to lay out the seat. Draw a centerline through your seat blank and lay out its width and depth. If you want to add an overhang to the front edge of the seat (1" or so) now is the time.

Accurate scraps. I'm using some garbage to measure the width of the seat. The sticks are pointed, which allows me to get them right where I need them. Touch them to the insides of the dados. Remove them and record that dimension.

Two straight lines. The wooden straightedge represents the front edge of the seat. The perpendicular steel ruler determines the true depth of the seat.

CHAPTER 26

Not for CAD. I recommend you finalize your layout on the workpiece itself. After drawing this up a dozen times in CAD, I realized that direct experience was superior.

Saw the seat to shape and fit it to the dados in the assembled chair. You might have to thin the seat at the edges to get it to fit. Do this on the underside with a handplane. When the seat fits, temporarily screw the seat in place by driving a 3" screw through each side and into the seat.

Disassemble the chair and plane all the panels. Next is the fun part.

Curves

While the shape of the sides looks complex, it's not. The swoops at the top are made with trammel points set to 9-5/8". The centerpoints of the arcs are 18-1/4" apart. I don't have an exact layout to offer you. Play around with your trammels until you get something you like.

Unsung hero. I love my band saw, but I'll never own a band saw big enough for this. A jigsaw with a new blade makes this an easy task.

CHAPTER 26

Scrub it now. Even if you use hide glue, which is easily cleaned with water, it's easier to remove any squeeze-out while the glue is wet. Use a toothbrush and warm water to get in the corners.

Most people say they don't like the pointy bits at the front of the arms. I do, and they are found on a fair number of traditional chairs and settles. So adjust things around until you are happy.

Use a straightedge to lay out the angle of the feet. This angle is somewhat arbitrary, but I make the back feet 14" long, measured from the floor to the underside of the back. (Look at the construction drawing, which explains this better than words.) Now lay out the arc between the feet – it's a 7-1/2" radius or so.

Cut all these shapes with a jigsaw or a turning saw. Clean up the shapes with a rasp, spokeshave and sandpaper. This part of the project takes the longest. I also decided to add one more decorative detail to the sides – I cut a 1/4" x 1/4" rabbet on the curvy bits to add an additional shadow line.

Hide the geometry. It's easier to plane the 9° angle on the back after assembly instead of before.

CHAPTER 26

Final Assembly & Finish

Remove any machine marks left, then reassemble the chair, this time using glue in all the joints. Because of the grain orientation of the seat, glue the seat to the sides only in the front 6" of the dado. And don't forget to add glue between the seat and the back.

Clamp the back to the seat and use a toothbrush and warm water to scrub away any squeeze-out.

After the glue dries, plane the long edges of the back so they are in the same plane as the sides. This is quick work with a jack plane. Get close with a jack plane and finish the job with a smoothing plane.

Before finishing, break all the sharp edges with a bit of sandpaper. Dress the feet with a rasp until the chair sits flat on the floor.

I finished the inside of the chair with organic linseed oil. The outside is painted with a black acrylic. The idea was to make sitting in the chair similar to sitting inside a tree. While sitting inside, you are surrounded by natural wood. And the wood's light color reflects light, which is nice if you read books. The chair's dark exterior is supposed to represent the exterior bark of the tree and make the size of the chair diminish in a room. This is a huge chair.

There are lots of things you could do with this design. You could saddle the seat to add some more comfort. You could get the interior upholstered. You can make the chair into a rocker. These are all examples found in the historical record.

The one thing I couldn't accomplish is to create a version with a low back. I'm sure, however, someone out there is up to the task. Sadly, all my low-back examples looked like Klingon vacation furniture.

BOARDED SETTLE CHAIR

NO.	PART	SIZES (INCHES)		
		T	W	L
1	Seat*	1-1/4	26	20
1	Back	1-1/4	21-1/2	40
2	Ends	1-1/4	19	59
2	Back feet*	1-1/4	5	19

* Parts are oversized for fitting

BOARDED BOOKSHELF

CHAPTER 27

Do we need to adjust every shelf?

Trying to improve a simple set of bookshelves might seem ridiculous. But I think there are significant things to say about the warped state of bookshelf construction in the modern age.

What could be wrong about horizontal surfaces fastened to vertical ones? Plenty.

For starters, I'm not a fan of adjustable shelving. I think that if you gave enough monkeys enough mescaline, you might be able to come up with a plastic jig to drill the right number of holes for adjustable shelf pins that weren't a waste of time or space. But that's a lot of mescaline. Adjustable shelving is, in my opinion, mostly a cop-out.

Books come in fairly standard sizes. Heck, they once came in sizes that were based simply on how many times you folded a large sheet of paper. But thanks to the miracle and wastefulness of modern book manufacturing, we now have some bizarre sizes to deal with.

These odd books are at the extreme ends of a bell curve of book shapes (called "form factors" or "formats" in the design world). You can find books out there that are 18" wide and 10" high (yup, a book on billboards). But if you are someone who reads woodworking books, novels and nonfiction (and not art books on Estonian midget nudist wrestlers), then trying to accommodate whack-doodle form factors isn't necessary.

So I've always viewed adjustable shelving with great suspicion. Do we need to adjust every shelf in a carcase 1" up or down? I don't.

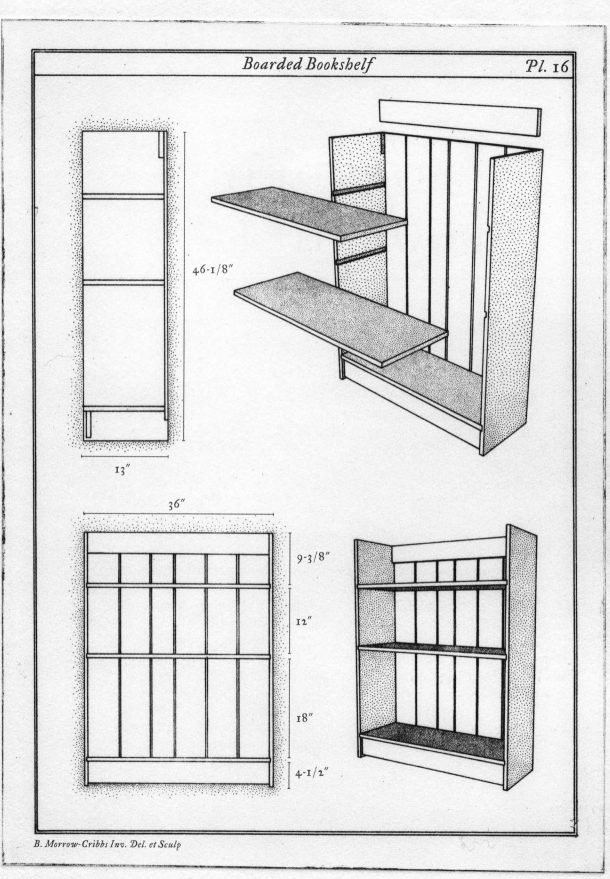

What Sizes are Important?

Go to any bookstore and you'll find that most books come in roughly three sizes: small, medium and large.

Small books are 6" x 9" or smaller – these are the novels and standard woodworking books of the 19th and 20th centuries. It's a convenient size for reading in the subway or the park. And they fit easily into a knapsack or shoulder bag.

The medium size is about 8-1/2" x 11" (slightly more if it's a hardback). This became a fairly standard size for how-to books in the latter 20th century and is economical to print. So you will encounter a lot of these books as you build your library. I find them to be a stepchild size. They are too big to travel with easily. Yet when I am reading them at home I always wish they were bigger.

The large size of book is 11" x 17" or some close variant. These books are uncommon in the modern age, unless you are into art books or old books. But when I find them they are worth the extra expense.

Many excellent old books on woodworking, including the 18th-century pattern books, were oversized folios. So I think it's worth making a place for them in a bookshelf. It might be wishful thinking, but so what?

So this bookshelf has shelf openings of three sizes: 18" high for big books, 12" for the medium books and 9-3/8" for the small ones. (However, the top shelf has no top, so you can fit taller books or whatever up there if you dare.)

"Artists and craftsmen too should deal

With good faith and with honest zeal;

Let each of them the other aid

With work well done and things well made,

And as he would be served, thus serve."

— Hans Sachs, "The Book of Trades (Standebuch)" (Frankfurt, 1568)

Other Advantages of this Form

So now that you know the typical book sizes, wouldn't it be sweet to provide just a wee bit of adjustability – up and down – for odd sizes? No, it wouldn't.

Fixed shelves are far stiffer than adjustable ones. You can nail a fixed shelf in place through the back of the carcase. This adds immense stiffness so the shelf won't sag. (And if you think that sagging shelves aren't a problem then you don't own enough books.)

The other advantage to fixed shelves is they add to the overall soundness of the carcase. If you have only two fixed shelves – which is typical in a commercial bookcase – the carcase is more likely to rack compared to a carcase that has multiple shelves that are nailed through both the back and the bookcase's vertical uprights.

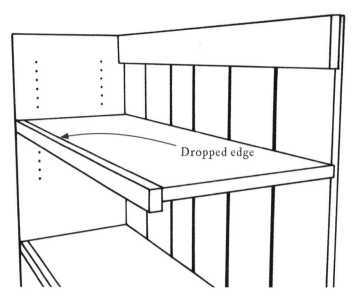

Dropped edge on a shelf.

One last thing I like about fixed shelves: They don't ever collapse or slide off their adjustable shelf pins.

How to Cheat

So let's say you think I'm full of crap or you pine desperately for adjustable shelves. Can you make a shelf unit that is stiff enough? Yup. Do these two things: Use a plywood back that is glued and screwed in place. That will stiffen the carcase. To make the shelves stiff, use what is called a "dropped edge" on every adjustable shelf. This is when you attach a strip of solid wood to the front and/or rear of the shelf to stiffen it.

A typical dropped edge is 1-1/4" wide and is attached to the front of the shelf. Note that the dropped edge can also be used to hide the fact that you used plywood for the shelves. (Naughty, naughty. Plywood isn't as stiff as solid wood – hence the name "solid" wood.)

If you look at the bookcase in this book, the "kick" (the horizontal strip affixed to the lower shelf) works exactly like a dropped edge. There's good reason for it to be attached to the lower shelf because it's designed to hold the heaviest books.

CHAPTER 27

Roughing it. These pine planks were almost 15" wide when I started flattening them. I dressed them with a jack plane by traversing the grain. After truing them up as best I could, I ripped them down and put them through my electric planer.

Or Build this Thing

This bookshelf is designed to hold the three standard sizes of books. It is made with a minimum of material. And it is dirt simple to build because it is nailed together with just a little glue and a few shallow grooves and dados.

With this particular example, I began building it Friday afternoon and was painting it Sunday night.

The only difficult part of the bookcase is finding wood that is 13" wide. A standard 1x12 is 11-1/4" wide, which is too narrow to hold the biggest books. So if you are using dimensional lumberyard stock, you'll need to glue up some panels for the sides and shelves. Using 1x8s is a good place to start.

If you find some rough pine that is wide enough, you are likely going to have to process it by hand. That was where I started on a Friday with a jack plane and a full head of steam.

One side. You can see how I use a fence and saw to cut a perfect wall for the dado. After sawing this first wall, don't remove the fence.

The pusher block. This is the same operation as above, but on the other side of the fence. Note the pusher block.

Use the shelf. The shelf is the best indicator of the second wall of the dado. Mark it in pencil then saw inside the line.

CHAPTER 27

Quick work. Knock the chisel with a mallet to remove the waste. Use the chisel bevel-down so you have more control over how aggressive the cut is.

Clean-up. The router plane will make the bottom of the dado perfectly flat and the same depth – even if the stock is a bit cupped.

Housed Joints for Shelves

The three shelves are held tight in six 1/4"-deep dados in the sides. Dados are easy to cut with hand tools, even if you don't have a dado plane (I don't).

The way I make dados is to saw the two walls of the joint using a handsaw and a fence made from a scrap clamped to the carcase. After sawing out the walls, I remove most of the waste with a chisel used bevel-down for the most part. Then I clean up the bottom of the dado with a router plane set for the final depth – in this case 1/4".

Use the construction drawings to set out and cut the six dados. The last little bit on the carcase sides is to cut two short grooves – also 1/4" deep – that hold the top rail of the bookcase.

These grooves are even easier to cut than dados. Mark them out using a knife or a marking gauge and define the walls with a wide chisel. With a narrow chisel – I used 5/8" – chop out the area where the groove ends.

Sawn walls. If you are in a sawing mood, cut the walls with a tenon saw.

Chiseled features. You can simply chop out most of the waste with a chisel, working across the grain for the most part. Be careful if you decide to chop parallel to the grain because you could split the entire case side.

If you are an assassin with a tenon saw, cut the walls of the groove. If you prefer the chisel, bust up the waste with that tool. Then follow up with a router plane, which will peel out the waste with ease.

Assemble the Carcase

Headed nails do most of the work in holding this bookcase together, though some well-placed glue can also help things stay together during the long term.

First fit all the shelves and the top rail into their housed joints. I prefer to plane down the shelves to fit the dados rather than adjust the dados. (That's because I don't own side-rabbet planes.)

Once all the shelves and the top rail fit into their housings you are ready to add glue.

CHAPTER 27

Tape guides me. I use a strip of painter's tape to lay out the location of the nails on the sides of my carcase. Once I lay out the pilot holes on the first joint, I mark the location of the pilot holes on the tape with a marker. Then I re-stick the tape to a new place.

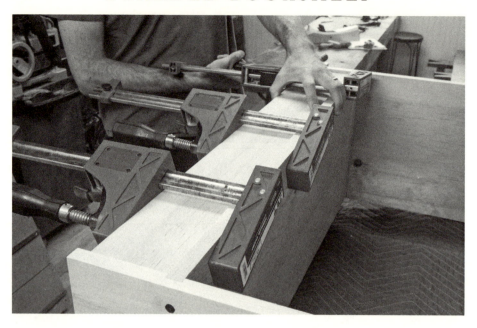

Long-grain kick. The kick is glued in place to the underside of the lower shelf. Then it is nailed in place through the sides of the bookcase.

If you own clamps, I recommend you glue the joints, clamp them up and wait for the glue to set before nailing the sides to the shelves and top rail. If you don't have clamps, the nails will be your clamps.

Paint glue on the end grain of the shelves. Let the glue sit for a minute. Apply more glue to the dry spots. Now paint glue in the housings and drive the shelves and top rail into place with a mallet. Add the other side piece. If you have the clamps to hold things in place, clamp the sides until the joints close.

If you don't have clamps, glue things up, drive everything home then nail the sides to the shelves with cut or wrought nails while the glue is still wet.

Before you drive the nails, lay out their locations on the case sides and drill pilot holes – the size and depth of the holes depends on the nails you're using. I used 6*d* nails for this joint but 5*d* would also have worked.

I used five nails to fasten each shelf in place. That's a bit of visual overkill, but the sides of this case will be painted, so I knew it wouldn't be a big deal. If you are going to finish this piece without paint, use only three or four nails per shelf.

Shiplapped & beaded. The backboards have a 1/4"-thick x 5/16"-long tongue on their long edges. On the tongues that face the viewer, I cut a 3/16"-wide bead to help conceal the joint between the backboards.

Add the Kick

Once the carcase is complete and the glue has cured, you can add the kick below the bottom shelf. This 4"-wide piece of pine helps prevent the carcase from racking and strengthens the lowest shelf, which takes the most abuse.

Shoot the end grain of the kick board so it fits snugly between the case sides. Glue it to the underside of the bottom shelf so it's set 1/4" back from the front edge of the shelf. Then nail the kick in place through the sides of the carcase.

The Back

The 1/2"-thick back strengthens the carcase and completes construction of the whole bookcase.

I used four back pieces that were slightly less than 9" wide and shiplapped. The shiplaps conceal any wood movement during the seasons.

"As to shape, it is contrary to their purpose of convenience and interior capacity, to make cabinets, cupboards, or other receptacles, with showy and spreading architectural details, such as cornices, architraves, columns, pediments, and the like. All these parts, which are laborious and costly in construction, are so many additions to its size, and make no more room inside to compensate for this expenditure. Cabinets should, in propriety, be as big and convenient inside as their size would lead us to expect."

— J.H. Pollen's essay on Furniture and Woodwork in "British Manufacturing Industries" (1877)

Secure the back. Nailing the back to the shelves helps prevent the shelves from sagging and the backboards from pulling away from the carcase.

I glued and nailed the two outermost back pieces to the case sides. The two interior bits were simply nailed in place. All four back pieces were nailed to the three shelves, which greatly increases the strength of the entire piece.

After cutting the shiplaps and beading the backboards, glue the outermost backboards to the sides of the carcase. Clamp them up and lay out pilot holes so you can nail the backboards to the back of the shelves. Drive two nails through the backboard into each shelf.

Finishing

For this bookcase, I painted the exterior of the sides with a brick red milk paint (sanding between coats with a #320-grit sanding sponge). Then I coated the entire thing with lacquer.

I took this tack because I didn't want to get any paint on my books. But I also wanted to use the dark paint to frame the light-colored interior of the case.

CHAPTER 27

Before cleaning up the case and leveling all the joints, I taped off the front and back edges of the bookcase and painted the case sides with two coats of paint. Then I removed the tape and used a block plane to level the front edges of the shelves and sides (and remove any paint that seeped under the tape).

With the details sorted and cleaned up, I broke all the hard edges with #220-grit sandpaper and finished the bookcase with two coats of lacquer. And I called it done.

BOARDED BOOKSHELF

NO.	PART	SIZES (INCHES)		
		T	W	L
2	Sides	3/4	13	46-1/8
3	Shelves	3/4	12-1/2	35
1	Top rail	3/4	4	35
1	Kick	3/4	4	34-1/2
	Backboards*	1/2	34-1/2	43

* Made up of multiple shiplapped boards

BOARDED BOOKSHELF

No Thanks, Billy

I'm easygoing for the most part. My friends are liberal, conservative, devout and agnostic. Homosexual and ammosexual.

But it annoys me when I see an IKEA Billy bookshelf in a woodworker's house. This 31-1/2" x 11" x 79-1/2" bookshelf is sold for a penny less than $80 at IKEA and seems like a great deal to people with a lot of books – my in-laws have almost a dozen of them. But the Billy is an abomination if you have any hand skills.

Yes, you get about 15 linear feet of shelving, plus a carcase that is ridiculously unstable. Only two shelves are fixed. So unless you secure the Billy to the wall (or other Billys), it will rack in short order.

The shelves are rated to hold 66 pounds each – which isn't bad if you read only paperback novels – but the shelves sag like crazy if you own old books with stout bindings.

I say this with experience. When my wife and I bought our first house, we actually drove to Virginia to visit the nearest IKEA and bought two Billy bookcases. I put them together and immediately felt wronged. After a few months I let them do what they do best: fall apart. Then I started building shelves for our home.

Apology: I pick on IKEA sometimes. Though I respect the company's good designs, the construction is sub par. And yes, I know there is worse joinery out there. See below.

This is why we fight. Typical interior "joinery" on a modern upholstered chair.

CHAPTER 27

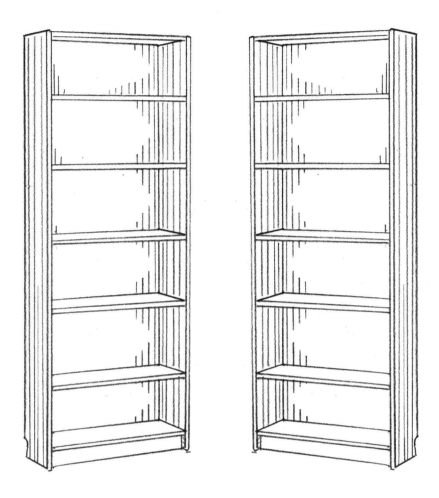

Billy, Billy wrong. The IKEA "Billy" bookcase represents everything that is wrong with bookshelf design. Yet even people who know better cannot resist the $79.99 price tag.

Photo by Al Parrish.

AUMBRY
CHAPTER 28

Both common & secular.

It is easy to forget that many of our favorite pieces of furniture are recent innovations. Forms such as coffee tables, bookcases and desks are – archaeologically speaking – recent designs brought on by incredible modern wealth.

When you cast your eye back on the furniture record, the forms become simpler, fewer in number and (in some cases) quite unfamiliar. One of my favorite types of early furniture is the "aumbry" – sometimes called a dole or livery cupboard. It is the honored ancestor of the bookcase, hutch, cupboard, armoire and common kitchen cabinet.

Today the word "aumbry" is typically used to refer to a liturgical piece of furniture or place in a church that holds the sacrament. But the word, and the piece of furniture, was both common and secular in the 1400s and 1500s. This enclosed cabinet held things that were precious – food for the most part – plus anything else that had to be locked up.

One of the defining features of aumbries is that the front of the cabinet is pierced by Gothic tracery. These piercings are not just decorative. They allow air to circulate inside the carcase, like a modern pie safe. To stop insects from getting inside the cabinet, the piercings are covered with cloth that is fastened to the inside of the case.

Aside from the pierced tracery, these cabinets are straightforward to build using simple tools. Most aumbries are knocked together using basic joints – rabbets, dados and nails made from wood or iron.

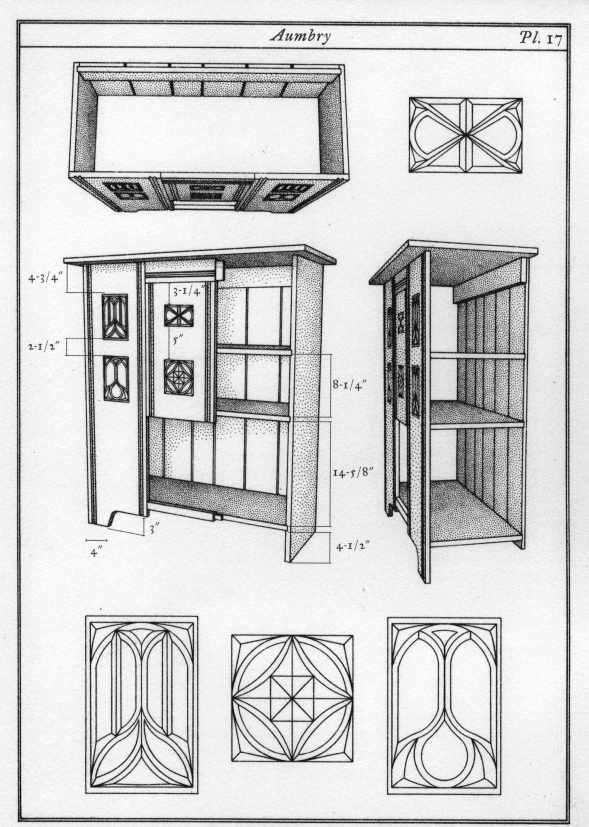

CHAPTER 28

First wall. Clamp a batten on your layout line and saw the first wall of the dado. Press the sawplate against the batten to create a vertical cut.

This particular aumbry is based on a circa-1490 piece that was part of the Clive Sherwood collection that was sold at a Sotheby's auction for more than $50,000. To make the piece more approachable, I simplified the tracery and removed some of the chip carving and knife work that festoons the original. Despite these simplifications, this aumby would look at home in any medieval English or French home.

It shares a lot of its design DNA with the boarded bookcase in the previous chapter. So if you can build that, you are well on your way to building this.

Start with the Oak

Most aumbries are made of oak. And because wide English oak is nearly impossible to get, I chose quartersawn American white oak for this aumbry. The original was made with planks that were 12" to 14" wide – a tall order. So I glued up the sides, top, stiles, shelves and door from two narrow pieces, taking care to match the grain and color.

Because I built this aumbry almost entirely by hand, I took care to

"Now, in order to have anything good made in stuff, or in hard material, we must seek out the artist to provide us with a design, and then a workman to carry it out as mechanically as possible, because we know that if he puts any of his coarser self into it he will spoil it."

— Ralph Radcliffe Whitehead (1854-1929), founder of the Byrdcliffe colony, in "Grass of the Desert" (1892)

Don't measure. Use the mating shelf to strike the second wall of the dado. Use a pencil or knife to mark this wall.

also make sure the grain direction in the panels was consistent among the boards in each glue-up. This detail makes life a lot easier for those who prepare wood for finishing with a handplane.

The case itself is as simple as it gets. The shelves are nailed into dados in the sides. The face frame, backboards and top are nailed to the carcase. The only complex bits are the mortise-and-tenon joints that hold the face frame's rails and stiles together.

And then there are the Gothic piercings. These are simple to make with a drill bit, a chisel and a couple rasps. Don't be intimidated by them – they are easier than they look. To get started on your aumbry, glue up the panels for the entire case, then cut the two sides to their final size and get ready to cut the carcase joinery.

CHAPTER 28   505

Second wall. Because of the set of the saw's teeth, clamp the batten so it covers your layout line for the second wall. This will ensure your dado isn't too loose.

Handmade Dados

The 1/4"-deep dados in the sides that hold the shelves are simple to make with a handsaw, chisel and a router plane. Begin by laying out one wall of each dado on the side pieces. Then clamp a scrap right on the layout line and use it as a fence for your saw. Saw down 1/4" into the side to create the first wall of the dado. Do not remove the batten.

Then place the mating shelf up against the batten and use it to lay out the second wall of the dado. Reposition the scrap so it covers the pencil line, clamp it in place and saw the second wall of the dado on the waste side of the line.

Remove the majority of the waste with a chisel then flatten the bottom of the dado with a router plane. Check the fit of the shelf. If the dado is too tight, rabbet or bevel the end of the shelf. If it's too loose, make some wedges to knock into the gap at assembly time.

Cut all the dados, fit all the shelves then prepare all these boards for finishing, inside and out. Assemble the case using hide glue and 6d rosehead cut nails. Cut nails were invented a few hundred years after the

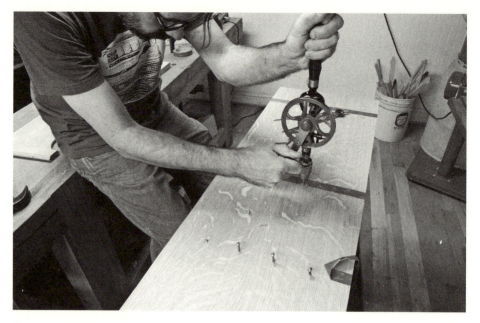

Square nails. Use wrought nails or rosehead cut nails to fasten the sides to the shelves. Use tape to remind yourself where the nails go – the tape is easier to remove than a pencil line.

original aumbry was built, so they aren't authentic to the core. However, because blacksmith-made nails are expensive (about $1.50 to $2 apiece) and the roseheads look (fairly) authentic, I decided to use them on the side pieces.

A second authentic option would be to fasten the sides to the shelves using glue and "trenails" or "trunnels," which are tapered oaken nails.

A Rail for the Backboards

To make the carcase a bit sturdier, add an interior rail to the inside of the case. This rail, which is located at the back of the carcase, helps hold the backboards in place. To hold the interior rail in place, cut 1/4"-deep stopped grooves for the rail. Make these grooves just like you did your dados: Saw the walls, chop the waste and clean the floor with a router plane.

CHAPTER 28

Chop & stop. The stopped grooves for the interior rails are made the same way you made the dados for the shelves.

Knock & nail. Drive the interior rail in place. Then fasten it from the outside of the case with two 6d rosehead nails at each end.

Rack the back. Here I'm pulling the case square with two clamps. Then I nail the backboards in place. When I release the clamps, the carcase will remain square.

Add the Back

The back of this aumbry is assembled using several narrow boards. On many originals, the backboards were merely butted against one another and nailed on. This works, but you will have some ugly gaps back there when the boards shrink during the dry season.

To avoid those gaps, cut shiplap joints or tongue-and-groove joints on the long edges of the backboards. I used shiplaps.

When attaching the backboards with nails, first use clamps to pull the carcase square. Then nail the backboards to the shelves and interior rail using 4d rosehead nails. The nailed-on backboards will hold the carcase square, making it easier to fit the face frame and the door.

Build the Face Frame

The pieces that adorn the front of the aumbry are much like a modern face frame. The wide stiles join the narrow rails with mortise-and-tenon joints. I chopped the 1/4"-wide x 1-1/4"-deep mortises

Chapter 28

Simple moulding. After plowing two grooves in the stiles, shape the interior bit into a curve with a rabbet plane. Then finish up with a small hollow plane.

first, then I sawed the tenons to match.

With the joints fit, you can cut the "crease moulding" that runs parallel to the long edges of the stiles and top rail. This is easy to make with simple tools. The crease moulding begins 3/4" from the long edge of the board and is 3/4" wide.

To begin, plow a 1/8"-wide x 3/16"-deep groove on either side of where the moulding is located. Then shape the material between the grooves with a rabbet plane and – if you have one – a small hollow plane, such as a No. 6.

The last bit of work on the face frame before the piercings is to saw out the feet. Cut them with a frame saw and clean up the cuts with rasps.

Gothic Tracery

The geometric pierced shapes in the stiles are easy to make, even if you've never carved before. You don't even need carving tools to do the job. Here are the tools I used:

• A 1/2" Forstner bit to poke holes in the waste.

Pattern & piercings. Apply the pattern with spray adhesive and drill out the waste with a 1/2" Forstner bit.

- An electric jigsaw to remove most of the waste.
- A coarse cabinet rasp to shape the openings.
- 1/4" and 1/2" chisels to bevel the edges and make the triangular chip carving.
- A fine rasp to clean up the details.

Apply the pattern directly to the work using spray adhesive then bore out most of the waste with a drill.

After sawing out the waste, clean up the openings with a cabinet rasp. I used a 10" rasp with hand-stitched teeth that were fairly coarse – a 9 grain. The goal is to make the walls square and the lines fluid.

With the openings shaped, bevel their interior edges with a 1/2" chisel, working bevel-down for the most part. The bevel should be only about 1/4" deep to create the three-dimensional effect. If you are using oak, you should sharpen the chisel frequently for the best results.

Then clean up the cuts with a fine rasp, shaping the bars of the Gothic windows. I used a 7" modeler's rasp with 13-grain teeth. Follow up with sandpaper if you like.

Many of the corners of the tracery have triangular chip-carved details.

CHAPTER 28

Saw out the windows. Use a jigsaw set with minimal orbit to remove waste as close to the line as possible. I used a standard jigsaw blade for this. I tried using a narrow blade intended for scrollwork, but it deflected too much.

These are easily made with bench chisels. Chop straight down on the three facets of the detail. Then pare out the waste toward the chops. Repeat these two operations until the detail is as deep as you want it – mine are 3/16" deep.

With the piercings complete, glue the face frame together and attach it to the front of the carcase with 6*d* wrought nails. Because the wide stiles will expand and contract significantly, I would not glue the stiles to the sides of the carcase. The wood movement might crack the carcase.

If you do want to use glue, apply it to the shelves near the door opening only.

The Door

Most aumbries have a single door. There is evidence that this aumbry had two, and the lower one is missing. I like the open space below, so I made only one door that enclosed the top two shelves.

Rasping right. It's easier to rasp vertically if you hold the handle with one hand and the tip of the rasp with the other. Check your work with a square until you get a feel for the operation.

The door is just a slab of oak with two geometric piercings. Make the crease mouldings and piercings using the same techniques as on the face frame stiles. I used a blacksmith-made lock and H-hinges, which were installed with wrought nails.

Installing hardware with nails is a bit stressful at first, but you'll get over it. Finally, nail the top in place with 6d headed nails.

The finish is simply boiled linseed oil. Apply thin coats and allow each coat to dry thoroughly before adding another. After five or six coats, add a coat of beeswax and buff it out. That's the traditional finish for early pieces such as this.

CHAPTER 28

Quick chips. The triangular depressions at the corners of the piercings are easy to make with a chisel and mallet.

"*The joiner's craft was transformed during the seventeenth century, after wood ceased to be thought of purely as a constructional material. Until the middle years of the century, the colour and texture of the wood were disregarded, their decorative possibilities ignored, and their surfaces were made acceptable to the eye by painting, carving or inlaying. Interest in the natural color and marking of the wood was aroused by the rediscovery of veneering....*"

— John Gloag, "A Social History of Furniture Design: From B.C. 1300 to A.D. 1960" (Crown)

AUMBRY

Tracery patterns. All tracery patterns are full size.

CHAPTER 28

AUMBRY

CHAPTER 28

Nail job. The pilot holes for the nails should be about two-thirds the length of the nail. That will give the nail the holding power it needs to keep the face frame on.

Remove the slop. All hinges have a little play between the barrel and the leaves. When you decide where the pilot holes should go for the nails, press the hinge leaf toward the floor to remove downward slop. Then mark your pilot holes.

Nailed it. Nailing in hardware isn't as difficult as you might think. If you have taken the same care as you would for screws, then it's easy. Here I'm clinching the tips of the nails.

Install the lock. Sometimes a through-mortise is the best way to install a handmade lock. Begin the layout process by tracing the lock's shape on the door.

CHAPTER 28

First coat of oil. Though all the authentic aumbries I have seen are black from age, they started out the color of raw oak with perhaps some oil.

More blasphemy. The tops of many early pieces were simply nailed on. Who are we to argue?

CHAPTER 28

If you want more protection, consider adding a little varnish and mineral spirits to the oil to make a wipe-on oil/varnish blend. It's not traditional, but it will offer more protection and still look the part.

And speaking of looking the part, if you want to go 100-percent authentic, cover the interior piercings with some undyed linen that is secured with iron tacks.

Several woodworkers have asked me about the utility of this piece of furniture in the modern home. Something like: Isn't it a huge pain to store stuff behind the panels and have to fish them out through the small door in the front?

After using this piece for about a year, the answer is: Not really. This aumbry holds all the office supplies for our business – paper, toner for the printers and the things we need to keep the scanners and computers clean. All of these items are somewhat hidden behind the front panels, which is nice, but we can also see at a glance when we are running low on something.

We've never stored bread or foodstuffs in there, but the piece works on the same principle as a modern refrigerator. It protects stuff that you don't want to have to look at all the time.

AUMBRY

NO.	PART	T	W	L
			SIZES (INCHES)	
1	Top	3/4	17-1/4	40
2	Sides	3/4	14	42-1/8
2	Stiles	3/4	12	42-1/8
1	Door	3/4	12	20
1	Top rail	3/4	3-1/4	14-1/2*
1	Bottom rail	3/4	1-1/4	14-1/2*
1	Interior rail	3/4	3-1/4	35
3	Shelves	3/4	13-1/2	35
	Backboards**	1/2	34-1/4	39-1/8

* 1-1/4" tenon on both ends, 1/4" thick
** Made up of several boards

You cannot. You can't build a table with this sort of joinery and use it for a tough task such as butchering. Can you? There's only one way to find out, and it doesn't involve your mouth or a keyboard.

FEAR NOT

CHAPTER 29

I did, & you can.

I'm talking about shellac with a couple of experienced woodworkers and one of them remarked about an old employer:

"This guy made us make our own shellac," he said with a sense of wonder.

"He made you go to India and beat the trees?" I asked, a tad confused.

"What? No," he replied. "We had to mix it up with flakes and alcohol."

"Wait, how else can you do it?" I replied honestly.

After an awkward pause, the other woodworker said: "Next you're going to try to convince us to make our own glue out of animals."

He's right. I was.

I wouldn't call myself a traditionalist or a purist. I wear modern underwear. I use all manner of hand tools and machines. I'm fascinated by historical techniques, CNC, 3D printing and how technology (old and new) could change furniture making for the better. It is more accurate to say that I'm an explorer.

If someone told me I could make my own paint from beer, I'd try it that night. (I did, and you can.) And if someone were to tell me you could shrink beech biscuits in the microwave, I'd try that, too. (I did, and you can't. They only catch fire.)

The point is that woodworking is most interesting when you open yourself up to new techniques, no matter how crazy or daunting. I am always surprised at how easy most things turn out to be in our craft. The most difficult part seems to be to work up the courage to begin.

This is not a new problem. It is an old one that was at times state-mandated.

During the last decade I've had the privilege to work in Germany with talented journeymen who completed their formal training both in school and in the real world, earning the right to build furniture for a living.

As you would expect, these men and women are tremendously skilled and knowledgeable. They can cut joinery by hand or with power tools with equal facility. They can finish setting up an enormous spindle moulder then pick up a handplane.

It's a bit humbling for someone who hasn't been through the German program.

But then one year I taught a class over there that involved some simple turnings for some chair legs. And I was surprised that none of them had ever turned a spindle or carved a leg. They had never even really considered trying it, even though they had a sweet lathe in their shop.

Those tasks were reserved for people in the turning or carving programs. So their teachers never showed them even the first thing about the lathe or other woodworking disciplines.

I taught them to turn. They loved it. And because of all the other skills they had learned as joiners, they picked it up remarkably fast.

So the next time someone tells you that you can make your own liquid hide glue with a hot plate, try it – if only to prove that you can't.

CHAPTER 29

COFFIN
CHAPTER 30

You have the right.

When people hear that I made my own coffin at the age of 46, they react one of two ways: "You are so strange and morbid. That's just weird. Who does that?" Or, "I have always wanted to make my own coffin."

As a furniture maker, I can't imagine asking some other woodworker to make a crate for my final remains. Or, even worse, asking my family to buy a mass-manufactured coffin when I can put one together from home-center pine.

Yes, this is legal. The Federal Trade Commission's "Funeral Rule" is specific about it. You have the right to:

Provide the funeral home with a casket or urn you buy elsewhere. The funeral provider cannot refuse to handle a casket or urn you bought online, at a local casket store, or somewhere else – or charge you a fee to do it. The funeral home cannot require you to be there when the casket or urn is delivered to them.

Make funeral arrangements without embalming. No state law requires routine embalming for every death. Some states require embalming or refrigeration if the body is not buried or cremated within a certain time; some states don't require it at all. In most cases, refrigeration is an acceptable alternative....

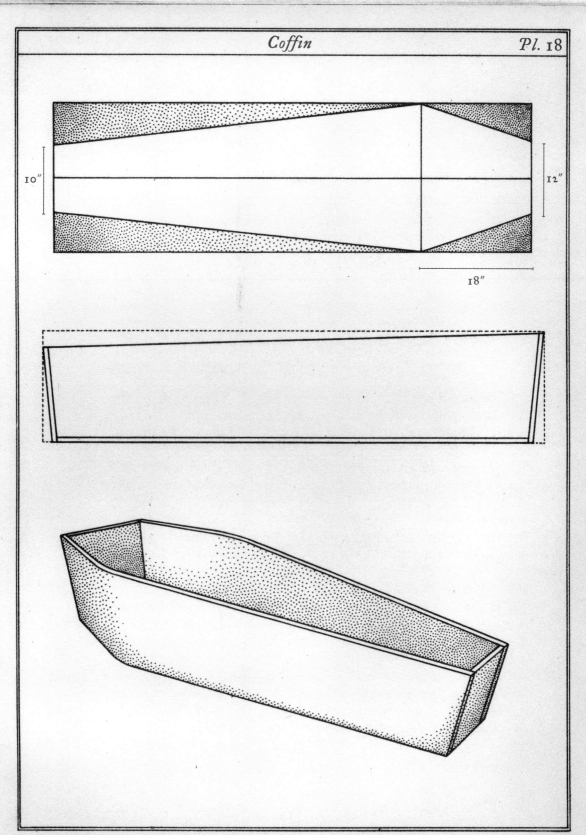

CHAPTER 30

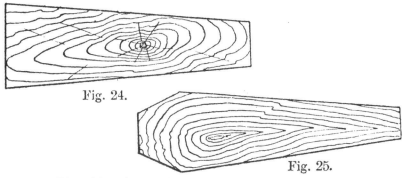

Figs. 24 and 25.—American Patterns of Coffins.

Not the only shape. Paul Hasluck's book on coffins also features this image of coffins in the American pattern in the early 20th century.

Every state has different details about exactly how it works, but the short answer is: Yes, you can do it.

But Why Now?

I'm not terminally ill, and I hope to be around for several more decades. So building a coffin now might seem a waste of storage space. I have the opposite opinion: It creates storage space.

This coffin has removable shelves. So it will hold books (or record albums or bourbon bottles) until I die. Then it will hold me. It's also a great yard decoration during Halloween – my wife's favorite holiday.

Surprisingly, there is not much literature out there about making coffins. If you want to read more about the details of the process in 19th-century England, I recommend "Coffin-making & Undertaking," edited by Paul Hasluck (Cassell & Co., 1913).

"Coffin-making & Undertaking" details construction of two types of coffins: the Lancashire pattern and the Southern Counties pattern. The Lancashire form uses sides that are bent around the bottom board using a fire lit inside the coffin. The Southern Counties form uses sides that are bent around the bottom using saw kerfs to help encourage the bend.

In the summer of 2014, a group of friends and I built coffins using both methods. While the Lancashire coffin was more exciting to build,

Glue up. If using dimensional wood, you'll need to glue up at least two boards to create the bottom, sides and lid. My coffin was less than 23" wide – just enough to squeeze by with two 1x12s.

it was tricky to make the bend with kiln-dried wood. We had to soak the parts for a long time – and get a team of people to manage the fire and the bend. Even then, it was touch-and-go. One of the coffin's sides split badly during the bend on our first attempt. (Our second attempt went much better.)

Just like with making chairs, green wood or air-dried wood is better for bending. Because getting wide planks of green or air-dried pine is difficult in the city, I recommend you try the Southern Counties coffin. It is easy to make with home-center wood and with minimal assistance.

Lay Out the Bottom

Historically, shops that made coffins would keep a series of templates for the different sizes, from infant all the way up to a full-grown

CHAPTER 30   533

Bigger at the top. The top and bottom of the coffin toe out about 6°. Cut this bevel on the ends by eye with a handsaw. Plane the ends smooth.

adult. Unless you are going into the coffin-making business, you can skip the template and use your height and some standard measurements.

Take your height and add about 2" to set the length of the bottom board. Measure your width at your shoulders (mine is shy of 22"). Add 1" to that number – the breast of the coffin – and that measurement is the width of your bottom board.

Draw a centerline down the bottom board. At the head of the bottom board, mark its width as 12". Measure 18" down from the headboard and draw a line across the width of the bottom board. That point is the maximum width of your bottom board (just under 23" in my example – two 1x12s). Down at the foot of the bottom board, mark the width as 10".

Then it's connect-the-dots. Join the headboard to the line across the breast. Join the line across the breast to the footboard. The layout is done. See the plate on page 530 for an illustration of the layout.

Two coffins. The boat shape of a coffin smoother is ideal for fairing the curves on the long edges of the bottom board.

Shape the Bottom Board

Cut out the long edges of the bottom board but don't cut the bottom board to its finished length. Those two cuts are angled slightly to make the headboard and footboard of the coffin toe out slightly.

Hasluck's book says the headboard and footboard should toe out about 6°, so cut a 6° angle at both ends of the bottom.

Now you need to do a little planing on the long edges of the bottom to smooth out the sharp corner at the breastline. If that area is gently curved, the sides will bend a lot easier around the bottom.

Hasluck says you can use the sidewall of a coffin smoothing plane to lay out this shape. We tried this and it worked quite well. Clean up the long edges of the bottom board.

Before moving onto the walls of the coffin, you should clean up the broad faces of the bottom board, especially if the coffin is going to be used as furniture in the interim. If the coffin will be lined with cloth or pitch, skip this step.

CHAPTER 30

Prop it up. Hasluck suggests propping the bottom up on a scrap to make it easier to nail on the headboard and footboard. Good call.

Coffin Walls

The sides of the coffin taper in width from about 16" at the head to 14" at the foot. So that means the headboard and footboard are different lengths. The headboard should be 3/4" x 12" x 16". The footboard should be 3/4" x 10" x 14" (standard adult sizes).

Once you have cut these two pieces to size, nail them to the bottom board with 6*d* headed nails – about five or six across the width. After those bits are nailed on you'll need to plane their long edges to match the angle on the bottom. This is easily done with a jack plane.

The sides of the coffin start about 12" longer than the bottom board. After they are kerfed and nailed on, you'll trim them flush. The extra length is handy because it gives you leverage and something to hold onto while you make the bend.

Glue up panels for the two sides then taper them in width from 16" (maybe a little more) at the headboard to 14" (maybe a little more) at the footboard. Note: This taper is cut on only one long edge. The other long edge remains square to the ends.

Not calculated. You don't have to know the exact angle of where the bottom meets the headboard or footboard. Just make them match.

Easy jack work. Mark the 2" taper on one of the long edges of the sides. Remove this material using a jack plane. Plane the second side to match the first.

CHAPTER 30

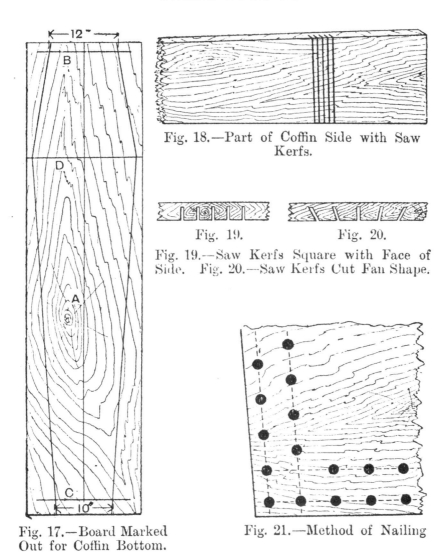

Fig. 17.—Board Marked Out for Coffin Bottom.

Fig. 18.—Part of Coffin Side with Saw Kerfs.

Fig. 19.—Saw Kerfs Square with Face of Side. Fig. 20.—Saw Kerfs Cut Fan Shape.

Fig. 21.—Method of Nailing

Coffin advice. Here you can see Hasluck's drawing for the Southern Counties coffin, including the two different ways to kerf the sides.

"*In order to create something that functions properly – a container, a chair, a house – its essence has to be explored; for it should serve its purpose to perfection, i.e. it should fulfill its function practically and be durable, inexpensive and 'beautiful.'*"

— *Walter Gropius (1883-1969), founder of Bauhaus*

Now you can lay out the kerfs that will allow the sides to bend around the bottom board. Coffins typically use five kerfs that are spaced 1/2" apart. The center kerf sits on the widest point of the breastline.

Several sources suggest there are two ways to cut the kerfs: straight down or at an angle that radiates from the center. All the sources I could

Perfect kerfs. To make sure we got the kerfs right on the first try, we used a fence to guide the saw.

find suggest that sawing them straight down is the way to go. I haven't tried the angled kerfs so I cannot say if the advice is bunk or not.

Saw the kerfs and leave 1/8" of solid wood remaining.

Attach the Side Pieces

If you have carefully prepared the bottom and the sides, then this part is easy. Nail one side to the footboard and the bottom board below the area that needs to bend. (Use 6*d* headed nails, of course.)

Once you get half the side nailed down, take a break for tea. The bend will be easier if you pour a teakettle full of boiling water over the kerfed section. The heat and moisture make it much less likely that the sides will crack when you bend them.

Pour the scalding water over the kerfs – both inside and out. Then immediately press the side down. It should move without too much complaint. Hold it in place and tack the side in place with 6*d* nails.

Flip the coffin over and repeat the process for the other side piece.

CHAPTER 30

Transfer around. If you want to be careful with your kerfs, transfer the cutlines from the inside faces of the sides to the outside. Then trim the sides flush to the box.

Drive nails in about every 2" if you want the thing to be bulletproof. Space them every 3" if you are resigned to being worm food.

Once the sides are nailed on, you can trim them flush to the headboard and footboard with a handsaw.

After that, you simply need to flush all the joints and level the top edges of the carcase so everything is in the same plane. The lid is a simple panel – you'll likely have to glue up three boards to create it. After you

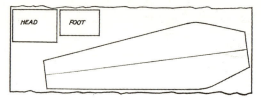

Fig. 3. How bottom was marked out with templet.

Fig. 4. Bottom nailed to head.

Fig. 5. Foot added and bent out.

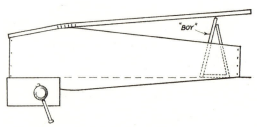

Fig. 6. Side being nailed down supported by "boy".

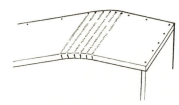

Fig. 7. Facets caused by kerfs to be planed out.

Five steps. Here is Charles Hayward's drawing of how his family built coffins (Hayward says his first project as a child was a coffin he built as a bed for his kitten).

CHAPTER 30

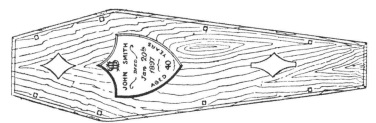

Fig. 92.—Coffin Lid with Screws and Furniture.

In the end. Traditional coffins would look like this before they went into the ground.

get the panel glued up, put it on your workbench and lay the carcase upside down on the panel. Trace around the carcase. Saw the lid to shape.

You don't need the lid just yet, so clean up the saw marks and get it ready to nail down when the time comes.

Many simple coffins included a bit of moulding around the base or some sort of faux finish to comfort the grieving that they weren't complete cheapskates. Don't fall for it. No one cares if you were able to afford miters or a fancy finish.

In the Meantime

If the coffin is for immediate use, it should be given a coat of raw linseed oil, according to Hasluck, then covered entirely in boiling pitch. Then the exterior of the coffin is covered in plain blue dress material that is affixed with tacks.

If the coffin will be for an occupant in the distant future you can finish it like furniture. You can add shelves to the interior to hold books, record albums or liquor bottles. This part is up to you. If you are going to make it a bookcase, check out the chapter on bookcases for advice on the three most common sizes of books you'll need to accommodate.

I finished my unit to hold vinyl albums. The shelves are spaced about 15" apart to allow plenty of room for 12" albums. It was difficult to space the shelves precisely because the sides of the coffin are tapered. Not only that, the pine had warped a bit since assembly. So getting a precise fit was a fun exercise with a bevel gauge and a block plane.

The shelves are tacked in place through the coffin sides with *6d* headed nails to make them easy to remove. Then I also tacked in angled cleats above and below each shelf for some Soviet-style over-building.

I painted the outside then asked my daughter Katherine to paint a few images from some of our favorite records. She chose some awesome artwork from Queens of the Stone Age.

The coffin hangs on a French cleat. Each cleat is 1" x 3" x 17" and is made using hard maple. The cleat on the cabinet is bolted through the case with 5/16" x 2" carriage bolts, large fender washers and nuts. The cleat on the wall is attached to two studs with 3/8" x 3" lag screws. I can climb this thing like a ladder, so I'm certain it will hold my records.

That will do nicely until the coffin and I need to take a dirt nap.

MY COFFIN

NO.	PART	SIZES (INCHES)		
		T	W	L
1	Bottom	3/4	22-1/2	78
1	Headboard	3/4	12	16
1	Footboard	3/4	10	14
2	Sides	3/4	16	90*
1	Lid	3/4	25	90*
16	Cleats for shelves	3/4	3/4	11
1	Top shelf**	3/4	11-1/8	19
1	Second shelf**	3/4	11-1/8	19-3/8
1	Third shelf**	3/4	11-1/8	16-1/2
1	Bottom shelf**	3/4	11-1/8	12-3/4
2	French cleats	1	3	17

* Overlong; trim to fit
** These shelf lengths are for my coffin. Yours may vary. These are a starting point.

CHAPTER 30

What's important. With a few removable shelves, you have a spacious bookcase that can hang on a French cleat attached to the wall. The shelves rest on nailed-on cleats. The French cleats are bolted to the case so the unit will hold a lot of weight.

THE ISLAND OF MISFIT DESIGNS

CHAPTER 31

An examination of odd stools (and other) samples.

When one of my designs is a failure, my immediate urge is to hide it like an embarrassing injury.

For many years I'd quickly dismantle the offending object and recycle its parts into something productive (jigs, swords for my children or kindling). While I was at it, I'd destroy any photos of the piece for a good shot of catharsis. I thought that purging my bad designs ensured that I wouldn't get labeled as a bad designer.

The problem is that we all start out as "bad designers." I have yet to meet anyone who was born with an unerring sense of proportion, line, value and color. These things are learned. And after designing hundreds of pieces of furniture for publication or sale, I've concluded that you can learn a lot through your failed designs.

At some point in my career I stopped burning by failures and started studying them. And I learned a lot by asking hard questions such as: Why is this not working? What would I change?

This chapter was the most difficult one to write for this book. I hope it will prove useful. Or that at least you can get a good laugh at these designs. Note: This is but a small sample of failed or near-miss designs for the book in your hands. If I published the entire lot, it would be its

MISFIT DESIGNS

"There's a price to be paid for working only on commission. I don't own any of my carvings. If you walk through my house you won't guess my profession.... Around here carving is a verb (well, a gerund), not a noun. Nouns leave the house."

— *David Esterly*
"The Lost Carving"
(Penguin)

A regular stool. This homage to historical milking stools turned out to be too predictable to be interesting. Also, it needs more splay.

own book. (Now, that would be a bestseller – "62 Projects You Shouldn't Build! Amazingly Awkward Designs for Dumpsters, Sink Holes & Bonfires.")

Sir, There's a Problem With Your Stools

I have lost count of the number of low stools I have drawn and built for this book. As I am typing this sentence, I still don't have a publishable design. So let's discuss the derelict and flaming heaps of crap that I assembled while on my way to … whatever is in the pages elsewhere in this book (hopefully inspiring).

The green stool (left), as I call it, was an attempt to make a full-on casual milking stool. These stools crop up everywhere in the historical record. I adore them because they look so thrown together. Like the farmer was drunk on clotted cream when boring the mortises. The legs and drilling angles aren't consistent. The seat is a weird chunk of something that doesn't have a shape you can put a name to. "Polygon" implies it might have sides. "Amoeba" suggests it's a shape found in nature.

Anyway, these irregular stools (a good band name) are difficult to design because the best ones are divorced from a pattern or plan or explanation. They look good because the maker found some legs and a seat that were somehow suited for one another.

My design brief for my stool was "rounded seat and swollen legs." I think the design failed because of a couple things. One, the components were too regular for a form that is supposed to be irregular. Two, the legs needed to be splayed out more. Maybe 5° more would have done it. Who knows? When I first mocked up the stool in half-scale, one of the people in my shop said it looked totally wrong. And I listened, which I have learned is the wrong thing to do when prototyping.

I like this failed stool enough that I keep it in the shop, for now.

For the Fish

This stool looked so good on paper that I built it twice (almost three times) – refusing to acknowledge that it was a stinker. This stool is supposed to be like a post-and-rung chair, with lots of structure to keep it strong and stable through the long haul.

One problem is that I crammed a lot of hand-cut joinery into too small of a space. Each joint's insignificant inaccuracy stacked up in the stool's 20 (!!) joints. Getting it assembled took a good deal of grunting

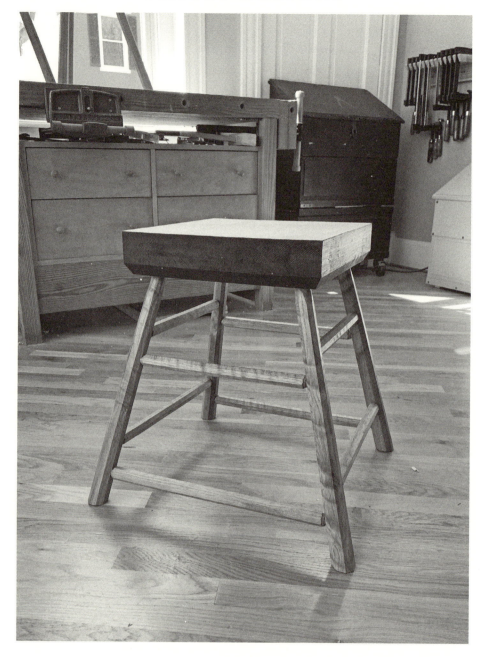

Too many tenons. My first version of this stool had so much internal tension that it tried to tear itself apart. This version wasn't much better. Twenty tenons is too many.

CHAPTER 31

and core strength.

Aside from the technical problems, I think the square seat is a loser. Yes, it reflects the square shape of the undercarriage. But surprisingly, that's not how a lot of chairs and stools are made. Their seats have curves, or they are round or half-round. A square chair seat is somewhat unusual (though it does happen, and I've built some).

I hated looking at this stool – even out of the corner of my eye – and had to get rid of it. Luckily, the local window washer needed a low bench to use for cleaning fish he caught in the Licking River. So, this stool now stinks – both for real and as a design.

Tabling This Design

The pine and poplar worktable on the following pages is another piece I had high hopes for. Based on tables in the "Tacuinum Sanitatis," a book on Medieval health practices, it seemed the perfect breakfast table. The splayed legs add stability to its small tabletop. And there's not a lot of joinery – two sliding dovetails and four holes for the legs.

The first design failure is in the legs. They are too bulky and need to be slimmed down. Plus, the transition between the tenon and the octagonal section is too abrupt – it makes the tenon look weak or, at least, out of place. This is caused mostly by the chunky legs. Once I slimmed down the legs for future versions, the transition didn't look so jarring. And I could use thinner stock, which saved some money.

The biggest problem is the shape of the table's top. It's square. Like the stool above, there is something not right with a square top or seat in these instances. Part of the problem with a square top is that it doesn't let you know which side is the front and which is the side. They look different – from one view the top looks thin and from the other view the top looks thick, thanks to the dovetailed battens.

So, when I walk up to this table, it looks different about half the time. I don't know which is "right," and this is disconcerting. It might be a personal problem. But once I made the top a rectangle and thinned the legs, the design snapped into place. It had a front face and a side.

In my head this is how architecture works. We are confused by buildings that don't have a well-defined entrance. If the table doesn't tell you how you are supposed to look at it – what is front and what is not – we are left unsure. Or we dismiss it.

MISFIT DESIGNS

At least the cat approves. This worktable has several flaws. Here you can see how the tabletop appears quite thick when viewed from this angle.

CHAPTER 31

Another view. Here the tabletop looks thin. Maybe too thin. And look at those chunky legs. It hurts me.

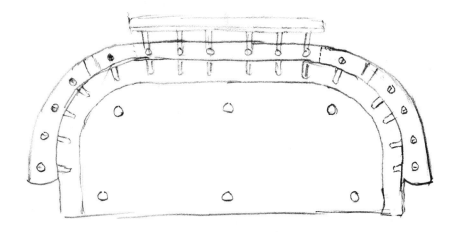

Widebody. Stretching the width of a chair to create a settee might work in some instances, but not here.

CHAPTER 31

Before the stretching. This is where the settee started, before the Silly Putty approach.

The Same, But Worse

At times it is tempting to take a good design and scale it up or stretch it in one dimension. This rarely works for me.

So welcome to the Settee Section of Shame in which I fail to produce a satisfactory settee design for this book. It's not for lack of trying. My sketchbook is stuffed with doodles. I just haven't doodled superbly, I suppose.

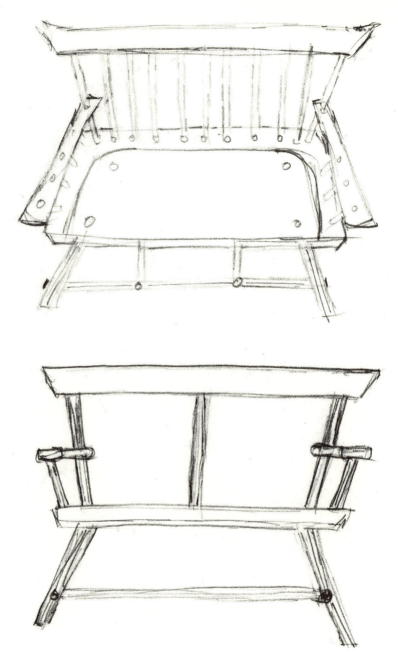

A failed fix. Making the crest rail longer might have made the settee more comfortable to sit in, but I wasn't happy with the overall look.

CHAPTER 31

One approach I took was to stretch my armchair design into a settee or settle. This seemed reasonable. Many Windsor settees use design elements from sackback and fanback chairs. But this strategy doesn't quite work with a stick chair.

When I mocked up this design, I quickly found the folly. It looks OK but sits like crap, especially when there are two people perched on it. The ends of the crest rail bite into the center of each sitter's spine. And one shoulder blade is left unsupported.

The only way this design works is for a single sitter who happens to be 2.5 times as wide as a normal sitter.

To fix this, I extended the length of the crest rail to completely support the backs of both sitters. But this design looked ungainly and created a lot of construction problems. So, I am back to being unsettled.

Bigger Stool Problems

Designing the tall staked stool in this book took about 10 iterations, and it would get really boring (for me and you) to review the entire evolution from mudskipper to hominid. The general arc of the design was a typical one for me. The stool's components started out too heavy. And the details were too fussed-over.

The cherry version on the next page (at least I think it's cherry) shows this problem.

The legs are too chunky and they double-taper. The tapers begin at the point where the stretchers meet the legs. Then they taper both up and down. But they don't taper enough. In fact, you have to really look for the tapers. The front stretcher (also bulky) also has a double-taper.

This design started to look better when I removed about 1/4" from the legs and 1/8" from the stretchers. And I simplified the tapers on the legs to be a single taper. Lighten and simplify.

The seat isn't bad. The curve along the rear is nice. But it's too bulky overall. A chamfer on the underside of the seat was the fix.

The shallow curve on the front edge of the seat, however, is lame. It's vestigial. In fact, I think it distracts from the dramatic sweep of the bigger curve. Plus, it doesn't offer any comfort. And it's more work.

The mahogany stool below was a later iteration. Here I still need to lighten the legs. I also somehow made the stretchers worse. I made them too thin and turned them round. They look like pencils. After making this stool I went back to octagonal stretchers and found a good balance between pencils and billy clubs.

Too thick & curvy. This stool needed to go on a diet. And lose the curve on the front of the seat.

CHAPTER 31

Wow, even worse. Shrinking the spindles and turning them definitely wasn't the fix.

Better. Here the simple tapers have kicked in and the stretchers are proportional to the rest of the piece.

CHAPTER 31

Cute, but ouch. I love the look of this chair but it is otherwise a torture device for the human body.

Armchair Misadventures

The armchair was another project that was almost a breech birth. I sketched about 20 chairs for this book and built about 10 of them to get to a design that I am (honestly) happy with. Let's take a look at some of the lowlights.

Above is where I began. It's an adaptation of a lovely chair (prob-

Comfort isn't everything. While this chair looks as inviting as a dentist's chair, it actually sits quite well. Too bad it looks its best with a flaming blanket over it.

ably Welsh) that I spotted in England one summer in an historic home. Though it has nice lines, it's uncomfortable. The back is almost straight-up 90°, and the seat is too small. The chair feels like it's hugging you (if you are slim) or trying to squeeze your guts out (if you are like the rest of us).

I also wanted to try to simplify the construction when it came to attaching the arms to the back spindles (remember lighten and simplify?), but I went too far.

I first decided to make the arms separate from the back. This would make it easier to drill the sticks for the arms and the back because they weren't all attached. I also used a less-traditional seat shape.

The result was just terrible. The chair sits great. The back tilt is just right. The arms slope nicely back. The chair is super easy to build. But it looks like a dog's dinner. I tried reshaping the arms (they are too rectilinear as shown in the photo), but I concluded the problem is that having the arms separate from the back makes the chair look weak. And just wrong.

So, I went back to the way I built armchairs in about 2003 and started from there, trying to refine those designs.

That meant steam-bending the armbow and the crest rail. I knew this chair wasn't going to be the final design for the book because I wanted to avoid any difficult steam-bending. Avoiding a long or tricky bend would make the chair more approachable for a beginner. But I hoped that if I built this chair, then the next iteration might come to me.

I was right. This chair has a nice flow to it and is light in color, much like an early chair I built in David Fleming's class in Cobden, Ontario. And that vague memory of that old chair did the trick. I decided to use an armbow that was built up from three pieces, just like Fleming (and many old Welsh makers) did.

In fact, before I owned a steam box, I used to make chairs with a three-piece arm all the time. But I had blocked them from my mind for some reason. After that little jolt, the chair design came together in just a few days.

Transitional. This chair was the bridge I needed to build to get back to the designs I was building in 2003 and 2004.

CHAPTER 31

Hey (drunken) sailor. This table never looks the same twice. I must have taken 20 photos of it to try to understand its failure to charm others.

The Tipsy Table

This simple maple end table derived from an early morning sketch. I drew it over coffee and had it built by supper. Then I showed it to a few friends. Most treated me warily, like when you show up at high school wearing red leather pants. A couple people laughed out loud. No one but me liked the thing.

Because of the angled legs, it looks unstable, but it's not. Thanks to the placement of the feet, the top is well supported, even when you press hard on a corner.

The table is a bit disconcerting to look at – it changes in appearance radically as you walk across the room. Sometimes it looks like a ballet dancer. Other times it looks like a frog trying to square dance.

My friends had suggestions as to how to change the design to make it more conventional. I decided to leave the table as it was and abandon the design. My oldest daughter uses the prototype as a nightstand. It has survived well, despite its radical geometry.

There are many more failures I could discuss. But writing this short

We'll call you, promise. It's hard to believe this is the same table in all of these photos.

chapter has been painful enough. I look at some of these designs and think I should have my woodworking license revoked. Oh wait, I don't have a license (but I do have all my vaccinations!).

The good news is that design is learned, not granted by a moistened lady or a tarnished lamp. Even if your designs start out as bad as mine, there's a good chance that you can improve them. With work, they might look like something that someone will swoon over. (Or at least not put to the torch.)

AFTERWORD

One more word on 'that word.'

There is great power in naming things, but there is also violence.

A few years ago I was driving to dinner with a fellow furniture maker, and he asked me this question: "Do you consider yourself a writer or a woodworker?"

I hate this question, but I also hate looking like a wanker.

I replied, "I'm a writer who builds furniture."

"Ah!" he said. "You said the word 'writer' first. So that's more important to you?" He raised the tone of his voice at the end of the sentence like it was a question. But it wasn't.

So I bristle a bit when people tell me what I am and what I am not. At times I build cubbyholes, but I won't be put into one. After writing "The Anarchist's Tool Chest" in 2011, a fair number of blowhards declared that I wasn't an anarchist. Anarchists, they explained, are explicitly anti-capitalist. They seek to overthrow the government. They embrace violence.

Saying that you have to be committed to violence to be an anarchist is like saying you have to oppress Africans to be a Christian, or you have to own a gun to be an American. It's nonsensical.

The truth is, I barely discuss my beliefs about the world in "The Anarchist's Tool Chest" and this book. There might be only two or three people in this world who have heard my unfiltered thoughts on how the world works, and I plan to keep that number in the single digits as long as I live.

Do I have problems with authority – liturgical, corporate and governmental? Absolutely. Do I routinely disregard laws and mores because I think they're at odds with human decency? You bet. Am I going to write about my behavior in a book that is already quite difficult to ship to military bases because of its title?

Do you think I'm stupid?

So if I don't espouse the full details of my personal belief system, why bring up anarchism at all? Two reasons.

It's the right word to describe me. I'm an anarchist and here is a book about my tool chest. Here is a second book of my furniture designs. Beyond those simple declarations, the goal of the books is to point to a path that doesn't get discussed much in Western society. During my training as a journalist we were urged to tell "both sides of every story." After working as a journalist, the problem I discovered was that there are usually about a dozen sides to every story. It's just that most of those ideas aren't discussed at the country club.

Ideas such as: Organizations dehumanize and homogenize us. Modern production methods enslave us to a cycle of making nothing and consuming everything.

But these ideas, which I discuss in both books, are only starting points. If you have a brain it's easy to see where the trail head leads. Like working with hand tools, it can be a difficult path to travel, but it can take you almost anywhere.

The second reason I couch these simple ideas inside work-a-day books on tools and building furniture is that I refuse to become part of the circle-jerk clique of writers who obsess on discussing Craft, its Demise and How to Fix Things.

In my 25 years of hanging out with woodworkers, I've never once heard someone say: "I just finished reading David Pye's 'The Nature and Art of Workmanship,' and now all I want to do is carve bowls." It just doesn't happen.

Don't get me wrong. Discussing craft is important. I just don't think you should talk about it much until you have done it – a lot.

The solution to "fix" everything – for lack of a better word – is not in words. It's in your fingers. Pick up the tools, and the answers to these questions will become apparent. Make something, and you will understand more about craft than all of the books written about its doom.

Yesterday I had a tape measure clipped to my pants pocket, and a young woman in a store asked me what I did for a living. When I told her I made furniture, she gushed at length about how that was all she'd ever wanted to do. As a child she built all of her Barbie furniture. Now she watched television programs and read books about woodworking every night, but she didn't want to go back to school to train as a furniture maker.

"You don't have to go back to school," I told her.

"But how will I learn it?" she asked.

"By doing what you did when you were a little girl: Pick up the tools and use them."

Every word I write is aimed at one thing: To make you crazy to pick up the tools. They are the answer to everything that's wrong with our lives and with our world. With tools you can fix things. You can make things. You can escape from a job that is slowly killing you. With tools you can build a life that doesn't depend on your next annual review and whether or not you managed to wear out the knees in your pants while groveling for a raise.

I don't care if you call that anarchism or not. In fact, I recommend that you don't.

So stay tidy. Be friendly. Build things instead of buying them. You'll know what to do next.

Christopher Schwarz
Fort Mitchell, Kentucky
February 2016

APPENDICES

A: TOOLS YOU NEED

The tools are neutral.

I wrote my first book in 1995 on a Macintosh Centris 610. The story was about a carpenter whose life is saved when he joins a religious cult teetering on the brink of collapse and violence. The book was titled "Fisheye" because once you can actually see the world around you in all directions, it becomes distorted and difficult to interpret. Think of a fisheye lens for a camera.

The book completely sucked. I burned the manuscript in 1998.

What's important about the first paragraph of this tale is the model number of the computer. It was the same machine I used at my newspaper job. There my editors assigned me about 300 stories a year on everything from the machinations of the zoning board of appeals to a local duck that had fallen in love with a neighbor's dog.

I am grateful that most of that work went to wrapping fish, starting fires and stuffing the coats of mountain hermits.

In neither case was the Centris 610 to blame for the resulting drivel. It was caused by the stupid bag of meat between my ears. Yet there is a key difference between the two similar stories above. At the newspaper, I used my Centris 610 to make money for my employer. When I wrote my doomed novel, I used the Centris 610 to attempt my escape.

It's the same in woodworking. The tools – hand, power or digital – are neutral. What makes them terrifying or liberating is how they are wielded. You can use a table saw to make MDF tchotchkes for a mass-market retailer, or you can use it to build something for yourself – a table, a chair, a business that exists outside of the corporate world.

It's too easy to anthropomorphize our tools with political, social or emotional traits. In the end, all tools are just rocks. You can use one to scoop out a tree trunk for a canoe or bash in your neighbor's head.

So why do hand tools seem more subversive than a random-orbit sander? It's probably because you don't find many handplanes on the factory floor anymore. So owning a backsaw instead of a chop saw makes you feel like you are thumbing your nose at industry or society. But the truth is that until you put the saw (either saw) to the wood, you are just picking your nose with the wrong digit.

Tools are interesting. The things we can make with them are far more so.

In that spirit, I'd like to introduce some of the critical tools (and a couple machines) that will help you build the projects in this book. This chapter is not an infomercial. All of these tools here are mine, and I paid full price for them. You might not even be able to purchase some of them because of where you live in the world or because you are reading this book in the prison library run by our squid overlords in 2174.

So don't sweat it. There are lots of good tools out there. This chapter will show you what to look for.

16 oz. Hammer

Hammers are essential to woodworking. Anyone who tells you otherwise is selling dovetail jigs. But which hammer is basic to building furniture?

The furniture-maker's hammer has a 16 oz. head, a smooth and slightly domed striking face, a wooden handle and the balance of a trapeze artist. A 16 oz. tool allows you to drive 4*d* and 6*d* nails for furniture with a few strikes and without wearing you out. A domed striking surface lets you set the heads of nails flush without "Frenching" the work.

A wooden handle is warm in your hand and won't vibrate your arm apart like some metallic or fiberglass hammers.

Lots of people talk about the "balance" or "hang" of a tool, but it's difficult to describe. You will not know it when you first pick up the hammer. You will not know it after you drive a nail. By your thousandth nail, however, you'll know. And the knowledge will never leave your fingers.

Lump Hammer

In the last few years I've become fond of using what the English call a "lump hammer" to assemble casework and chairs. Here in North America, it's called a sledge, blacksmith or engineer's double-face hammer. But none of those names does the tool justice quite like "lump hammer."

I like one with a head that weighs between 2 lbs. and 2-1/2 lbs. (in metric land, look for a 1,000-gram head) with the tool's total length about 10-1/2". You might have to cut down the handle; this will improve its balance and finesse.

The lump hammer offers gentle whacks when you lift it and let it fall a few inches. And if you put any swing into it, you can knock almost anything home, even a dovetailed carcase that is locked-in mid-assembly because the glue has swollen the joints.

That's how I came to love the lump hammer – I had one in my tool kit to rescue student work that was on the brink of failure. But I came to appreciate it as a tool of great subtlety; I use it for mortising and setting holdfasts, too. Plus beautiful vintage ones are cheap and plentiful.

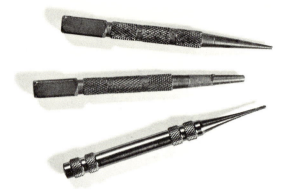

Nail Set

Sometimes called a "nail punch," these are goofily named but important tools. If you want to drive, set or punch a nail head 1/32" below the surface of the wood, you need them. Buy good ones or undamaged vintage ones. They typically come in three sizes. Get all three.

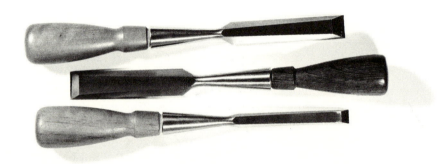

A Few Bevel-edge Chisels

A "few" might be more than you need. For most work, a 1/4", 1/2" and 3/4" chisel will handle most everything.

Don't worry about the tool's steel or how long it keeps an edge. That's fairly irrelevant. If a chisel is garbage, you'll figure that out and exchange it. Most, and by most I mean 90 percent, chisels have steel that's better than you need.

Focus instead on the handle and determine if the chisel is handle-heavy, which will wear out your wrist. I prefer a lightweight wooden handle – most plastic-handled chisels are too heavy. The chisel should feel like something you want to hold all day, like a pencil.

The long edges of the chisel's blade should be beveled so you can get into acute corners. These bevels also reduce the tool's overall weight.

There are lots of other details in this simple tool, but if you buy a wooden-handled bevel-edge chisel, you can make any necessary modifications yourself.

Mallet

Mallets are as personal as hammers. I have a 16 oz. round-head mallet for light chopping with chisels, mostly. You can make your own if you like. Wooden mallets are great because they can be easily modified or repaired by a woodworker (you).

Jack Plane

The jack plane is by far the most common handplane in woodworking, and for good reason: You can set it up to hog off material, straighten surfaces or provide the final surface for finishing. For many years a jack was the only bench plane I used.

A vintage (the older the better) metallic jack plane with wooden handles is a fantastic choice. My Stanley No. 5 cost less than $20 and is still going strong after 20 years of constant use.

There are so many resources out there for picking and restoring planes that it can become a hobby unto itself, though that's not my bag. Get the tool working and improve its condition every time you disassemble it for sharpening. That's my best advice.

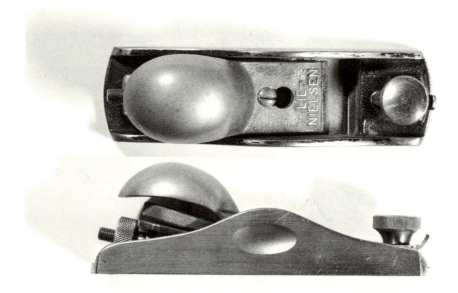

Block Plane

The second plane I use the most is a low-angle block plane. You basically have two choices with this tool: Buy an old one and restore it or buy a premium new one. Inexpensive modern block planes are good for rock fights or adding ballast to a bag that you're trying to sink to the bottom of the lake – little else.

I like a tool that has an adjustable mouth and fits easily in one hand. I'm not a fan of monster block planes.

Router Plane

Router planes are essential to every hand-tool shop for installing hinges or making dados or sliding dovetails. The larger size – based on the Stanley No. 71 – is the most useful if you can buy only one. I like a "closed throat" router, or a tool where the throat can be temporarily closed.

Premium router planes include a depth stop, a handy feature. Don't worry about having all the different irons; you'll do 99 percent of your work with a straight iron.

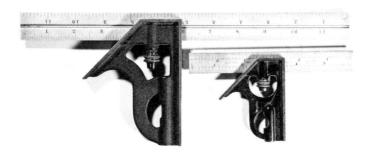

Combination Square

Though originally designed as a metalworking tool, a good combination square is outstanding for woodworking. I use the 12" and 6" models. You get what you pay for with combination squares; cheap tools are frustrating and quality versions are not.

Pick up a Starrett or a Brown & Sharpe and you will be spoiled.

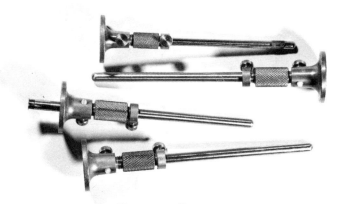

Cutting Gauge

Cheap marking gauges that use a dull pin to abuse the wood are frustrating. You need to file the pin to a sharp, flattened point that is angled slightly away from the fence and make sure the beam and fence lock so everything is at right angles.

Or buy a good cutting gauge and get to work. There are lots of good ones available. Look for one that has a fixed (not rotating) wheel to make the cuts. Keep it sharp.

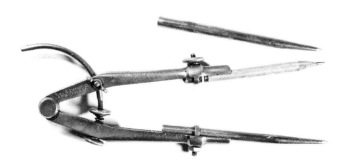

Compass

Woodworking has more to do with geometry than mathematics. So a compass is essential for layout – not just arcs and circles, but for many straight-line layouts as well. I have a nice Starrett compass I purchased (finally) after struggling for years with a draftsman's compass. The Starrett is built like a tank and allows me to swap out one of the points for a pencil – it's perfect.

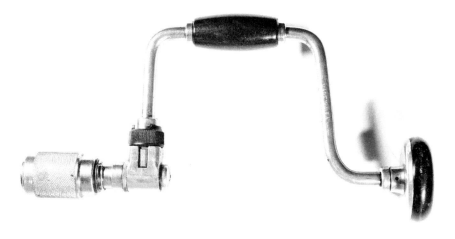

Brace

If you are ever going to build a piece of staked furniture, you need one good brace with an 8" or 10" sweep. I'm not picky about brand names. Instead, I nitpick the tool's condition. You need a chuck that has its springs, closes tight on the bit and has crisp – not worn-out – jaws. The brace's pad at the top shouldn't wobble much, if at all. The handle, where you grab the tool to crank it, should spin freely.

Hand Drill

If you are going to use nails or screws, a hand drill is essential. Just like with the brace, don't shop by brand name. Shop by the tool's condition. The chuck should be in perfect working order. The tool's gears should engage and turn freely. A little lubrication in the tool's oil ports will work wonders. Oh, and the crank's handle should be firmly affixed and not weirdly bent. All the other features – detachable side handle, multi-gear transmission, bit storage – are tits on a tomcat.

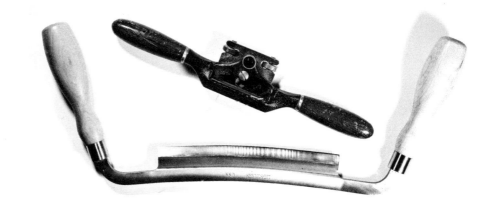

Spokeshave or Drawknife

To create the rough shape of a round tenon for staked furniture, a spokeshave or drawknife is essential (if you don't own a lathe). A drawknife works faster than a spokeshave, but it is more difficult to sharpen and learn to use.

If you buy a spokeshave, I recommend ones based on the Stanley 151 model. These have two spinwheels that let you adjust the tool's cutter. Beginners have much better luck with these tools compared to ones without mechanical adjusters. Spokeshaves come with either a flat sole (like a handplane) or one that is slightly bellied from front to back. Both are useful.

Coping Saw

For sawing tight curves, a coping saw is ideal. Most of the modern ones are shoddy; vintage ones are much better. Look for tools that accept pinned blades.

More important than the tool is its blade. Good blades make the difference. I use Swiss-made Pegas blades. If you are having difficulty finding them, that is because I have hoarded a lifetime supply. Apologies.

Rasp

Rasps are invaluable for curved work. I use them for smoothing the cuts made by the coping saw or drawknife. For the projects in this book, you need only a small, fine-toothed half-round rasp. Look for rasps with random, hand-stitched teeth. They are (a lot) more expensive, but they cut smoothly and leave a better surface behind.

Backsaws

For cutting pieces to final size or cutting joints, you need a backsaw or two. Most woodworkers end up with three backsaws: a 10-point tenon saw filed with rip teeth, a 14-point carcase saw filed with crosscut teeth and a 15-point dovetail saw filed with rip teeth.

You can get away with just buying a dovetail saw at first. Look for one that is lightweight and fits your hand in a glove-like manner.

Handsaw & Buckets

For cutting pieces to length, a handsaw and two plastic 5-gallon buckets (thank you Mike Siemsen for that advice) are the ticket. Good vintage handsaws that are ready to work are difficult to find or expensive. So buy a hardware-store saw with induction-hardened teeth. This tool will last you about 10 years. Yeah, the handles are plastic or uncomfortable, but the tools cut surprisingly well and cost almost nothing.

Sharpening Stuff

Entire books have been written about sharpening gear, so reading one of those books is (eventually) a good idea. What's more important than your equipment or your technique is that you choose one sharpening system and stick with it. Sampling all the systems is expensive, confusing and another hobby entirely.

I use a side-clamp honing guide (sometimes called an Eclipse guide) and waterstones.

Bottom line: It's more fun to make tools dull than it is to make them sharp.

USEFUL STUFF AT THE BACK

Some Brand-name Stuff

I hate to do this to you. But here are some of the tools where the brand really makes a difference. It is worth searching for these specific tools.

WoodOwl Auger Bits

In 2013 I switched to WoodOwl Ultra Smooth Augers after working for years with vintage augers. These Japanese-made bits are the best I've found. They cut fast and clean, and they clear chips with ease. Plus you can get them sized by kinda-16ths. Yes, they are technically metric. No, it doesn't technically matter.

I use the 5/8" WoodOwl in a brace to bore the initial hole for the mortise in all the staked furniture pieces in this book. If you can't find a WoodOwl, find the best 5/8" auger you can.

Large Veritas Standard Tapered Reamer

This Canadian-made reamer works incredibly well in a brace, corded drill or drill press. That's why I prefer it to Veritas's professional reamer, which can be used only in a brace. I'll get about a dozen chairs out of an edge before I need to stone the edge, which I do with a diamond paddle.

My only gripe about the tool is it doesn't have to be this long – I plan to grind off the first 3/8" of the reamer for my work.

I usually drive this reamer with a heavy-duty corded drill. My second choice is using it in a brace.

Veritas 5/8" Tapered Tenon Cutter

This is the matching tenon cutter to the reamer above. It works like a giant pencil sharpener. Simply shave (or turn) your tenon near to its finished size. Then take it for a spin in the tenon cutter and you will have a tenon that matches the tapered mortise.

The blade is easy to remove and sharpen – it's about the size of a spokeshave blade.

Vesper Tools Sliding Bevel

I have an incurable case of Chris Vesper Fever. He is one of the best two or three living toolmakers I've ever met. His stuff has the precision of Karl Holtey – and I can afford it on my salary. I use the small one for chairmaking and staked furniture because I can sneak it right up next to the auger bit or reamer. The blade of a large bevel can get in the way during these operations.

USEFUL STUFF AT THE BACK

Oh, & Electric Things: Corded Drill

For building chairs and staked furniture, I use a corded drill to ream the mortises because it has an endless supply of torque. You might as well spend the extra money and buy one that has a 1/2" chuck, a side handle and a long power cord. Don't worry if the drill is heavy – you're not a contractor who has to hoist it all day.

14" Band Saw

If you're making furniture for yourself (not for a living), a 14" band saw is likely more useful than a table saw. It cuts both curves and straight lines, it's safer, quieter and takes up less space. I like vintage U.S.-made band saws that have little (or no) plastic parts. They are better machines and are less expensive than new. My Delta/Rockwell band saw was made in the 1970s – so you don't have to hunt down the ancient stuff.

Portable Thickness Planer

The portable thickness planer is the single-most important woodworking machine in my shop. It saves immense amounts of time and labor and produces a better surface finish than most industrial machines. The knives are simple to change. It can be stored under a workbench.

Most woodworking texts recommend you use an electric jointer in tandem with your thickness planer. And for a production shop, that's the correct advice. In a home shop, however, you can flatten one face of a board with a jack plane then run it through the planer to create two parallel faces.

Yes, you need a dust collector. No, it cannot be a shop vacuum.

And Perhaps a Lathe

I enjoy turning, so I use a lathe in some parts of this book to make tenons or add details to legs. You don't have to own a lathe or learn to turn to make furniture – you can use a spokeshave or drawknife to create round shapes.

If you want a lathe, I recommend a solid benchtop model (sometimes called a "midi" lathe) that can accept a bed extension. You want to be able to chuck up a 30"-long table leg in the machine. Anything less is for turning pens.

ON HIDE GLUE
B: FURNITURE'S NEVER BEEN THE SAME

This fact sucks.

Most of us grew up with yellow glue or white glue, which is known commonly as polyvinyl acetate (PVA). This polymer was discovered in Germany in 1912 by Fritz Klatte. By the late 1940s and early 1950s there was a series of U.S. patents filed for PVA wood glue or cement from a variety of companies, including Borden.

Furniture has never been the same.

PVA has many merits that appeal to the modern mind, so it's easy to forget that it has a huge and fatal flaw: It does not stick to itself. So repairing furniture made with PVA requires you to scrape off all the old PVA, and likely take some wood away in the process.

As furniture maker David Savage said to me, "We have created an entire generation of furniture that cannot be repaired."

And this fact sucks.

Let's Backpedal

From pre-Egyptian times up until the mid-20th century, the most common furniture glue was made from animals. Though the animals in question (cows and fish, for the most part) never intended it, their bodies made an ideal glue that has yet to be surpassed by modern chemistry.

Animal glues:

1. Are reversible with heat and moisture.
2. Are easily repaired by applying more glue.
3. Can be easily modified to stick to metal, be water-resistant or do a variety of other tricks.
4. Act like a lubricant when knocking together joinery. (PVA causes joints to seize.)
5. Are transparent to many common wood finishes. (PVAs reveal themselves as a white stain on wood when they haven't been scraped away.)
6. Offer a darker glue line that doesn't show up when joining walnut, cherry or other domestic woods that are brownish.
7. Doesn't creep. Creep can be good or bad – think of it like a rubbery bond that can shift with the seasons. Sometimes it's a good thing (think wide tenons in a leg). Other times it is sub-optimal (think of a tabletop where the boards shrink differently, leaving raised ridges at the joints).
8. You can create glues that are stronger or more elastic. You also can manipulate the glue's open time so it is really short or as long as 45 minutes.

But lest you think that I don't know PVAs intimately, I do. I grew up with this glue and know its advantages. PVA glues:

1. Are available everywhere.
2. Don't have as short a shelf life as hide glue, which can spoil if treated poorly.
3. Are cheap.
4. Are premixed and ready to use.
5. Can be purchased already formulated to be water-resistant.
6. Offer a light-colored glue line that is suitable for joining light-colored woods.
7. Dry on a more predictable schedule – natural glues are more… natural. They are more susceptible to humidity and temperature.

If you are a beginner, I recommend you try "liquid hide glue" – the starter drug of the hide-glue world. This stuff is premixed and works like PVA in that you just squeeze and go. It also has all the advantages of hide glue, including a bond that is reversible.

USEFUL STUFF AT THE BACK

Liquid hide glue is not a new thing. These glues have been sold commercially since the early 20th century. And you can make your own liquid hide glue if you want by combining hot hide glue and salt (or urea).

But I'm getting ahead of myself. Go buy a small bottle of liquid hide glue at a local family-run hardware store (I've never seen it for sale at a home center). Check the "use by" date on the back of the bottle. Use it up.

You'll either be amazed (because you're used to PVA), or you'll say, "Big deal" (because this is the way that furniture glues should behave).

Really scrubbed. I used a soap finish on the top of this worktable. Four coats of soap resulted in a low-sheen finish.

ON SOAP FINISH
C: DOES IT WORK AS A FINISH?

Yes. Absolutely.

Finishing a piece of furniture with soap is no stranger than covering wood with a bug excretion (shellac), tree sap (varnish), bee stuff (wax) or rendered flax seed (lacquer).

All finishes seem odd when you consider their sources. So when I first learned that soap was a traditional finish for floors and furniture on light-colored woods in northern Europe, I was intrigued because of what soap is and is not.

Of all the things that will harm you in woodworking, finishes are at the top of the list. Take a look at the material safety data sheet (MSDS) for lacquer thinner. Now do you have the courage to spill the stuff on your skin or inhale it?

I don't.

I'm not a safety nut. Woodworking is dangerous, and I embrace that. Cut yourself or don't – that is a concept we all get. But when it comes to chemicals that silently build up in my body without me noticing, I'm cautious. I know people who were professional finishers who walked out of a spray booth one day and dropped dead after years of inhaling volatile organic compounds.

So soap – a treatment of a natural oil with an alkali solution (such as ashes) – is comforting.

Does it work as a furniture finish? Yes, absolutely. Is it as durable as a lacquer or urethane? Absolutely not. But that is the trade-off with safer

Soap flakes. Simple soap flakes have no detergents or fragrances added – that's what is best for a soap finish.

finishes such as natural oils, waxes and soaps. They require maintenance, and I'm OK with that.

What is a Soap Finish?

You can't just rub a bar of Irish Spring on a chair and call it finished. (Wait, maybe you can. Try it for yourself.)

A Danish soap finish uses natural soap flakes that are mixed with hot water. Soap flakes are a pure form of soap that doesn't include additional detergents, fragrances or other modern chemicals. It is simply an oil that has been mixed with an alkali solution to create a salt of a fatty acid. Our ancestors made soap by pouring tallow (animal fat) onto the ashes from a fire.

You can still buy this important and elemental soap from a variety of sources all over the world. Look for companies that specialize in "natural soap flakes." You'll find a bunch.

The flakes are white and soft to the touch. They don't have much of a

Soap & hot water. A solution of water and a little soap will make a soupy mix that doesn't look like much at first.

smell until you mix them with water. Then they will smell just a wee bit. Your nose will register the smell as "clean."

If you mix these flakes with hot water you will produce a solution that is somewhere between whipping cream and a soft wax. Then you can rub this solution on your work to give it some protection and a little sheen.

The trick is deciding how much water to add to how much soap.

Two Solutions

When I first started to dig into the recipes for a soap finish, I found two types. One used a lot of water and a little soap – a couple spoonfuls of soap and a liter of water was a typical recipe. Then there were recipes that used equal parts soap and water.

I tried both.

When you mix equal parts soap and boiling water you end up with a waxy solution that gives furniture a semi-gloss sheen and mild protection.

Wax on. With equal parts water and soap, you'll quickly create a stiff mixture that can be immediately applied to the work.

When you mix a little soap and a lot of water you make a mayonnaise-like solution that is easy to apply and gives furniture a matte finish with mild protection.

Neither soap finish is bullet-, baby- or waterproof. But both are easily applied, repaired and renewed.

To mix up a watery solution – what I call "soap soup" – boil four cups of water and pour that into one cup of soap flakes. Stir vigorously. The result looks like bathwater after a long soak. Don't throw it out in frustration (like I did the first time I made it).

Put the solution in a jar to let it cool and set up. After a few hours, the liquid turns an opaque white and becomes a bit stiff like shaving cream or mayonnaise. After 24 hours, the stuff is ready to use on furniture.

To mix a hard solution, begin with a cup of boiling water and a cup of soap flakes. Pour about half of the boiling water on the flakes and mix. Add water bit by bit until you get a stiff whipped-cream-like solution. Let that cool and set up. After about an hour it will be waxy and ready to use.

Soap soup (later). After 24 hours the "soup" firms up into something like mayonnaise. This can be easily ragged onto wood.

Application

Applying the soap soup is easy. Rag it on so that the wood is wetted and a bit foamy. Let it stand for a couple minutes. Then take a clean rag and wipe off the excess. Let it dry for an hour then sand the surface – I use a #320-grit sanding sponge – and repeat.

After four coats you will start to see some sheen build up. Stop whenever you like the way it looks. Two coats is not unreasonable – nor is 10.

To renew the finish in the coming months, apply more soap solution to clean it and create the original soft sheen.

The waxy solution is applied more like a wax. Get a clean cotton cloth and scoop a single dip-sized dollop into the middle. Wrap up the soap and twist the cloth around it to create a ball of rag and soap.

Squeeze the rag and the soap will begin to leach out of the rag. Rub the rag on your work and a small amount of the waxy soap will flow onto

Soap's on. The thin soap finish rags on like a soft hand cream.

the wood. After you finish a leg or seat or door of your project, come back with a clean rag and buff out the soap solution. It will polish up to a semi-gloss sheen like any wax polish.

Repeat the process a couple times until you get the look you want.

This soap polish can be renewed at any time. You can use either solution at any point – use the watery solution over the waxy solution if you want to experiment with a flat look. Or vice versa.

It's a great finish, but it requires upkeep. If you are happy with the ease of melamine or the durability of bartop, you probably won't like a soap finish.

USEFUL STUFF AT THE BACK

The whole ball of soap. Spoon the soap into a rag and wrap it around the ball to create something similar to a "rubber" when French polishing.

Rub-a-dub-dub. Your body heat and friction will start to melt the soap and it will flow through the rag.

A soap shine. The waxy soap finish produces a medium sheen.

USEFUL STUFF AT THE BACK

What Happens if…

Many people wonder if water, stains, heat or nasty solvents can hurt a soap finish. Yes, but the finish can be easily renewed with more soap. So don't worry about it.

Can you use it over other finishes? Sure, but it's best on raw wood. I've applied it over milk paint, cured oil, varnish and other finishes. If you aren't sure (or don't trust my advice) then try it on a sample board. You'll get your answer.

No finish is perfect. But when it comes to a finish that is safe, easy to apply and easy to repair, soap is hard to beat.

What About the So-called 'Scrubbed' Finish?

Many dealers in vernacular antiques will describe a table as having a "scrubbed" finish on its top. Scrubbed tops are typically dead flat in sheen, nearly white and the subject of much controversy.

What made them look like this? Lye? Oxalic acid? A white pigment stain?

Chances are that a true scrubbed finish is created like this: You buy a table that has a finish – wax, oil, paint, whatever. It's washed and scrubbed every day with household cleansers, bleach and a slightly abrasive pad. Over the course of years the original finish wears away and is replaced by cleanser and bleach.

As this finish is desirable, antique dealers have a reputation for faking it by stripping off the top coat on a tabletop and bleaching out the wood's color with oxalic acid or another kind of bleach.

Woodworkers can create a scrubbed finish by simply leaving off the topcoat and start cleaning the wood. Then leave the rest to the client. The best description of a scrubbed finish is in Alan Peters' book "Cabinetmaking: The Professional Approach, 2nd edition" (Linden). As I cannot say it any better, here is a lengthy quote from that book about the topic:

> *At times this (a flawless finish) disturbs me, for the surface that some admire and some craftsmen strive to satisfy has little to distinguish it from a piece of plastic laminate; for that is precisely what the surface has become, after the grain has been filled and endless coats of plastic film*

Scrubbed? Who knows if this 100-year-old tabletop is a true "scrubbed" finish. But this is what it's supposed to look like.

have been applied and painstakingly rubbed down.

Natural wood finishes, such as oil and wax, are very susceptible to marking in their early stages and do require care and attention. Frankly, this dilemma of finding wood finishes that leave the material looking like wood, resist marking, and improve rather than deteriorate with age, has dogged me and often defeated me these past 20 years....

For example, a scrubbed finish to an oak dining table, so favoured by the Cotswold School, is a beautiful surface, immensely practical in use, improving with age and developing a wonderful surface texture that would look fine in many situations, especially in the older farmhouse or cottage-style dwelling, and for most of the time it requires no more than a wipe over with a damp cloth after a meal.

However, it is also virtually colourless, just a bland uniform silvery grey. It has none of the colour variations of say a rosewood veneer or an oiled elm surface, and it is this richness of colour and grain that many of us find attractive about wood, so one has to move in this instance to a finish that heightens and preserves these characteristics....

> *Ten years ago on moving to Devon I needed to make a pine kitchen/ dining table quickly for our own use. Today, it is a beautiful golden colour similar to old stripped pine with not a bruise and hardly a scratch to be seen. We do not use a table cloth, only place mats, and we have never treated it at all gently. Yet, all that it has received in treatment or finish is a regular wipe over with a damp cloth after use and, once a month perhaps, it is thoroughly washed and scrubbed with hot water and household detergent. The hot water raises any bruises and scratches and the table looks like new, or rather, even better than new, for it has acquired a lovely patina now. There is no comparison with the treacly, bruised and scratched polyurethane surfaces so often encountered with modern manufactured pine tables.*
>
> *A scrubbed finish is not restricted to pine, and I have used it for dining and kitchen tables and sideboards in oak, chestnut, pine, cedar and also sycamore. In the case of the latter, if an occasional wash with household bleach is substituted for the detergent, a beautifully white spotless surface will result.*
>
> *My only regret is that I cannot persuade more of my customers to have this finish.*

I couldn't agree more. My personal dining table was perfectly finished for about one day. Then my youngest daughter spilled fingernail polish remover (acetone) on it, cutting right through the lacquer and discoloring the wood.

During the next decade, the table saw many more injustices than that little spill. Now it looks like hell. The lacquer is crazed and lifted in places. Areas of the finish are down to bare wood.

I am on the verge of stripping off the lacquer on the tabletop and starting fresh, clean and naked. It seems a bit like revisionist history, like something Stalin would do if he were a woodworker. But I don't envision this tabletop looking any better in my lifetime unless I remove the film finish and start over.

ON MILK PAINT

D: LIKE A COLORED WATER

You can make your own.

First thing, milk paint is essentially a myth… I have never seen anything called 'milk paint' advertised in period publications (of the nineteenth century), it doesn't show up on probate inventories or other historical records and is apparently entirely a made up 20th century idea.

— Stephen A. Shepherd, "Shellac, Linseed Oil, & Paint" (Full Chisel Press, 2011)

The milk paint used for in-door work dries in about an hour, and the oil which is employed in preparing it entirely loses its smell in the state to which it is reduced by its union with the lime. One coating will be sufficient for places that are already covered with any colour….

— Henry Carey Baird, "The painter, gilder, and varnisher's manual …" (M. Taylor – London, 1836)

Milk-based paint has been around a long time – I've found dozens of sources that describe how to make it from the 1800s and earlier. It was inexpensive, didn't smell, dried fast and could be made with commonly available materials – milk and lime. Some recipes added linseed oil, pigment, egg yolks (to give the paint more sheen) or white pitch (to make it weather-resistant).

I've used it for almost 20 years now on furniture and can attest that milk paint looks good, wears well and is not going to expose you to nasty solvents. You can make your own – there are lots of recipes online – or you can buy a commercial powder that you mix with water. If you live in the United Kingdom, casein-based paints are available from stores that cater to the restoration trade.

Most beginners will opt to buy the commercial powder because it's foolproof and comes in lots of nice colors.

If you go this route, here are my instructions for mixing the stuff:

1. Throw away the manufacturer's instructions.
2. Mix the paint 2:1 – warm water to powder.
3. Mix your proto-paint for 10 minutes to ensure all the lumps get dissolved.
4. Let the paint sit for 30 minutes. It might thicken a bit.
5. Strain the paint through cheesecloth and into your paint tray or bucket.

After that, it's just like using a very thin paint. It's not like latex or oil paints that have a lot of body or oiliness. It's like applying colored water.

It dries quickly, so I apply the paint with a small foam roller then use a natural-bristle brush to push the color into the details and corners. Then I "tip off" any flat surfaces.

After one coat, you will have a translucent colored surface. If you applied the paint with any skill, you can stop painting here if you like the look (I do).

If you want things more opaque, then sand the first coat with a #320-grit sanding sponge, dust off the project and apply the second coat.

This coat should obscure most of the wood grain, but not all. Repeat the sanding and painting if you want a third coat.

Once the color is laid on, you have a choice: Do you add a topcoat of some other finish to it or not? The raw painted surface will be dead flat. If you like this (I do), you can smooth the painted surface with a folded brown paper bag and call it done.

If you want some sheen or a deeper color, smooth the paint with the paper bag and add a coat of boiled linseed oil, wax or varnish. This will make the finish look less chalky.

As always, make a sample board if you are unsure of the look you want or if you are unfamiliar with a finishing product. I know you won't do this, but I am obligated to beat my head against this particular wall.

USEFUL STUFF AT THE BACK

Cheap sandpaper. A folded paper bag is a great tool to smooth a milk-painted surface. And it won't cut through the color.

TENONS BY HAND

E: NO LATHE?

No problem.

Throughout this book I rough out the tapered tenons for the legs on a lathe then finish them with a Veritas tapered tenon cutter – basically a big pencil sharpener.

But not everyone has a lathe to get the tenon to rough shape. To be sure, there are lots of ways to rough out the tenon without a lathe, including a drawknife, spokeshave or even a hatchet. But the method I prefer uses a jack plane, block plane and a tapered tenon cutter.

Boiled down, the technique involves simply marking the finished diameter of the tip of the tenon on the top of the leg then planing the tenon to shape with planes. Then using the tenon cutter to show you where more material needs to be removed.

Jack Does the Job

Most of the wood for a tapered tenon can be removed with a jack plane. But first you need a target to plane to. Mark the center point of the leg and drill a shallow 5/8" hole in the top of the leg. That's your target. Now clamp the leg in your vise and tilt the tenon's end up above the benchtop a bit. Then use a rank-set jack plane to make tapering cuts down to the 5/8" target. Here's how to do that.

The tapered tenon for the projects in this book is 2-1/2" long. You'll need to start the taper farther back than that. How far back depends on

Set your target. A shallow 5/8" hole becomes the tip of your tenon.

Jack the waste. A coarse-set jack plane makes short work of this oak leg. Here I'm removing half the waste around the tenon. Then I'll finish the job on my next go-around.

USEFUL STUFF AT THE BACK

the thickness of your stock. For 1-3/4" legs that are straight and untapered, for example, I start the taper about 6-1/2" from the end of the tenon. With thinner stock you won't need to start that far back from the tip. You'll get a feel for it after you do it once or twice.

Begin removing material. I skew the jack plane quite a bit during this operation. Skewing helps remove material quickly without the plane's long sole interfering with the cut.

To help keep the tenon centered on the stock, first remove about half the material all around the tenon's tip. For example, for the tenon shown in these photos, the leg was 1-3/4" square. I removed a bit more than 1/4" all around on my first time around the tenon. Then I went around again and removed another 1/4" from all the facets to get to my 5/8" target.

Once you reach your target, get the tenon cutter out to refine the shape to a perfect taper.

Let the Tenon Cutter be Your Guide

Crank the tenon into the cutter (I'm using the Veritas Tapered Tenon Cutter). It should cut a short distance then stop cutting. Press the tenon hard into the cutter. This won't hurt the tool or the tenon, but it will do something valuable.

The metal mouth of the tenon cutter will mark on the tenon where you need to remove material. You'll feel the high spots left un-tenoned by the tool. And the tool will mark the high spots in black for you.

All you have to do is now remove those high spots and put the tenon into the tenon cutter again. Here's how I do that.

Like chairmakers Chris Williams and John Brown I clamp a block of wood in a bench vise and press the tip of the tenon against it. Make sure the block of wood projects up from the vise less than the diameter of your finished tenon. If the tenon is 5/8" in diameter, for example, set the block so it's 1/2" above the jaws of the vise.

Then use a block plane to shave off the high spots. Try to prevent the block plane from cutting into the area that the tenon cutter has already shaped (you do this by simply lifting the heel of the plane as it gets near the tenon).

After some work, put down the block plane and crank the tenon into the tenon cutter again. You should make some more progress and then the tenon cutter should stop cutting – just like before. And just like before, press the tenon hard into the mouth of the tool.

Where to cut. The tenon cutter tells you where you need to remove material.

Remove the bulk. A rank-set block plane removes the high spots pointed out by the tenon cutter.

USEFUL STUFF AT THE BACK

And just like before you will have little black marks that you need to remove with your block plane. Open the mouth of the tool and set the blade for as thick a shaving as you can while still keeping control of the cutting action. Skew the plane during cutting to make the tool easier to push (skewing reduces the tool's effective cutting angle). Repeat this cycle until you get a full-length tenon. The joint is done, but the component might not be.

Final Shaping

If the component needs to be tapered over its full length, this is the time to do that job. Place the leg (or whatever it is you're working on) in a V-shaped cradle to taper its facets using a jack plane.

This technique was born out of necessity – I had to teach 12 students in a remote workshop how to make tapered tenons without a lathe. All we had were workbenches, jack planes and my tenon cutter. We made it through the project just fine. After a few years of working with the above technique, it has become my favorite way to make this component without a lathe.

MACHINE TAPERS

F: THIS LOOKS DANGEROUS

It's not.

Cutting tapers on legs with a jack plane and a smoothing plane is simple work if you have only a handful of legs to do. But if you need to do a production run of legs – 10 or more – you might want to switch gears.

One way to speed the plow is with a band saw. Saw the leg square and tapered on the band saw. Then finish the job with a jack plane.

But the easiest way to do it is with an electric jointer.

The first time I learned this process from woodworker Troy Sexton in the 1990s, I thought it looked dangerous. It's not. I've used this procedure for more than 16 years in production work without a single incident. But if you are skittish, skip it.

Troy told me that this operation came to him in a dream. He's one of the smartest woodworkers I know, and after you try it, I think you'll agree with me that it is brilliant.

Here's an overview of the process.

1. Decide how much material you want to remove from each face of the leg at the foot. Let's say it's 1/4". So you need to set your jointer to take half that amount (an 1/8"-deep cut). Lock it. You are done setting the jointer.

2. Decide how long the taper needs to be. Let's say you have a 30" leg and you want the taper to be 26" long. Divide that in half (13"). Clamp a stop-block to your jointer fence so it is 13" away from the top dead

A foot at first. If this is your first time out, mark the finished foot size on the leg.

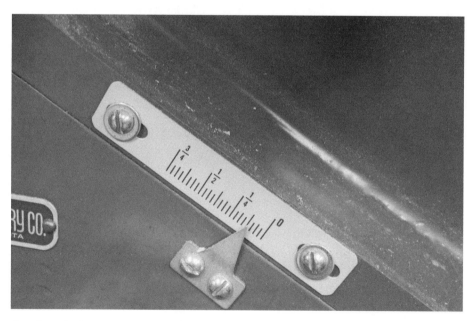

Set the infeed table. If you are going to taper a face of a leg by 1/4", set the infeed table to remove 1/8".

USEFUL STUFF AT THE BACK

Set the stop. The leg should stop halfway along the taper.

First cut. Push the foot of the leg into the cutterhead. Stop at the stop. Lift the leg off the machine. Repeat for every face that needs to be tapered.

First-cut results. It looks wrong, but it's right.

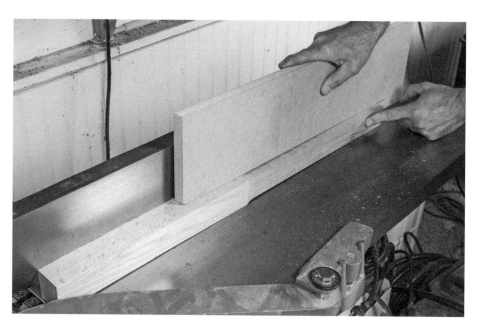

Pop the wheelie. A substantial push stick will push the leg into the correct position for the second pass. This time the top of the leg is first across the cutterhead.

Final results. This leg is tapered almost perfectly to the lines drawn at the beginning. Finish the job with a handplane.

center (TDC) of your jointer's cutterhead. You are done setting stops.

3. Take your leg and push it into the cutterhead foot first until it touches the stop-block. Lift the leg off the jointer's table. Repeat this process for all the leg faces that you want to taper.

4. Remove the stop-block.

5. Now push the leg through the jointer a second time. This time the top of the leg goes in first. And you need to press the leg down against the table so the top of the leg "pops a wheelie" (for lack of a better expression) as you push it across the cutterhead. Cut all the faces this way and you will have a perfectly tapered leg in just a few minutes.

Note that this process is far safer than using most commercial tapering jigs for a table saw. Those jigs are designed to remove fingers as much as create tapers.

SEAT TEMPLATES

G: MAKE YOUR OWN

Simply study the drawings.

When I took my first class in making Welsh stick chairs in 2003, the instructor asked if we wanted to trace his seat and arm templates.

It would be fair to say that John (the other guy in the class) and I freaked. We quickly grabbed cardboard, paper and pencils and began tracing all the templates. I still have those templates down in the basement, but I've never used them.

When I returned home from the class, I took a good look at the templates and realized that almost everything about the templates could be described with rectangles, squares and simple arcs. The rest could be easily sketched in with French curves.

Since that realization, I've always made my own templates. And I would rather show you how to make your own templates instead of providing a silly gridded drawing or something that has to be blown up 478 percent on a photocopier then printed on a plotter.

Here are the tools you need:

1. A big sheet of paper (I use cheap newsprint sheets). You also can draw these templates directly on thin MDF
2. Trammel points with one end being a pencil
3. A yardstick
4. Drafting triangle
5. Pencil

APPENDICES

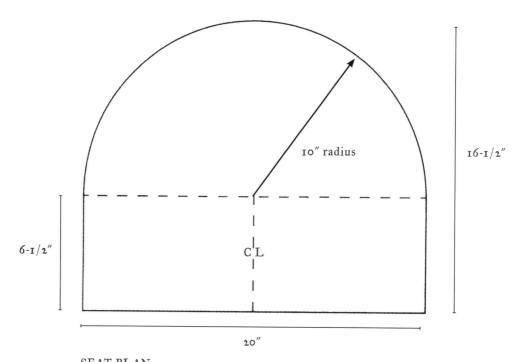

SEAT PLAN

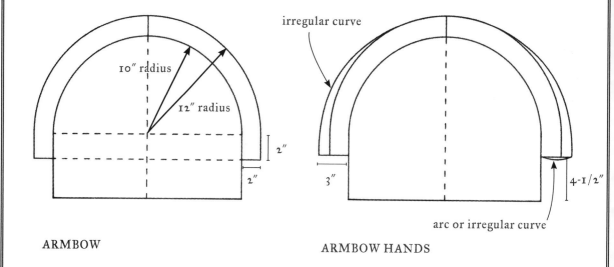

ARMBOW

ARMBOW HANDS

USEFUL STUFF AT THE BACK

Draw the Seat

Most of my chairs use a D-seat, which looks like a more complicated shape than it really is. It's simply a rectangle with a half-circle attached to one edge. To make the seat, draw a rectangle that is 20" wide and 6-1/2" high. Draw a centerline though the rectangle's 20" width.

Set your trammel points to a 10" radius. Scribe the half-circle arc where the centerline intersects one edge of the rectangle. That's it.

All of the other parts of the chair – the arms, doubler and the crest – all evolve from the seat shape. So, I've shown the seat in the illustrations to make this clear.

Make the Arms

The arms for my stick chair are 2" wide and start about 4-1/2" back from the front edge of the chair. Here's how to lay them out. Start with the seat plan you just drew. The first arc is a half-circle with a 10" radius – just like the seat. Scribe that. Then adjust the trammels to describe a 12"-radius circle and scribe that on your paper.

Now add 2" x 2" squares to the front of your arms to make them longer and to match the shape of the seat. The illustrations show this clearly.

Now you have the basic shape of the armbow. You can alter this shape to suit. I decided to widen the arms at the front and add a curve to the front area of each arm. This part of the armbow is called the "hands."

Create the Hands

I made my hands 3" wide at the front. Then I wanted the additional 1" to flow into the original arm so the armbow ended up 2" wide at the back.

This is the only difficult part of the exercise. I used French curves to create this irregular curve. You also could draw an ellipse, but using French curves is faster (for me). Then draw the arc at the front of the hands. It can be a simple arc or an irregular curve. Your call.

The Doubler

The "doubler" is a piece of wood that beefs up the armbow and helps strengthen any short grain. It has the same basic shape as the armbow but is only 12" long. Scribe the two arcs – one at a 10" radius with

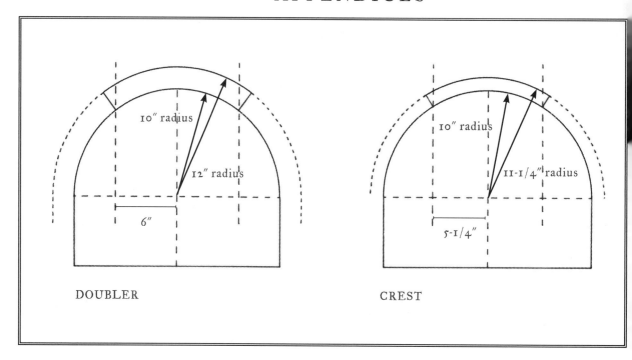

the second at 12". Then use your yardstick to create endpoints that are 12" apart. Use these endpoints to connect your two arcs.

The Crest

The crest begins just like the doubler – by scribing a 10" arc. Then set your trammels to draw an 11-1/4" arc. Use your yardstick to create endpoints that are 10-1/2" apart. Join the two arcs using the endpoints as a guide.

All the text above is much more difficult to follow than is simply studying the drawings. Everything flows out of the 10"-radius arc that is the back edge of the seat. Once you get that in your head, everything else is easy.

After you make your templates, you can transfer them to MDF or hardboard. Cut them out and smooth the edges with files and sandpaper. And put them in a safe place. While templates are easy to make, remaking lost ones is a grumpy affair.

Buzz II. Briony Morrow-Cribbs, etching and watercolor, 12" x 9", 2013

ACKNOWLEDGMENTS
WE WERE BEING CONNED.

Words, bread and whatnot.

This book began to take shape when my friend Narayan Nayar became impatiently hungry after a photo shoot. We were seated across from one another in a bistro one chilly night, and I could see that his nerves were on edge – a rare sight with this normally impossibly placid man.

So I turned to the table at my left and asked if I could steal some bread to feed a famished Narayan. The two women agreed, and after he stuffed a couple bits into his bread-hole we returned the favor with some of our appetizers.

After some small talk, we learned the following things: One of the women was a furniture maker. The other made copperplate etchings.

At first I thought we were being conned.

After a lot more words, bread and whatnot, we exchanged contact information at the restaurant. A week later, I convinced Briony Morrow-Cribbs, the copperplate artist, to make the etchings for this book.

If it weren't for that encounter, this book would probably not be the thing you are holding in your hands. A visit to Briony's studio and a long look at her work convinced me that I could combine my love of traditional process and contemporary design. And that an off-kilter visual presentation of traditional material could work in the normally boring world of how-to books. (To experience the same hot-beef injection of tradition into contemporary, visit her site: brionymorrow-cribbs.com.)

ACKNOWLEDGMENTS

For many years I've been at odds with the idea that traditional tools should be used ideally for traditional work. That a vintage try plane is best suited for making only traditional pieces of furniture – highboys, lowboys, anything with "boys" in its name.

This idea makes sense on many levels. Traditional tools were indeed designed for making the work of the time. Gouges were sized to match radii in carvings or mouldings of the period. Bench planes and benches were sized to deal with standard carcases. Moulding planes were sized to reflect Greek or Roman shapes in architecture.

The tools seem to drag us back to making "classics."

This book, and Briony's work, is proof that traditional methods are ideal for much more.

In addition to Briony, I would like to thank the following people who helped me with this book without any recompense (and at times without knowing they helped):

Narayan Nayar, for photography and setting me straight.
John Hoffman, the other half of Lost Art Press.
Megan Fitzpatrick, for listening to my BS.
Suzanne Ellison, the indexer, researcher and never-ending help.
Katherine Schwarz, for monkeys.
Ty Black, a lab rat, and for representing the non-English speakers.
Dr. Tim Henriksen, lab rat and bartender.
Dr. Sean Thomas, lab rat, physician and scone eater.
Raney Nelson, for thinking with his clothes on.
Jameel Abraham, a lab rat, proofreader and breakdancer.
Jason Thigpen, for proofreading and wrestling knowledge.
Deneb Puchalski, proofreader and lab rat.
Brian Clites, proofreader.
Andrew Lunn, lab rat and destroyer of plumbing.
Mark Firley, unit 2 photography and clamps.
Roy Underhill, for proof that this can be done.
Peter Follansbee, for research and general bad-assery.
Richard O. Byrne, for research I didn't know I needed.

SUPPLIES

NOTHING FOR FREE

And without reservation.

None of these companies supplied anything for free or at a discount for this book or to be listed here. They are here because I use them every day in my business of making furniture and writing about it. I recommend all of them without reservation.

Lee Valley Tools
leevalley.com
Tapered reamers, tapered tenon cutters, general woodworking tools and supplies, cut nails, hide glue, WoodOwl bits, Auriou rasps

Lie-Nielsen Toolworks
lie-nielsen.com
Woodworking hand tools, Auriou rasps and supplies

Tools for Working Wood
toolsforworkingwood.com
Shellac Tiger Flakes, general woodworking tools, hide glue pearls, cut nails

Highland Woodworking
highlandwoodworking.com
Woodworking hand tools and general supplies

SUPPLIES

Peter Ross, Blacksmith
peterrossblacksmith.com
Handmade locks, hinges and nails

Horton Brasses
horton-brasses.com
Brass and iron hardware, including hinges for chests

Tremont Nail Co.
tremontnail.com
Cut nails

Dictum
dictum.com
Machine-forged nails, general woodworking supplies

McMaster-Carr
mcmaster.com
Hardware: bolts, nuts, washers, screws etc.

Blacksmith Bolt
blacksmithbolt.com
Unplated slotted screws and other awesome hardware bits

Whitechapel Ltd.
whitechapel-ltd.com
Iron hardware, including crab locks

Old Brown Glue
oldbrownglue.com
Liquid hide glue

Titebond/Franklin
franklininternational.com
Liquid hide glue

The Real Milk Paint Co.
realmilkpaint.com
Milk paint

Pure Soap Flake Co.
puresoapflakes.com
Soap flakes for finishing

Dieter Schmid
fine-tools.com
Wood-threading tools, general woodworking tools and supplies

Easy Wood Tools
easywoodtools.com
Lathe turning tools

Blue Spruce Tool Works
bluesprucetoolworks.com
Marking tools, mallets, chisels

Infinity Tools
infinitytools.com
MaxiCut Forstner bits

HyperKitten
hyperkitten.com
Vintage woodworking tools for users

INDEX

Page numbers in italics refer to illustrations.

A
American anarchism, ix-x
aumbry
  carcase, *502*, 504-509, *520*
  cutlist, 521
  door and hinges, 511-512, *517, 518*
  finish, 512, 521
  Gothic tracery, 501, 509-511, *513-516*
  history of, 501
  nails, 505-506
  wood for, 503

B
backstool. *See under* chairs
battens. *See under* joinery
Bebb, Richard,
  "Welsh Country Furniture," 236
  "Welsh Furniture 1250-1950," 238
bed
  assembly, 176-180
  battens, 170-171, *173*
  cutlist, 182
  finish, 182
  legs, 171, 174, *180*, 181
  mortises, 173, 175
  slats, 175-176
  woods for, 169
bench
  assembly, *370*, 375-378, 379
  cutlist, 381
  as a good first project, 369, 371
  finish, 378, 380
  legs and aprons, 372-374
  nails, 371, 378, *381*
  seat, 371
  shelf, 378
  wood for, 371
bending. *See* steam-bending
bookshelf
  assembly, *486*, 492-496
  back, 495-496
  carcase, *486*, 489-492
  cutlist, 497
  finish, 496-497
  shelves, 485-489

wood for, 489
Brown, John
  on chair seat thickness, 144
  on chair seat tilt, 247
  influence, 238
  method for tenons by hand, 607-611
  "Welsh Stick Chairs," 235
Byrne, Richard, 151

C

chair design for comfort, 242-249
chairmaking skills, 277, 278
chairs
  armchair
    armbow, 297-300, 309-314
    assembly, 328-333, 335
    crest rail, 333-335
    cutlist, 302
    drilling jig, *316*, 317-319
    finish, 300, 337
    legs, 301-302, 305-307, 335-337
    mortises, *298*, 303-305, 316-319
    saddling, 322, 323, 324-326
    seat, 302, 303
    spindles, 298, 309, 320-322
    templates for, 619-622
    wood for, 300-302, 315
  backstool
    assembly, 272-274
    crest rail, 264-269
    cutlist, 274
    design, *20*, 23, 26-27
    finish, 274
    legs, 259, *260*, 261, 274
    mortises, 255-258, 262-263
    saddling, 270-272
    seat, 255, *256*, 257, 259, *260*
    spindles, 262-264, *265*
    stability, 252-253, 255
  prototypes, 308, 559-562

settle chair
  assembly, *468*, 475, 476, 481-483
  back feet, 468, 477
  chair angles, 469, 474
  cutlist, 483
  finish, 483
  seat, 468, 469, 477-479
  sides, 470-477, 479-481
  wood for, 469
side chair
  assembly, 289-290, 292-294
  crest rail, 281-283
  cutlist, 294
  finish, 294
  as a good first chair, 277, 279
  legs, 281, 285-289
  mortises, 284-285
  seat, 279, 281, 283-285
  spindles, 285, 290-292
  templates for, 619-621, 622
  wood for, 279
chests
  mule chest
    assembly, 455-465
    carcase, 444-455
    cutlist, 448
    design options, *446*
    drawers, 451, *452*, 453, 462-465
    finish, 465
    lid, 459-462
    origin of name, 443, 445
    wood for, 445
  six-board chest
    assembly, *431*, 432-433
    carcase, 422-432, 435
    cutlist, 438
    cutting plan, 418-422
    finish, 438
    lid, 436-437
    marriage marks, 427-429

mouldings, 433-435
nails, *415*, 416-417
wood for, 413-416
tool chest
  assembly, 385, 388-391, 393
  carcase, 384-388, 393-395
  cutlist, 403
  finish, 402
  interior trays, *399*, 400-402
  lid, 396-398, 399, 401
  lifts, 395, *396*
  rot strips, 385, *394*, 395
  wood for, 385
coffin
  alternative uses, 531, 541-543
  assembly, 538-541
  "Coffin-making & Undertaking" (Hasluck), 531, 537
  coffin patterns, 531-532, 537
  cutlist, 542
  finish, 541
  FTC Funeral Rule, 529, 531
  kerfs, 537-539, *540 fig. 6-7*
  lid, 539, 541
  sides, 535-537
  sizing the bottom, 532-534, *530, 537*
  traditional use, *348-349*, 529
creepie, 85, 87

D
dados. *See under* joinery
design
  chair comfort and, 242-249
  historical sources, 12-19, 149, 152, 238
  "Human Dimension & Interior Space" (Panero and Zalnik), 10-12
  inspiration, 21-23, 141-145, 236-238, 404-407
  leg angle models, *21, 22-25, 47-53*

by trial and error, 544-564

E
end grain
  and nailing, *391*, 457-459
  sizing with glue, 377, 388, *390*

F
finishes
  milk paint, 603-605
  scrubbed, 599-601
  "shou sugi ban," 114-115
  soap finish, 590-599
Fleming, Dave, 30, 237, 238
furniture
  knock-down, 116-137, 168-183, 186-227
  staked, 28-39
  utility, 295
  vernacular, 3-5, 8, 12-19, 81-83
  See also specific furniture pieces

G
Galbert, Peter
  "Chairmaker's Notebook," 238, 324
  influence, 238
  leveling chair legs, 74-76
glue, 587-589
  and end-grain sizing, 377, 388, *390*

H
Hayward, Charles
  coffin construction, *540*
  octagonal leg tapers, 78-79
  utility furniture, 295

J
jigs
  armbow and chair seat drilling, *316*, 317-319

INDEX

for compound-angle mortises, *58*, 59-60
joinery
  battens
    clenched, 205-207, 436-437
    screwed, 396-399
    and sliding dovetail, 155-160, 165-166
    to strengthen a thin surface, 149-152, 413
  dados
    angled, 470-473
    with batten cutting guide, *503*
    for boarded carcases, 429-430, 490-492
    sawing tip, 445-448
  grooves, 491-492
  mortises
    blind with battens, 153, 160-161
    dummy leg for test fits, *62*, 63, 221
    by hand or power, 56-60
    jig for compound angles, *58*, 59-60
    reamers, 60-63, 583
    for stretchers, 93-97, 109-112, 196-199
    See also under specific furniture pieces
  rabbets
    cross-grain cutting, 386-388, 430, 431-432
    with batten cutting guide, 453-455
    for drawers, 167, 462, 465
    for ease of assembly, 422
  shiplaps, 495
  tenons
    cutters, 66-68, *583*, 584
    dummy leg for test fits, *62*, 63, 221
    by hand, 65-68, 607-611
    wedge and tenon assembly, *68*, 69, 72, 331
    wedges for, 69-70, 327-329
  tongue-and-groove, *392*, 393, 395

K
Klint, Kaare, 14
knock-down furniture
  bed, 168-183
  drinking tables, 116-137
  trestle tables, 186-227

L
Langsner, Drew, 47
legs
  angles and models for, *21*, 22-25, 47-53
  chair devil for shaping, *260, 320*
  leveling methods, 73-76, 180-181, 223, 335-337
  octagonal, *64*, 65, *163*, 165
  and the staked joint, 35
  tapering
    by hand, 78-79
    by machine, 613-617
  tenons, 65-68, 607-611
  wood for, 33, 54

M
marriage marks, 386, 427-429
milk paint, 603-605
Morrow-Cribbs, Briony, *624*, 625
mortises. *See under* joinery; *specific furniture pieces*

N
nails
  clenching, *207, 363*, 365-367
  dovetailing, 390-391
  driving and setting, 364-365
  and end grain, 457-459
  nail cabinet, *360-361*
  orientation, *362*
  penny size, 358-359
  pilot holes for, 359, 362, 364
  tape template, 451, *452, 456*, 493

USEFUL STUFF AT THE BACK

types and naming, 352-357

R
rabbets. *See under* joinery
rake and splay, 44-45, 47-49
resultant angle, 49-51, *53*

S
saddling a seat
  bodger trick, *270*, 287
  for chair comfort, 242-243
  tools for
    adze, *322, 323*
    jack plane and card scraper, 270-272
    scorp, *323*, 326
    spokeshave, 325
    travisher, *324*, 326
  See also under specific chairs
sawbench
  assembly, 53, 68-72
  cutlist, 78
  finish, 76
  legs, 52, 54, 64-68
    angles, 44-45, 47-51, *53*
    leveling, 73-76
    tapering, 78-79
    tenons, 52, 65-68
  mortises, *46*, 56-64
  top, 54-56
  use in the shop, *76*, 77-78
  vs. sawhorse, 41-42
  wedges, 68-70
Sexton, Troy, 345-346, 613
shooting board, 371, *372*
"shou sugi ban," 114-115
sightlines for leg angles, 49-51, 53-56
  See also resultant angle
soap finish, 590-599
spindles
  armchair drilling jig, *316*, 317-319
  assembly, 292-294, *331*, 332-333
  dowels for, 301, 315, 320-322
  layout on a chair seat
    armchair, *298*
    backstool, 285
    side chair, 262-263
  length, 290
  making, 263-264, 290-292
  spindle deck, 309, 323
  wood grain, 263
split repair, 134-137
steam-bending
  crest rail bending form, 267, *282*
  kitchen oven set-up, 268-269, 281-283
  steam box, 266-268
stools
  creepie, 85, 87
  high stool
    assembly, 113-114
    cutlist, 115
    design, 105
    finish, 114-115
    legs, 106
    mortises, 107-108, 109-112
    seat, 105, 106-17
    stretchers, 108-109, 112-113
    wood for, 105
  low stool
    assembly, 97-99
    cutlist, 99
    finish, 100
    legs, 89-92, 99-100
    mortises, 89-90, 92-97
    seat, 88-89
    stretchers, 97
    wood for, 87, 89
  prototypes, 546-549, 555-558
stretchers

assembly, 98-99
making, 97, 109
mortises, 93-97, 109-112, 196-199
tapering, 112-113
to do or not to do, 31

T

tables
 drinking tables
  assembly, 117, 119
  cutlist, 131
  finish, 131
  legs, 131
  mortises, 124-128, 130-131
  six-legged variation, *120*, 133-134
  split repair, 134-137
  top and subtop, 119, 121, 123-124, 129-131
  wood for, 133
 gateleg vernacular tables, *15-18*
 historical design sources, 149, 152
 prototypes, 549-551, 563-564
 trestle tables
  Mughal-stretcher trestle
   assembly, 221-222, 225
   cut-list, 227
   finish, 226
   legs, 217-218, 223
   mortises, *193*, 219-221
   stretcher, 217, *224*, 225, 226-227
   tabletop, 225-226
   trestle, 217, 219
  plain trestle
   cutlist, 212
   finish, 212
   legs, 189, 191-193
   mortises, 193-197, 199
   stretcher, 195, 196
   top with battens, 205-210
   top with wooden screw, 189, 199-205
   trestle, 191, 210-210
   wood for, 189, 200
 worktable
  assembly, *164*, 165-167
  battens, 149-152, 155-160
  cutlist, 167
  drawer, 167
  legs, 162-165
  mortises, 160-161
  top, 153, 155
templates
 aumbry Gothic piercings, 514-516
 chair components, 619-622
 Mughal-trestle stretcher, 227
tenons. *See under* joinery
tool chest. *See under* chests
tool set
 electric, 585
 hand tools, 572-584

W

Weber, Don, 30, 238, *270*
Williams, Christopher, 111, 238, 607
wood grain
 interlocked for seats and tops, 33
 nail orientation and, 362
 for spindles or sticks, 263, 301, 315
 for staked furniture legs, 33, 37, 54, 301
 and wedged tenons, *68*, 69, 114
wood movement
 soft vs. hard woods, 413-416
 in staked furniture, 19, 35, *36*
 "The Wood Handbook: Wood as an Engineering Material" (U.S. Forest Products Laboratory), 35
wooden key, 134-137

ISBN 978-1-7333916-1-0